Inventing Fear of Crime

Inventing Fear of Crime
Criminology and the politics of anxiety

Murray Lee

WILLAN
PUBLISHING

Published by

Willan Publishing
Culmcott House
Mill Street, Uffculme
Cullompton, Devon
EX15 3AT, UK
Tel: +44(0)1884 840337
Fax: +44(0)1884 840251
e-mail: info@willanpublishing.co.uk
website: www.willanpublishing.co.uk

Published simultaneously in the USA and Canada by

Willan Publishing
c/o ISBS, 920 NE 58th Ave, Suite 300,
Portland, Oregon 97213-3786, USA
Tel: +001(0)503 287 3093
Fax: +001(0)503 280 8832
e-mail: info@isbs.com
website: www.isbs.com

First published 2007

Hardback
ISBN-13: 978 1-84392-175-2

Paperback
ISBN-13: 978 1-84392-174-5

British Library Cataloguing-in-Publication Data

A catalogue record for this book is available from the British Library

Project managed by Deer Park Productions, Tavistock, Devon
Typeset by GCS, Leighton Buzzard, Bedfordshire, LU7 1AR
Printed and bound by T.J. International Ltd, Padstow, Cornwall

Contents

Acknowledgements

The writing of this book has been a labour that goes back some 10 years. No doubt in that time the work has become a collective effort to the point that it is difficult to acknowledge the input of every individual colleague, friend and family member. Thanks to the efforts and patience of all who contributed their time, ideas and emotional support, and apologies to anybody I have forgotten to mention.

Without the early guidance of Kerry Carrington and Russell Hogg this project would never have been undertaken. Their feedback and input into early versions of what became this text helped etch its intellectual terrain and give it its critical focus. I remain indebted to their commitment. I also want to acknowledge the early inspiration provided by Andrew Johnson whose friendship and collegiality were greatly appreciated as this project took shape. Likewise, I greatly appreciate the constructive feedback on earlier versions of this text provided at various times by John Pratt and Tony Jefferson.

This book would not have been written without the enthusiastic prompting of Stephen Farrall. His feedback on earlier concepts and ideas remain central to the book. I also acknowledge the increased match fitness provided by Stephen's guided mountain bike tours through the wilds of North-East Wales and the Peak District on my visit to Keele University in 2005.

Likewise, Jason Ditton and Furzana Khan provided me with astute advice, ideas and feedback on a visit to Glasgow while researching this book. I'm particularly indebted to Jason for his hospitality and whistle-stop tour of the Glaswegian crime sights. Gabe Mythen also proved a most hospitable intellectual sounding board on a brief visit to Manchester – though no doubt his backhand could do with some work before our next 'court' visit. Reece Walters, Keith Soothill and Shadd Maruna, as peer reviewers of the original proposal for this book, provided valuable and constructive feedback which I've attempted to incorporate. I hope the finished product measures up to expectations. Thanks to Brian Willan who has not only had faith in the project but who patiently awaited the arrival of the manuscript well after the due date.

Kelly Richards, John Gaffey, Alyce McGovern and Lynette Aitken have all worked on research projects related to this book. Their efforts are greatly appreciated. My colleagues Denise Weelands, Moira Carmody, Elaine Fishwick, Adam Possamai, Leanne Weber and Craig Osmond have all provided me with inspiration and support over the period of writing this book. I am additionally grateful to Craig and Elaine for providing feedback on chapters herein. My great friends from Ancient Marinators – Mark, Bruce, Tom and Adam – provide me with a weekly reality (or perhaps hyper-reality) check without which I would probably go clinically insane, although I'd sleep easy in the knowledge that categories of insanity are simply constructs of the knowledge/power of the psych-sciences, being a good Foucaultian.

I would additionally like to thank Mark Hetherington for allowing me to use his wonderful painting 'The Fear of Crime' on the cover. Mark's work can be viewed online at the Ray Hughes Gallery http://www.rayhughesgallery.com

My parents Beth and Brian Lee and my grandparents Alice and Arthur Billett have furnished me with ongoing love in life and support in my work. I remain indebted to them. I was fortunate to grow up at a point in history when a working-class kid from the suburbs of Newcastle NSW could make it into a university – albeit as a mature student with a bit of 'life experience'. As we continue down the – inevitable, we are told – road of 'user pays' education in Australia such opportunities are quickly evaporating. If I were starting my journey now I fear I would never have made it through the gates of a university let alone be set loose to teach and research in one.

Wendy Lee has supported me in my work and my life in ways too numerous to detail. The book would not have been written without her. Nor would I have made it to the end without the support and patience of our children Manon and Tate. Perhaps Manon was right when she said, 'Dad, why didn't you just write a little kids' book?' Anyway, if there are any publishers out there I've got an idea about a dinosaur and a lion scared of becoming victims of crime. The lion says to the dinosaur, 'Would you feel safe in the park after dark?', and the dinosaur replies, 'I don't really go out in the dark to the park.' But perhaps it's time to move on, I might get stuck in a rut. And anyway, the thought of writing a children's book terrifies me, they are always the most insightful and rigorous of critics.

Murray Lee

Chapter 1

Introduction

> There is an almost endless number of still-to-be written histories
> of concept formation in criminology: Concepts that were invented
> in this culture, by thinkers in those strata, in that period of time,
> for these reasons, and with those effects. (Beirne 1993: 9)

This is a book about a concept, its formation and its effects. The concept
under discussion here is fear of crime.[1] This is a history of how fear of
crime has been problematised and pathologised, how it has assumed
an empirical validity and a social scientific respectability, and how it
became normalised as a socio-cultural term used to describe an element
of life experience in late modernity. Piers Beirne notes in the introduction
to his book *Inventing Criminology: Essays on the Rise of Homo Criminalis*
(1993), from which I have paraphrased the title of this book, that there
are an almost endless number of histories of criminological concepts to
be written. This book constitutes one such history.

Over the past four decades the fear of crime has become an
increasingly significant concern for criminologists, victimologists, policy-
makers, politicians, policing organisations, the media and the general
public.[2] Indeed, fear of crime has been identified by researchers as being
responsible for an ever-increasing number of social maladies.[3] Growing
interest in the fear of crime 'problem' from policy-makers across the
political spectrum (Reiner *et al.* 2000) has led to an extraordinary
proliferation of research and literature in this field with one team of
researchers even humorously suggesting that fear of crime has become
bigger than General Motors (Ditton *et al.* 1999a).

For example, it is now possible for government criminologists using
data from the British Crime Survey (BCS) to state that:

> The BCS shows ... the level of worry about violent crime has also increased, whereas worry about car crime has remained stable ... The proportion of adults who have a high level of worry about violent crime increased from 16 per cent to 17 per cent. (Povey *et al.* 2005: 8)

Similarly, research conducted by the Australian Institute of Criminology could claim that 13 per cent of men and 41 per cent of women felt somewhat unsafe 'walking alone in the local area after dark' (Johnson 2005: 45). Again in the USA the Bureau of Justice Statistics could report that 38 per cent of men and 62 per cent of women said that there was somewhere within one mile of their home where they would not walk alone at night (US Bureau of Justice Statistics 2006). The picture is similar in New Zealand, where

> ... more than two-thirds (68%) of the women (compared with a third of the men) said that they did not walk alone in their neighbourhood after dark, and almost three-quarters (72%) of those aged 60 and over said they did not walk alone in their neighbourhood after dark, compared with over a third (37%) of those aged 17 to 24, more than two-fifths (44%) of those aged 15 and 16 and almost a half of those aged 40 to 59 (46%) and of those aged 25 to 39 (47%). There was a little difference on this dimension between New Zealand European/European and Pacific participants (51% and 48% respectively said that they did not walk alone in their neighbourhood after dark). (Morris *et al.* 2003: 216)

Examining the plethora of data being produced about fear of crime one could conclude that there has all but developed a fear of crime industry. This industry does not just include academic researchers, government criminologists and policy-makers, but also private security providers, insurers, and other public and private institutions and functionaries. To get some perspective on the rapidity of the growth in interest in crime fear we need only follow the ever-expanding paper – and increasingly cyber – trail. Chris Hale in 1996 noted that over 200 reports on the subject were available and a more recent online search by Ditton and Farrall (2000a) located 837 entries. I repeated the exercise in researching this book and dragged up 242,000 fear of crime entries using the Google search engine. Not only has the amount of information about fear of crime expanded at a staggering rate, but it is also being democratised. Fear of crime, as a concept used to explain a range of psychological and/or social reactions to the perceived or symbolic threat of crime, is no longer, if it ever was, simply a domain of academic or government criminologists and other social scientists. Fear of crime is now a 'prominent cultural theme' (Garland 2001: 10).

Today local and national newspapers conduct fear of crime surveys, politicians comment on the problem of crime fear, and then use it in their campaigns, and many policing organisations are committed to reducing the fear of crime amongst other terms of reference. The UK Home Office even publishes an online 'fear of crime toolbox' aimed at helping to reduce crime fear in communities (UK Home Office 2006). This also provides instructions on how to conduct local fear of crime audits and surveys, making the governance of crime fear a local government responsibility. A UK-based women's website hosts a 'fear of crime quiz' that assesses whether the participant overestimates UK crime rates and so overestimates their risk of victimisation.[4] If we believe all the surveying and quantifying, fear of crime is almost everywhere and affects almost everyone – although, we are told, to wildly varying degrees. Firstly, the previously victimised are said to be more fearful of crime.[5] Secondly, women are apparently more fearful than men despite lower levels of victimisation.[6] Thirdly, the elderly report fear of crime more than younger people who, likewise, are ironically more at risk.[7]

This recurring theme of lower risk/higher fear has been termed the fear/risk paradox. The implication is that fear of crime operates quite independently of crime itself (Maxfield 1984). Specifically, there is seemingly no identifiable statistical relationship between those who are the most at risk of becoming victims of crime, and those who report being the most fearful (Hough and Mayhew 1983). As I will suggest in later chapters there are complex reasons for this discovery. In light of such findings there has been an ongoing debate as to whether the fear of crime is a rational or irrational fear.

While currently the UK perhaps leads the way in the preoccupation with crime fear as a problematisation for government and object of enquiry, the problem of and focus on fear of crime seems to know no geo-spatial boundary. Fear of crime research has proliferated in the United States, Australia and New Zealand, and has more recently been expanding in popularity in Europe.

What of the socio-cultural context of this expansion? Generally, we are increasingly said to live in what Barry Glassner (1999) has called a 'culture of fear', and in socio-spatial realms that Mike Davis (1998) has termed the 'ecologies of fear'. Fears apparently abound in relation to our children, schools, paedophiles, terrorism, HIV-AIDS, asylum seekers, food, global warming, water supply, meteorites, earthquakes, volcanos, tsunamis, bird flu and, of course, the seemingly perennial fear of the late modern Western world, fear of crime. Recent decades have witnessed the growth in gated communities, private security, security hardware and software, and of course prison populations. Risk theorists such as Ulrich Beck (1992) have suggested that we live in a 'risk society' in which we organise our lives around the distribution of 'bads' as opposed to the industrial world that was organised around the distribution of goods. Here the anxiety produced by probabilistic calculation – increasingly our own but also those of the experts – implores us to follow the path of least riskiness (see also Giddens 1990). We seek out information on the distribution of risks and their probability, and organise our lives accordingly. However, as Glassner and others have argued, the risks or 'bads' that concern us most are often – on any objective measure – the wrong ones. David Garland suggests that the 're-dramatisation of crime' has led policy-makers to shift their emotional temperature 'from cold to hot' and that this is partially responsible for the growth of what he terms a 'culture of control' where political populism jostles for legitimacy with new administrative measures that rationalise and define down the goals of police and other state organisations (Garland 2001).

The politics and problematisation of fear of crime

While being a problem for government, fear of crime has also become political. It is now seen by many researchers and policy-makers as being as serious a problem as crime itself (Hale 1996; van Dijk and Mayhew 1992; Wilson and Kelling 1982) and just as, if not more, debilitating (Braithwaite *et al.* 1982). Walklate (1995) suggests that in the 1980s the 'process of invoking the imagery of the crime victim' became the basis for policy formation, thus increasing the political and theoretical debates around fear of crime and indeed interest in research into the subject. This is echoed by Williams *et al.* (2000) who suggest that criminologists have also come to recognise that victimisation is an important 'dependent variable' in their field of expertise. However, the fear of crime literature has extended well beyond being simply an element of the study of victimisation: fear of crime has itself become an independent field with its own body of expert knowledge. Indeed, this body of knowledge has gradually expanded to include research into almost every conceivable socio-economic group, gender category, ethnic origin, sub-culture and age group we might like to imagine. No 'variable' has been left wanting. If the imagery of the victim has expanded such that in the eyes of many researchers and policy-makers we are all imagined as potential victims, to paraphrase Alison Young (1996), the corollary is that we are now also potential fearers.

Fear of crime literature and the research that has driven it has developed from numerous, and often competing, ideological and theoretical positions. Significantly, debate has raged around what fear of crime might actually be,[8] how it might be measured,[9] what its causes might be, and how it might be remedied. Indeed, there has been a broad range of theoretical and methodological approaches applied to these problems. In the search for causation alone an increasingly long and complex list of variables has emerged, from the psychological to the social, the economic to the geographical and the symbolic to the real. To suggest that there has been methodological confusion over how to measure fear of crime is an understatement. Maxfield (1984) has suggested that there are two reasons why it is important to think critically about how fear of crime is to be measured. Firstly, criminologists have long argued about *how* it should be measured and what types of fear might be worth measuring. Secondly, at the level of public policy it is important to understand *relative* levels of fear in terms of where and how policy might be directed. Surveys asking respondents about 'fear for personal safety on neighbourhood streets [are] not well suited to access anxiety about burglary or other household crimes' (Maxfield 1984: 6).

Hale argues that the confusion over measurement is in part a result of a lack of a specific definition of what the fear of crime might actually be. He suggests that many of the debates about the rationality of fear are due in part to the lack of clarity in being able to distinguish between 'risk evaluation, worry and fear' (Hale 1996: 84). Williams *et al.* (2000) argue that the term fear of crime remains vague and that it is perhaps preferable to substitute the concept of 'worry'. Ditton *et al.* (1999a) argue that although numeric historical measures of fear of crime have been increasingly refined, conceptual development has stagnated. On a more optimistic note, Ditton *et al.* also suggest that in more recent times because of the consistency of the instrument operationalised in the British and Welsh crime surveys, and indeed their Scottish equivalents, these now constitute a unique data source. They argue that the retention of identical survey questions in successive sweeps and across geographic borders means it is now possible to speak with confidence about trends over time. However, the question of what these trends are measures *of* remains unclear. All this has driven Farrall *et al.* (1997: 676) to suggest that:

... the results of fear of crime surveys appear to be a function of the way the topic is researched, rather than the way it is. The traditional methods used are methods which seem consistently to over-emphasise the levels and extent of the fear of crime. It seems that levels of fear of crime and, to a lesser extent, of victimisation itself, have been hugely overestimated.[10]

Sparks (1992) has suggested that the fear of crime has not only become the focus for 'empirical disagreements' but has 'assumed a heavy polemic charge' in both political and theoretical disputes. Weatherburn *et al.* (1996:1) argue that:

> public opinion about the risk of criminal victimisation is probably more influential in shaping state government spending priorities in law and order than the actual risk. If public concern about crime is driven by an exaggerated assessment of the risks of victimisation then strategies need to be in place to address the problem.

Thus, crime fear can shape the way we treat crime and those we criminalise; it can have effects on the machinations of the justice system. Ditton *et al.* (1999a) argue that the recognition that the fear of crime had political power was almost instant following the first National American Crime Survey.

Some researchers suggest that what people fear most is the 'shadowy stranger', the unpredictable and unknowable criminal other, whose victims are randomly selected for no apparent reason other than their availability and vulnerability (Bauman 1993; Young 1996). Such conceptualisations have indirectly, and perhaps unintendedly, fuelled the rational/irrational fears debate, especially given the statistical reality that most serious offences occur within the walls of the family home and among friends, acquaintances and family members. As Shapland and Vagg (cited in Pratt 1997: 151) note:

> It would seem that the kinds of images evoked by the question of fear of crime are not the typical or known, but generally the unusual and unknown ... those that were fearful seemed fearful of everywhere beyond the view of their own windows.

Pratt (1997: 151) suggests that the 'threatening forces of modernity' and the neo-liberal ideal make the horizons of life seem infinite and more exciting than the limited possibilities of the 'welfare era'. However, it also creates new fears and uncertainties through the erosion of traditional support structures like the family. Dangerousness now has a freedom to roam and feed off our fears and insecurities (Pratt 1997).

Obviously, this book has a focus that extends well beyond fear of crime as it has generally been understood. If we are to understand the birth of fear of crime as a concept we must understand the underlying conditions of this birth – its conditions or surfaces of emergence. To achieve this aim a variety of knowledge bases in which fear of crime has been historically enmeshed will be explored. Criminology as an academic discipline and an administrative enterprise of government has perhaps been the most influential of these bases of knowledge, although it is certainly not the only one. I will argue that shifts in criminological thought and the field of criminology have been vital to the invention of fear of crime the concept; a concept that has since reached far beyond the discipline.

Criminology, and criminological research more generally, has proliferated in the past 40 years. While Rock (1994) described the late 1960s/early 1970s as a 'big bang' period for criminology, Maguire (2002) has more recently noted the 'explosion' of academic activity and the 'boom' in criminological research of more recent years. Similarly, Radzinowicz's *Adventures in Criminology* (1999) clearly identifies this 40 or more years of expansion. This growth is illustrated in an increase in membership in criminological bureaucracies (Walters 2003), in the huge numbers of students choosing to do criminology undergraduate programmes and, importantly, by the entry of specialised forms of criminological knowledge into ever increasing domains of government. Significantly, criminology's expansion owes much to its growing array of objects and fields of inquiry, objects such as fear of crime and fields such as victimology. This expansion in objects of focus, and the development of conceptual tools to understand them, has allowed criminological knowledge into new domains of government. I will argue that interest in fear of crime research has constituted part of this disciplinary, or perhaps more post-disciplinary, growth (see also Jackson 2004). The problematisation of crime fear has provided new domains for research and has also been a conveniently attractive object of inquiry for the growing 'administrative criminology'. That is, the problematisation of crime fear has allowed many researchers in university departments and elsewhere to secure consultancy work in an environment where external funding is becoming a requirement both within and outside the discipline of criminology (see Walters 2003).

The term fear of crime is a recent invention. Ditton and Farrall (2000) suggest it was 'discovered' in 1967. Apart from a smattering of references I will explore later, it certainly did not have linguistic currency prior to 1965. Indeed, prior to the 1960s the historical ledger is conspicuously light on references to fear of crime. This absence is not just evident in the criminological archive, but in every relevant domain; social scientific, governmental, and popular media. This begets a number of conventional historical questions. Was fear of crime simply not experienced or expressed prior to 1967? Was this fear of crime overlooked by social inquisitors and if so, why? Did we simply not have the tools to find or identify this apparently ubiquitous fear of crime? Did we previously name what we now know as fear of crime something entirely different? The following discussion is based on the premise that these questions are misguided and would only inform a partial, presentist, analysis. I suggest this for two reasons. First, it would seem incongruous to presuppose that populations did not harbour concerns about crime and victimisation prior to 1967. While fear of crime as a concept might not exist, and while fear of crime might not constitute a common discourse as such, many episodes of what we might now call fear of crime, albeit problematically as I have intimated, are easily identifiable in earlier periods. Second, to suggest that fear of crime is simply 'discovered' in the 1960s suggests the pre-existence of a phenomenon that continues in a-historical sameness. This privileges a teleological history of social scientific inquiry that imagines the progressive uncovering of the truth about the social world, the enlightenment myth of the march of scientific progress. It also essentialises fear of crime as if it had existed apart from and outside the social, cultural and historical conditions, institutions and interactions where it is apparently experienced and/or expressed. Rather, as I will suggest in later chapters, the modern (or late modern) concept we now call fear of crime is a product of particular socially, culturally and historically contingent assemblages of governmental and political rationality, and regimes of truth configured through social scientific knowledge and power. Further, that the conditions provided by these assemblages rendered fear of crime intelligible as a criminological problematisation, and that this intelligibility introduced it into a field of discursive possibilities. Fear of crime was not 'discovered' in 1965 or 1967. Rather, from about 1965 all the socio-political elements, paradigms of knowledge and truth, and anxieties fell into place that made fear of crime a social scientific concept and so a legitimate cultural theme.

Methods

The following chapters constitute an altogether different project from any of the research outlined above although they do take the arguments of some later critical research as a starting point (Sparks 1992; Stanko 2000; Hollway and Jefferson 2000; Ditton and Farrall 2000; Loader *et al.* 2000; Jackson 2004). This book is not interested in contributing new methodologies or new conceptual tools to the measurement of crime fear. It is, rather, a history or, more accurately, a genealogy of the concept of fear of crime. While I draw on a number of analytical traditions, Michel Foucault's (1991) related concepts of genealogy and governmentality are central to the overall argument.

Genealogy

The writing of a history is always a fraught practice. Dominant presentist narratives will invariably offer frameworks through which certain versions of history will emerge to the marginalisation of others. Garland (2002) rejects what he describes as the 'progressivist', 'presentist' view of many histories which conceptualise criminology as a science which was 'waiting to happen'. I would also suggest that many versions of criminological history present criminology's objects of inquiry as waiting to be discovered – somehow pre-discursive. This approach, as Garland argues, ignores the cultural and historical specificity of the discipline, its knowledges, reasoning and investigative procedures; it cuts from view other problematisations that historical records reveal, and forgets that the way in which we constitute 'crime and deviance are through established conventions rather than unchanging truths' (Garland 2002: 13).

Similarly, to paraphrase Rose (1988), authoritative 'textbook' versions of disciplinary history establish a unity among the subjects of the discipline and construct a 'continuous tradition of thinkers' who have attempted to grasp the truth of its subject matter. The objects of the disciplines are thus rendered 'a-historical and a-social'; as pre-existing any attempts to study them. 'These histories establish the modernity of the science. They ratify the present through its respectable tradition …' (Rose 1988: 180). Through such historical narratives disciplinary boundaries become clearly demarcated and disciplinary subjects become objectified and naturalised. The discipline establishes its 'regime of truth', its legitimacy and authority about its chosen topic while criticism is largely silenced or rendered 'unscientific'.

The methodological process followed in this book is one described as genealogical (Foucault 1984), a 'history of the present'. I begin with the assumption that the phenomenon to be explained is a present day phenomenon – fear of crime – and that my task is to trace its historical conditions of emergence, identify the intellectual resources and traditions on which it drew and give account of its formation and development – to closely paraphrase David Garland (2002: 14). Foucault's genealogical studies have focused on three interrelated concepts, *knowledge, power* and *the body*; these concepts are used to analyse particular 'structures' or regimes of domination (Garland 1990: 137).

Fear of crime is a phenomenon that invites us to think of it as a-historical and outside of discourse. Its very conceptualisation as an 'emotional response' – as effect – produces understandings of it as given, as 'social fact'. Its cause is always to be sought elsewhere, either in recorded crime rates, misinformed or irrational individuals or in the media – it invites a search for its causal origins. Genealogy on the other hand opposes the search for 'origins' (Foucault 1984). It does not attempt to capture the pure essence of things or postulate that things have protected or hidden identities. Rather, genealogy seeks to identify the details and accidents that accompany beginnings, the small deviations, the errors and complete reversals, 'the false appraisals and faulty calculations' that produced *things*, knowledges, and 'truths' that continue to have value in contemporary settings (Foucault 1984). Genealogy sets out to re-establish and identify the systems of subjection by tracing *continuities* and *discontinuities* in regimes of knowledge and power. In short, this book will ask how fear of crime research was made do-able, and how fear of crime became a recognised object of governance. It seems to me incongruous to suggest that this fear was simply dormant in populations waiting for the 'science' or disciplinary practices of criminology to 'discover' it. Yet, it is equally incongruous to suggest that fear of crime simply did not exist prior to the social scientific discovery of it. So genealogy undermines the taken-for-granted nature of objects of governance.

Of course, suggesting there are historical continuities to anxieties about crime would not come as any sort of surprise to readers of, for example, Geoffrey Pearson's *Hooligan: A History of Respectable Fears* (1983). Pearson's work shows with some clarity that episodes of panic about the dangerous classes and other 'hooligans' can be traced to every generation. Indeed, he even terms this fear of crime. However, the application of such terminology is, as we will see, only possible as a result of Pearson writing in 1983. The term was certainly never used prior to the twentieth century. Genealogy offers the tools by which fear of crime might be explored in an alternative way. It can help explain why these fears were problematised and then understood, experienced and indeed treated, differently in these earlier periods from the way they are today. Having said that, one must be careful not to equate the development of a language or lexicon around crime fear with a totalising argument around its development. As I will demonstrate, there are continuities and discontinuities in the history of the concept of fear of crime. Nonetheless, the development of the concept of fear of crime is more than simply the development of a lexicon.

So this history of the present will also take account of how the emergence of fear of crime is situated within particular temporal, social, political and cultural settings. That is to say, while I begin with the notion that fear of crime is a present day concept, I do not wish to underplay the historical, cultural and political context of its emergence. To this end I note Loader and Sparks's (2004: 19) concern for the need to examine, in specific sites of activity, how actors whose relations constitute the field – politicians, civil servants, practitioners, campaigners, think tanks and criminologists – mobilise behind particular ideas or 'solutions'. In other words, this book is not blind to the politics – both institutional and popular – of the emergence of fear of crime.

Governmentality

Throughout this book I also draw implicitly on Foucault's (1991) notion of government, or governmental power, and, perhaps more importantly, on the subsequent and growing body of 'govern*mentality*[11] literature that has offered a framework for its analysis. These provide a useful framework for understanding how fear of crime became problematised, and how this problematisation led to attempts to regulate and control it; attempts at its governance. This analytic technique avoids the reductionist or totalising tendencies of many other methods of analysing political power, which usually proceed by attempting to identify which agents or institutions hold or possess it (Dean 1999). That is, my aim is not to simply suggest that fear of crime is a political tool for the powerful, although it may well operate as such in some situations (Rose 1999). Rather, an *analytics of government* attempts to reveal how the exercise of governmental power depends on ways of thinking (rationalities) and ways of acting (technologies) as well as ways of subjectifying populations to be governed (Garland 1997).

Scholars of governmentality have termed 'government' the 'conduct of conduct' (Dean 1999; Foucault 1982; Gordon 1991). Here government is not to be understood as narrowly as simply political structures or the management of states; rather the term is used broadly to designate more or less calculated modes or programmes of action aimed at acting upon the field of possible action of others (Foucault 1982). Thus, government is the act and art of conducting (directing, guiding, calculating, reasoning) and the conduct of oneself (one's behaviours, self-guidance, one's moral self-governance). The fear of crime field has also been occupied with conduct of individuals; it asks: how is conduct shaped by fear of crime? This is illustrated in the almost universally deployed fear of crime (victim) survey question: 'How safe do you feel walking alone in this area after dark?' The fear of crime field is also interested in how fearful conduct can be shaped or governed. This is illustrated on the one hand in attempts to reduce fear of crime in populations and on

11

the other, in attempts to encourage individuals to reduce their risks of a variety of forms of victimisation. Both have developed around them a range of governmental programmes, practices and technologies.

There are a number of identifiable if overlapping rationalities or domains that are constitutive of what Foucault referred to as the governmentalisation of the state. Amongst these would rank *police*, *liberalism*, and *statistics*. Let me briefly unpack these as they provide a basis of my later analysis of fear of crime's prehistory.

Foucault's notion of police was not simply that of a special agency whose stated aim was fighting crime. Rather *police* or 'police science' was a more general programme of regulation or domestic order that emerged in Europe from the waning of the Middle Ages (Dean 1991) and in Britain in the late eighteenth and early nineteenth centuries (Garland 1997). This domain was about what we might now think of as intelligence (or knowledge) on the one hand and regulation on the other: a positive programme that could act on knowledge – much like what we now term policy (Rose 1999). This programme was not necessarily oppressive. Rather, it progressively aimed to regulate freedoms and normalise populations. Its stated aim was to act as a 'foundation of power and happiness of States' (von Justi 1760, cited in Rose 1999: 24).

Liberalism as a political rationality emerging in the nineteenth century stresses the limits of intervention and so is potentially at odds with the programme of police. However, we cannot simply characterise a shift from the centrality of a police science to a liberal political economy in Foucault's genealogy of modern governance; techniques of police – and later policing – also underlay the regulation of liberal freedoms. The market and economy require governmental regulation to remain open, the citizen requires laws and regulations such that freedom might be exercised. For example, the census, a technique sharing elements of police science, is paramount for the liberal political economy.

Another overlapping and vital component of modern government is the 'science of state', statistics (Garland 1997; Hacking 1990). In the last two centuries, in particular, changes in the rationalities of government have produced what Carrington *et al.* (1996) have described as the 'statisticalisation' of government. In turn, the development of statistics has had its effects on techniques of government; a 'de-restriction' of the art of government through revealing that 'population has its own regularities, its own rates of death and diseases, its cycles of scarcity …' (Foucault 1991: 111). Statistics allows the problems of population to be made manageable and knowable. It allows a relationship of reflection, analysis, assessment and, as a result, malleability and regulation to be established between the bodies that govern and bodies that are to be governed. As Garland (1997: 178) puts it, the governmentalised state is tied up with the development of new social entities (the population, economy) and the development of social sciences that produce knowledge on them. Again, there is obvious overlap here with the programme of police and the rationality of liberalism; however, each have separate if intertwining genealogies. The story of fear of crime is one that is tied to the development of both statistics, as I've already suggested, and the social sciences that delineates the way they are counted and analysed. I will later suggest that statistics makes fear of crime knowable, produces a calculable object where only uncertainty existed; the social sciences frame, analyse and assess this knowledge. Any exercise of power relies on knowledge of the target or object of governance, whether it be natural or human: its forces need to be understood, its strengths and weaknesses known. The more known it becomes the more it becomes controllable or regulatable (Garland 1990). Cruikshank (1996) has noted in another context that the social sciences can be seen as productive sciences; the knowledges, data and measurements they produce are constitutive of relations of government as well as the subjectivity of citizens.

While Foucault himself often dealt with topics that related to the development of liberal governmental rationalities, a number of scholars of governmentality have attempted to advance Foucault's analysis of governmental rationality to the exploration of welfarism and neo-liberalism (Miller and Rose 1990; Rose 1999; Stenson 1993b; O'Malley 2000) or advanced liberalism (Rose 1999). It is suggested that broad programmes of government in Western democracies over the past two centuries can be identified as emerging under particular conditions at particular historical moments; police science, liberalism, welfarism, and neo-liberal being four such identifiable programmes. Obviously simple historical characterisation of these in terms of epochs is over-reductive and programmes of government are made up of many often-competing rationalities that vie for legitimacy. Nonetheless this group of scholars places emphasis on analysing how modern government increasingly relies on the exercise of 'government-at-a-distance'. That is, governmental power is translated through 'centres of calculation' and chains of actors across time and space (Garland 1997: 182). One of the central tenets of Foucault's conceptual framework is that the self becomes the subject of one's own government. The art of government is premised on the notion that the problem of population can be overcome by the development of a grid of governmental techniques and tactics through which subjects are not only governed, but take an active role in their own governance (the conduct of conduct). Here 'active subjects' of governmental power (or bio-politics) are enlisted to cooperate in delineating their own freedoms via the rationalities of marketisation, entrepreneurialism, prudentialism and consumerism (as active citizens). Under neo-liberal rationalities we might think of this as a process whereby citizens are 'responsibilised' (O'Malley 1996). While scholars have applied the analysis of neo-liberalism to the problem of understanding the shift away from state-based or 'welfarist' forms of social provision and the declining influence of 'social criminologies', here I want to focus on how these rationalities have also produced active subjects whose fear of crime becomes one's own responsibility to govern. I refer to this phenomenon in this book as the development of *fearing subjects*. These 'active citizens' are both the imagined or 'made up' targets of forms of government-at-a-distance, but also the responsibilised citizen seeking *inter alia* market solutions to their fear of crime problem and the avoidance of risky situations.

Thus, governance should be understood as a set of practices that are not in themselves intrinsically good or evil, positive or negative, oppressive or libertarian. In this manner the analytics of government employed here run counter to other criticism such as Marxism, which conceives power as a largely oppressive force exercised by one group over another. That is not to argue, however, that governmental power may not be exercised in oppressive ways or in manners that make it such for some subjects. Indeed, governmentality as method or critique is largely about identifying the actualities of government and by doing so also identifying other conditions of possibility, silences and resistances. It is about how government is thought into being in programmatic form and what concepts are invented or deployed to make subjects governable (O'Malley *et al.* 1997). In practising government, as Gordon explains, 'everything is dangerous, with the consequence that things are liable to go wrong, but also that there is the possibility of doing something to prevent this ...' (1991: 46–47). My argument in this book is that when it comes to fear of crime and its governance, things have indeed gone wrong. In part this book seeks to identify the unforeseen and unintended consequences of the development of the concept of fear of crime.

Arrangement of this Book

This book is divided into two parts. Part 1 Invention (Chapters 2, 3 and 4) deals with the historical emergence of the fear of crime concept. Part 2 Governance (Chapters 5, 6 and 7) deals with fear of crime and political rationality, and fear of crime as a tactic or technique of government.

Chapter 2 is a brief prehistory of fear of crime beginning in the late eighteenth century. Here I trace the development of domains via which fear of crime would become intelligible, the discursive surfaces on which it would emerge. I also argue that while fear of crime was not a concept prior to 1967, there were considerable anxieties expressed about crime and that this anxiety was helping push the development of a 'science' of crime. While the chapter encompasses discussion of the 'birth' of criminology it is not intended as simply a recital of a textbook version of history. Indeed, there are significant elements of criminological history that are not of importance here. Nor is it my intention to re-evaluate this entire history through the rather more nuanced lens of Foucaultian-style genealogy – although my aim makes this partially necessary. However, other scholars have done significant work in this area (Beirne 1993; Garland 2002; Pasquino 1991a) and the domains explored by the authors of these genealogies are vital to my analysis and provide links to my own genealogy.

Chapter 3 explores the initial emergence of fear of crime as a social scientific concept. The chapter contains an in-depth discussion of the apparent explosion of crime fear in the US in the 1960s and its attendant research. It also explores the political machinations in the US during the 1960s at which point the political purchase of fear of crime was both revealed and exploited. Perhaps most importantly though the chapter traces the development of a line of social scientific thought that made it possible to speak about fear of crime as an objective *thing*; something out there in the social world to be decoded by the researcher and deployed by the policy-maker.

Chapter 4 has two aims. One is to trace the migration of the concept of fear of crime across the Atlantic to the UK in the 1970s. This migration can be traced through a number of exploratory surveys and shifts in criminological thought through to the development and subsequent deployment of the British Crime Survey in 1982. Second, the chapter explores how these shifts in criminological thought from the 1970s to the late 1980s helped increase the criminological significance of a fear of crime research agenda while it also elevated fear of crime as a political issue and a governmental problematisation.

Chapter 5 considers how the variables of the fear of crime research agenda have been paramount in both maintaining fear of crime as an object of inquiry and providing a focus for governmental interventions into the lives of what I have termed *fearing subjects*. Here I use the variable of gender as an example and illustrate how the gendering of crime fear, and the subsequent governmental focus on women in the crime prevention literature, has helped drive both a research agenda and a popular and political discourse on crime fear.

Chapter 6 explores fear of crime as a tactic of government. Here I explore a variety of texts aimed at crime prevention and argue that fear of crime has been employed as a technique of 'responsibilisation'. That is to say, fear of crime, in line with a broader set of neo-liberal governmental rationalities, has been a tactic or technique of governance-at-a-distance; of producing *fearing subjects* that govern their own risks and manage their own safety. However, I also suggest that this *governance-through-fear* opens up crime fear to the private sector as individuals look for other ways of ensuring their security. I conclude this chapter with a discussion of the growing fear of terrorism in order to demonstrate how the discourse of fear of crime offers a blueprint for both the expression of fears and their political deployment and also to illustrate the spectre of a feared *other* in fear of crime discourse.

Chapter 7 explores this private provision of security and argues that, within the private sector, an array of expertise and products has developed in order to service a fear of crime industry. I also suggest that in providing this service the private sector is only too happy to play on public fears in the pursuit of profit. The opening up of crime fear to the private sector has implications for how it might be governed, particularly if governing fear of crime is really about fear reduction.

Like fear of crime this book crosses many international boundaries. It first visits Britain and France, explores the initial emergence of crime fear in the United States, crosses to the UK, touches on Australia and so on. This seemingly arbitrary nation hopping might be judged problematic, not least because of the locations it excludes; and there is no doubt that such exclusions and inclusions probably lead to some over-generalisation in the pages that follow. However, this book is a history of discourse; of knowledge, concepts and ideas. And these often know little of national boundaries. This is not to suggest though that fear of crime is experienced or researched in the same way in all localities. Rather, it is to suggest that particular forms of knowledge emerge at different times in different places, and that it is often particular assemblages of these that enable concepts to form. That said, every analysis, every history, has its exclusions, this one being no exception. I only hope these exclusions will not necessarily be seen as faults but as invitations to others to fill in the gaps.

Notes

1   In the name of readability I have resisted a strong inclination to place the term 'fear of crime' in inverted commas throughout this book. There would be good reasons for this strategy as will become clearer throughout this text. In part this book sets out to disrupt and render problematic the concept of fear of crime, open it to a range of interpretations and meaning,

and generally remind the reader of its shaky foundations. Of course such a strategy could only be partially effective. For try as we might to retain an 'open finding' on what the fear of crime might be, my socio-cultural baggage as writer, and your socio-cultural baggage as reader, will inevitably and repeatedly attempt to reconstruct meaning and objectivity around it. For my part, I don't necessarily want to resist this reconstruction. Rather, I want to allow meaning to reconstruct itself in ways that recognise that no construction can ever be complete, finished or whole; that there will always be an excess of meaning, an outside, an other that cannot be reconciled with any particular reconstruction. Thus, our reconstructions should be deferred – to borrow from Derrida (1977). The project here should not be to know or understand the concept of fear of crime but to observe it with all its contradictions and incompleteness; to understand how it functions discursively; with what language, knowledges, rationalities and mentalities.

2 Chris Hale (1996) carried out a thorough review of the body of scholarly crime fear literature. In 2000 Ditton and Farrall (2000a) assembled a collection of key writings in the field of fear of crime. While there have been 'advances' in this literature since then there seems little point duplicating these reviews. While this book discusses many of these central debates many are also footnoted in Chapter 1.

3 Thus, the fear of crime is said to: make some public places no-go areas (Garofalo 1981; Maxfield 1984; Maxfield 1987; Williams *et al.* 2000; Wilson 1975); erode a sense of community and neighbourhood and create a suspicion of neighbours (Box *et al.* 1988; Conklin 1975; Maxfield 1984; Skogan 1986; Taylor and Hale 1986), even causing some residents to move out altogether (Dugan 1999), engendering in some locations a spiral of community decline; fuel the security industry, with the more wealthy able to take steps to protect themselves (O'Malley 1992), adding to the sales of firearms in the United States in particular (Edmondson 1994: 19; Jones *et al.* 1986); exacerbate racism and xenophobia, the threat of crime being often projected on to minority groups (Chiricos *et al.* 1997; Sibley 1995; Skogan 1995); energise the law and order debate, potentially resulting in more punitive criminal justice measures (Cohen 1996; Hogg and Brown 1998); have detrimental psychological effects (Gordon and Riger 1989; Skogan 1986); induce some people to change their everyday activities and habits because of the fear of victimisation (Braithwaite *et al.* 1982; Hough and Mayhew 1985; Jones *et al.* 1986; Keane 1995; Stanko 1990); actually increase levels of crime as a result of many of the above effects (Maxfield 1984; Skogan 1986; Skogan 1989); prevent many women from taking an active role in public life (Gardner 1990; Garofalo 1981; Gordon and Riger 1989; Stanko 1990; Walklate 1995); prompt people to avoid public transport (Reedy *et al.* 1994); constrain the liberty of the elderly (Akers *et al.* 1987; Golant 1984; La Grange and Ferraro 1987); and/or constrain how women dress and express themselves (Braithwaite *et al.* 1982; Smith 1986; Stanko 1990).

From a critical perspective it is worth pointing out, even at this early stage, that the first six points here have also been identified as having causal links with the production of the fear of crime; no-go public areas and physical decay may increase a fear of crime (Wilson and Kelling 1982); erosion of community may create suspicion of one's neighbours and increase the fear of crime (Krannich *et al*. 1985); the security industry may attempt to increase the fear of crime in order to increase its market share (Weatherburn *et al*. 1996); racism and xenophobia create fear and suspicion of possible criminal activity of minority groups (Sibley 1995); advocates of punitive criminal justice measures using scare tactics may increase the fear of crime (Hogg and Brown 1998); women being afforded less access to public life, and thus being dependent on men, may increase the fear of crime (Carach and Mukherjee 1999). That is, the causal direction related to crime fear is not altogether clear. Or to put it another way, the *components* of the fear of crime are also used as *predictors* (van der Wurff *et al*. 1989; Williams *et al*. 2000) and the 'independent and dependent variables have been arbitrarily transposed' (Williams *et al*. 2000).

But wait, there's more! Other factors that have been identified as having causal links in the production of the fear of crime are: lack of confidence in the police (Baumer 1985; Bennett 1994; Wilson and Kelling 1982, 1989); poor street-lighting (Grabosky 1995; Reedy *et al*. 1994); incivilities, such as groups of rowdy teenagers in an area, drinking in public places, beggars (Maxfield 1984; Skogan 1986), or graffiti and neighbourhood decay (Skogan 1986; Skogan 1989; Wilson and Kelling 1982); and media representations of crime (Gunter 1987; Heath and Gilbert 1996; Williams and Dickinson 1993).

Hale (1996) also identifies vulnerability, personal knowledge about victimisation and perceptions of risk as contributing factors. Of course, in addition to these more 'concrete' causes and effects of fear of crime there is the more general question of 'what crimes are people actually afraid of?' Thus, research has focused on whether respondents are afraid of assault, murder, robbery, theft, sexual assault, domestic violence, pub violence, harassment, hate crime, and any number of offences (Jones *et al*. 1986; Lupton 1999; Stanko 1990) and of course which sections of communities are afraid of which crimes (Janson and Ryder 1983; Madriz 1997; Yin 1982).

4 http://quiz.ivillage.com.uk.uk_politics/tests/crime.htm

5 One of the most consistently recorded statistical correlations in fear of crime research is that between fear of crime and direct experience of being a victim of crime (Smith and Hill 1991; Stafford and Galle 1984). However, as Maxfield (1984) argues, the effects of victimisation on fear also vary greatly according to the specific type of offence the victim endured. For example, the 1982 British Crime Survey results indicated that crimes which involve direct confrontation with a stranger, although very 'rare', were most likely to instil fear in the victim. Thus, crimes that involved the threat of physical harm, such as robbery or sexual assault, were likely to be the most fearful offences (see Maxfield 1984). There is therefore a range

of responses to a range of events that can here be placed under the fear of crime concept.

6 Much fear of crime research has found that women are less likely to become victims of crime, yet as a group express a greater fear of crime than men (Baumer 1978: 354–364; Furstenberg 1971: 601–610; Garofalo 1979: 80–97). Braithwaite *et al.* (1982: 222) in examining the findings of an early Australian study on fear even went as far as to suggest that '[t]he objective reality of rape, bad as it is, is surely of less importance to women than the way that fear hems them in to a protracted day-to-day existence'. Fear of sexual assault is said to regulate women's freedom of movement, self-expression, and social experience (Gordon and Riger 1989; Stanko 1990). The UK Home Office in one report described this restricted existence as 'living under curfew'. Younger women – those women most at risk of victimisation – are the least fearful. Fearfulness increases with age as a result of repeated victimisation and learned responses (Jones *et al.* 1986).

7 See for example Hough and Mayhew (1983), Maxfield (1984) and Skogan and Maxfield (1981). Vulnerability is once again said to be a factor (Hale 1996). Mugging – or more accurately assault – is the offence that is the most feared form of victimisation. This fear climbs steadily until after age 60 and then jumps sharply (Maxfield 1984).

It is also argued that older people's social circumstances may impact on their levels of fear. Most have lower incomes, lower levels of education and less social support from other family members than their younger counterparts. Walklate (1995) has more recently argued that when fear of crime for the elderly is positioned within the broader context of worries about finances, health and other problems, the fear of crime recedes in relative importance. This reading might suggest that the fear of crime for the elderly is often more an artefact of research design than a reflection of the lived realities of respondents. Alternatively, Ferraro and La Grange (1987) have suggested that the elderly only express higher levels of 'formless fear' and that on concrete measures of fear the elderly express no more fear of crime than other demographics.

8 Maxfield (1984: 3), for example, goes into some detail in attempting to define his subject. He argues that at its most basic, 'fear is an emotional and physical response to a threat'. When danger is posed, psychological changes occur automatically to help people cope with the threat, a 'fight or flight' reaction. Thus, for Maxfield, danger is a component of fear. Importantly, he suggests that fear is different from a 'more general concern' about crime in that 'it presents a threat to oneself', a personalised threat rather than abstract views and beliefs. He argues that one might be concerned about a rising crime rate but not be in the slightest way afraid of being personally attacked.

So for Maxfield anxiety is also a component of fear but risk assessment is a separate issue. Carach and Mukherjee (1999: 6) simply suggest that fear of crime 'refers to people's emotional response to crime'. For them the personalised threat element is seen as less important than the more general anxiety, quite at odds with Maxfield's definition. Similarly, but with a more individualistic focus, Taylor (1988: 384) defines fear as 'an emotional affective concern for one's safety'. The latter obviously includes at least some component of personal risk assessment and indeed management, thus also differing from Maxfield's definition. Ferraro and La Grange (1987) have argued that fear of crime, given its many divergent meanings, may have lost its utility altogether, although Ferraro argues in a later publication that fear of crime is 'an emotional response of dread or anxiety to crime or symbols that a person associates with crime' (Ferraro 1995: 4).

9   The most widely used measures of fear of crime are, despite the conceptual debate, those of the large-scale victim survey. This style of survey originated in the US but is perhaps best illustrated in the form of the questions asked in the British Crime Survey (BCS). Hale (1996) concludes that the measures taken in these surveys lack an emotional content and as such fail to give any indication of the rationality or otherwise of the replies, thus they are not measures of fear *per se*. Some of these surveys (Weatherburn *et al.* 1996) have discarded the notion of fear – at least explicitly – and specifically attempted to measure the respondents' personal assessment of their own risk. These studies use reported crime data to calculate the actuarial risk to individuals of becoming victims of specific offences and measure perceived risk in relation to this. Ferraro and La Grange (1987) would be critical, suggesting that measurements of fear of crime should tap emotional states of fear rather than judgements about crime concern.

Some researchers (Gomme 1986; Ollenburger 1981) have suggested that to accurately measure fear of crime the focus should be on the behaviour of respondents. The general argument is that the extent to which individuals alter their behaviour will indicate, or be a measure of, their fearfulness. However, others have argued that these changes in behaviours are consequences of fear rather than indicators, and as such they could be considered inconsistent across sample groups (Garofalo 1981; Maxfield 1987). Fattah and Sacco (1989), however, suggest that there may be vast divergences between how respondents really behave and how they say they behave, and that self-reported conduct can be vastly erroneous.

10   Some researchers have suggested that much fear of crime centres not on fear for the self, but fear that others may be victimised (Maxfield 1984; Reedy *et al.* 1994). Unsurprisingly, it has been mainly family households that have shown such a propensity. In the British crime survey of 1982 only 35 per cent of respondents who replied that they were worried about crime, were worried about being victimised themselves; thus their fears were projected on to significant others in their lives (see Maxfield 1984). Maxfield (1984) terms this 'other-directed' worry and suggests that it can be focused on other adults sharing the respondent's household (43 per cent) and the children of the respondent (22 per cent). Warr (1992) argues that women in particular experience 'altruistic fear', the fear of other family members being victimised.

11 Specifically, Foucault (1991: 102-103) defines governmentality thus:

> The ensemble formed by institutions, procedures, analyses, and reflections, the calculations and tactics that allow the exercise of the very specific albeit complex form of power, which has as its target population, as its principal form of knowledge political economy, and as its essential technical means apparatuses of security.
>
> The tendency which, over a long period and throughout the West, has steadily led towards the pre-eminence over all other forms (sovereign, discipline etc.) of this type of power which may be termed government, resulting on the one hand, in the formation of a whole series of specific governmental apparatuses, and, on the other, in the development of a whole series of *savoirs*.
>
> The process, or rather the result of the processes, through which the state of justice of the Middle Ages, transformed into the administrative state during the fifteenth and sixteenth centuries, gradually becomes governmentalised.

Foucault (1991) counterposes governmental forms of power to these sovereign forms of power. Sovereign power, he suggests, is exercised from above, with the provenance of God over men. Although sovereign power may well have as its aim the 'common good', in its ultimate circularity the common good is 'obedience to the law, hence the good for sovereignty is that people should obey it' (Foucault 1991: 95). Governmental power is distinguishable from sovereign power in that the former relies on tactics and technologies for arranging things, whereby the latter relies on laws. Governmentality is government through knowledge, primarily knowledge of the population whose government it seeks.

Part I

Invention

Chapter 2

Fear of crime: a selective prehistory

> The poor and vicious classes have always been and always will be the most productive breeding ground of evil-doers of all sorts; it is they whom we will designate as the dangerous classes. (Fregier, quoted in Chevalier 1973: 141)

> In a subject like the crime and vice of the metropolis, and the country in general, of which so little is known – of which there are so many facts, but so little comprehension – it is evident that we must seek by induction, that is to say, by a careful classification of the known phenomena, to render the matter more intelligible; in fine, we must, in order to arrive at a comprehensive knowledge of its antecedents, consequences, and concomitants, contemplate as large a number of facts as possible in as many different relations as the statistical records of the country will admit of our doing. (Mayhew 1862: 1)

To understand the invisibility of fear of crime up until the 1960s and its subsequent 'discovery', this chapter will explore both the epistemological underpinnings of early social scientific inquiry and also historically situated questions of how crime problems are/were made intelligible and governable beginning in the mid eighteenth century. It then explores criminological and sociological expansion in the early to mid twentieth century and the implications for the study of crime fear. Finally, it discusses twentieth-century media reportage that sees fear of crime increasingly become a topic of interest. The chapter draws on textual material produced via a number of seemingly disparate socio-political domains over almost a 200-year period; these include statistics, legal and moral philosophy, police, criminological and other social scientific texts, governmental and political proclamations, news media and popular representations. As this chapter will demonstrate there are continuities evident in the invention of fear of crime that date back to at least the late eighteenth century and are undoubtedly linked to the forces that gave rise to what we now call *modernity*. Ultimately, the chapter explores and identifies a variety of bodies of knowledge and thought which constitute discursive surfaces onto which the concept of fear of crime could and would eventually emerge.

Anxiety, power and the eighteenth-century 'science of police'

To feel fear in one form or other may be part of the human condition, however the concept of fear of crime is a much more recent socio-cultural construct. While this concept does not become fully formed (or conceptualised) until the 1960s, changes that begin in the mid to late eighteenth century no doubt lay the foundations of this formation. The processes associated with *modernity* were well underway by the mid eighteenth century and would accelerate over the course of the nineteenth. New modes of social life, new forms of social organisation (Giddens 1990) as well as the emergence of secular traditions based around scientific rationalities and Enlightenment philosophy were transforming Western European cities and nation states and undermining traditional feudal conventions and notions of divine right. An obvious historical point of reference for the emergence of the modern world is the French Revolution of 1789. The expansion of trade, industry and agriculture would lead to the massive growth of European cities just as it would lead to the dispossessed rural poor being gradually transformed into cheap or surplus labour. This labour would satisfy the demands of the Industrial Revolution into the nineteenth century (Burke 2005: 3). While burgeoning industrial activity began to create a new and powerful middle class its waste by-products, both human and material, began chocking up the infrastructure of cities, creating new risks and anxieties. Lack of appropriate housing, extreme poverty, overcrowding and disease made for squalid conditions for masses of the new urbanites. Unsurprisingly, these conditions saw increases – and perceived increases – in criminal and immoral behaviours as they almost simultaneously ushered in contradictorily new and exciting urban experiences (Hayward 2004). Meanwhile, space and time were being reconceived as more dynamic and changing (Ellin 1997). While the upwardly mobile bourgeoisie sought new ways to master this change and insecurity in technological terms – the wristwatch, personal calendars, timetables, town clocks and the like – they also became increasingly anxious about the lack of discipline and control in the poor and lower classes. Over time the technological rationality of the wristwatch and the timetable would have their equivalent in the development of the workshop, the workhouse, the school, the prison and the factory which attempted to master time, space and the human subjects within. This was a context in which traditional forms of social life were dissolving and new norms were also being forged. With new forms of freedom and control over one's life came new kinds of insecurity, not least the insecurity of change itself. Between 1750 and 1900 many of the elements that would later make fear of crime a thinkable concept began to assemble.

Was there fear of crime in the late eighteenth century? The question is probably not wholly answerable for it projects a modern-day concept and problematisation on to the past that would not recognise it. In this sense there was not. However, we can easily identify the contours of something we might now recognise as crime fear. Historian Clive Emsley (1987) amongst others gives a valuable insight into the anxieties and concerns in the era. Emsley argues that concerns about the level of disorder can be detected amongst the propertied classes of England following the Gordon Riots in 1780. Moreover, these fears then continued through the years of wars against Revolutionary and then Napoleonic France. This period of intense urbanisation and industrialisation saw food shortages, high prices, riots and social dissent in England. Tales of street massacres and guillotining in France, and the menace posed by British Jacobins, probably heightened these fears. In 1784 the *St James Chronicle* suggested that 'If robbers continue to increase, as they have done so for some time past, the number of those that rob will exceed those who are robbed' (cited in Emsley 1987: 61).

However, it was not just in the news media of the day that anxieties about crime were being expressed. In 1785 in *Thoughts on Executive Justice*, the conservative magistrate Martin Madan (cited in Emsley 1987: 61), suggested that:

> No civilised nation ... has to lament, as we have, the daily commission of the most dangerous and atrocious crimes, in so much that we cannot travel the roads, sleep in our houses, or turn our cattle into our fields, without the most imminent danger of thieves and robbers ...

These examples are illustrative of an anxiety about and urgency to govern criminal offending that would further develop. They also illustrate that behind this urgency to govern crime lay class-based anxieties and a will to ensure social order.

Contemporaneously, thinkers influenced by Enlightenment philosophies that we now regard as criminological 'classicists', such as Cesare Beccaria (1738–1794), Jeremy Bentham (1748–1832) and John Howard (1726–1790), were producing new programmes and strategies for the 'rational' governance of crime and punishment. Their work was informed by a concern for how a civilising state could regulate forms of behaviour it regarded as criminal through the administration of criminal law and the treatment of the criminal (Radzinowicz 1948) – a move from the relative *ad hoc* administration of justice at parish level conducted by elected officials. Many of their concerns constituted and were informed by a body of political knowledge known then as the *science of police*. Pasquino (1991b: 108–109) notes that the 'science of police' was the culmination of a vast literature which traverses the whole modern period supporting the construction of 'social order' since at least the Enlightenment. He suggests this body of knowledge was:

> known in the eighteenth century as both 'the science of happiness' and 'the science of government', which constitute[d] society as the object of knowledge and at the same time as the target of political intervention …

This secular science originated in German-speaking parts of Europe (*polizeiwissenschaft*), Italian states and France and was articulated as a political rationality from about 1600 to 1800 (Rose 1999). It is instructive that Beccaria held a Chair of Political Economy and Science of Police in Milan in 1769. The science of police was not articulated in the negative sense we understand police today, as an organisation charged with the prevention of crime and the maintenance of order. Rather, it was a positive programme (Dean 1991; Pasquino 1991b; Rose 1999) based upon knowledge which would act as 'the foundation of the power and happiness of States' (von Justi 1760–61 cited in Rose 1999: 24). It aimed to regulate public and political economy. Through the political rationality of *science of police* a range of technologies and techniques across a broad domain become intelligible as relatively coherent programmes of regulation; early statistical databases, programmes of moral improvement, workhouses, prison environments and the like all aimed to regulate through constituting population as an object or objects of government. Most of these strategies also dovetailed with mercantile aspirations to produce 'regularly labouring people' and so increase the 'strength of the country'.[1] By the time the term criminology came into common usage in the late nineteenth century, there were a number of 'ready-made' concepts or objects of inquiry upon which the discipline could and would focus (see Beirne 1993), many initially emerging as objects of regulation through a science of police aimed at maintaining the happiness of the state through the regulation of the indolent and threatening.

In 1751 George II (cited in Zirker 1967) made a direct request that England's sound financial position be directed to the attention of internal social order:

> Make the best use of the present state of tranquillity, for improving the trade and commerce of my kingdoms; for enforcing the Execution of Laws; and for suppressing the Outrages and Violences, which are inconsistent with all good Order and Government; and endanger the Lives and Properties of my Subjects.

For Henry Fielding, writer, magistrate, moral reformer, and regarded by many historians as a founder of modern Britain's policing system,[2] the 'immorality' of the lower class, social unrest and crime were all connected and very 'real threats to liberty'. While he notes in mercantile terms that 'the strength and riches of a society consists in the numbers of people is an assertion which hath attained the force of a maxim in politics' (Fielding cited in Dean 1991: 28) he also suggests that 'riots and tumultuous assemblies were dangerous to the public peace and a threat to civil government and all civilized life' (cited in McMullan 1998: 138). Indeed, the reformer's zeal, evident in writings such as his pamphlet *Enquiry Into the Causes of the Late Increase of Robbers* (1751), is accompanied by the equally colourful descriptions of the dangers of middle-eighteenth-century London, particularly in his fictional literary works.

Fielding and his brother John developed models for policing in London based – for the most part – on the premise that by reorienting and redeploying the hitherto diffuse law enforcement apparatus a more systematic and efficient body of knowledge could be collected. This knowledge would provide a basis through which *the poor* and lower-class immorality generally could be subject to new and more intensive forms of surveillance and regulation – both moral and legal. For the Fieldings' technical strategies were coupled with moral preventative measures that emphasised the need for education and forms of moral training and tutelage aimed at expanding the pool of available labour. Their policing reforms sought to use the apparatuses of government to gather knowledge of the population, knowledge through which regulatory power could be exercised employing both legislative reform and social interventions with the aim of producing new forms of moral subjectivity; a form of normalising subjectifying power. Like other moral reformers of his time, Fielding did not draw attention to the questions of abject poverty or class stratification and their links to crime and disorder; indeed he saw the poor as necessary to the 'happiness of the State'.

Fielding's reform strategies imagine the exercise of a form of what Foucault has termed pastoral power.[3] Foucault notes the importance of the eighteenth century in 'a new distribution' and a 'new organization of this kind of individualizing power' (1982: 783) as well as a 'derestriction' of government based on the newly identified problem of population (1991: 99). Administrative government was already rudimentarily familiar with 'statistics' within the juridical framework of sovereignty. However, with increasingly populated cities it was soon revealed that population had their own 'intrinsic' regularities including aggregative rates of poverty, disease and crime amongst other statistical certainties (Foucault 1991: 99); these were the new targets of government. The promotion of a secular form of moral salvation was becoming part of governmental rationality; individual health, well-being, security, protection against accidents were to be targets of government. Moral reform was being promoted by way of both identifying and attempting to overcome the potential of a threat within. These governmental strategies imagined the formation of subjects that could take up prescribed forms and the delineated freedoms that followed this normalisation (Rose 1999). Foucault suggests that pastoral power might be exercised through a range of state and private apparatus and institutions; the police, health authorities, welfare societies, benefactors, philanthropists, the family, medicine, hospitals. This power is focused on the development of knowledge of 'man' around two roles: one globalising and quantitative, concerning the population; the other analytical, concerning the individual.

Fielding's plans draw on this 'science of police' and speak to a form of subjectifying pastoral power; establishing as they did a knowledge nexus aimed at the location, supervision, disciplining and containment of the poor or lower classes which threatened the emerging social order. While we can identify the exercise of this new form of power and the rationalities that enable it in Fielding's plans, we can also identify that class anxieties were in turn, and in circularity, driving these developments. Fear of crime might not have been a concept but crime fear no doubt had a relationship to knowledge, power and indeed the development of proto-criminological thought. It is this relationship between the fear of a domestic threat of crime and attempts at its government through new modes of knowledge, calculation, and the exercise of power which makes the mid eighteenth century a useful starting point to trace this continuity in fear of crime's genealogy.

By 1795 the London magistrate, moral reformer and once Glaswegian merchant Patrick Colquhoun (1799) was able to argue strenuously that London's 'evils' were debilitating for a society which valued liberties. Colquhoun used this argument to justify his calls for law reform, recommending *inter alia* the development of a more professional and centralised preventative police; a 'new science ... in the prevention and detection of crime' (cited in McMullan 1998: 147). But, as with Fielding, the moral improvement and regulation of the masses were never far from his mind. Indeed, he saw idleness, depravity and working-class passions as the target of his version of 'police science'. Colquhoun's reforms conferred upon his 'new police' a new and more restrictive definition, to 'protect' and 'detect crime' (1799) and conceived an apparatus completely separate from judicial power. These shifts in the rationalities of governing crime become more intelligible with the knowledge that Colquhoun's systematic and economical approach to prevention and detection were strongly influenced by his close relationship to Jeremy Bentham (Dean 1991). Moreover, Colquhoun provides colourful testimony to the form concern about crime took in the period. He suggested:

> ... all ranks must bear testimony to the dangers to which life and property are at present subjected to by the number of criminal people, who ... are suffered with impunity to repeat acts of licentiousness and mischief, and to commit depredations upon individuals and the public. In vain we boast of those liberties that are our birthright, if the vilest and most depraved part of the community are suffered to deprive us of travelling upon the highways, or of approaching the Capital from any direction after dark, without risk of being assaulted and robbed; and perhaps wounded or murdered ... if we cannot lie down in our habitations, without the dread of a burglary being committed, our property invaded, and our lives exposed to imminent danger before the approach of morning. (Colquhoun 1799: 2)

So Colquhoun, like Fielding before him, described in some detail the problems and anxieties that were exercising his thought and motivating his work. Moreover, his reforms coincided with the period of scarcity in England that intensified a focus on the plight of the poor. The problems he described were at the heart of the emerging liberal rationality and posed in those terms – 'all ranks', 'liberties'. Moreover, Colquhoun was in the business of finding answers to, and producing knowledge about, the crime problem:

> If, in addition to this, the peace of Society can, on every specious pretence, be disturbed by the licentious clamours or turbulent effusions arising from ill-regulated passions of vulgar life, surely it becomes an interesting inquiry, worthy the attention of every intelligent member of the community … where is a remedy to be found for so many accumulated evils. (Colquhoun 1799: 3)

Colquhoun's invitation to inquiry again exemplifies how what we might now call fears were partially responsible for mobilising both inquiry into and new strategies of governing crime. But we need to be clear. This was not fear of crime as we understand it today. It was never referred to as fear of crime in the literature of the day and it was certainly not conceptualised as some kind of broadly measurable phenomenon despite concepts like 'happiness' being an inherent part of the science of police. While a range of European thinkers turned their attention to the measurement, regulation and governance of numerous objects of inquiry, essentially constructing the body of knowledge about problematisations that would later become criminological, they never once attempted to know the nature of, measure, or enumerate, crime fear.

David Garland (2002: 20) instructively lists the concerns that 'classical' proto-criminological thinkers occupied themselves with: 'modern' concerns about the legal institutions, which he notes, were also becoming 'recognisably modern'; concerns about the systematic arrangement of criminal laws and procedures aimed at promoting social policy goals; about sentencing choices; about police organisation and conduct; about the design and purpose of prisons and their regimes. They questioned the psychology of offending, the nature of motivation, the possibilities of deterrence, and appropriate ways for state institutions to regulate individual conduct. As Garland points out, these were concerns of a newly modernising world. They were thinkable only as a consequence of the emergence of a new administrative state, new state apparatus, a market society and a will to develop new modes of governing and regulating these and the individuals and populations that constituted them. It is instructive to the discussion here that fear of crime, or indeed any notions of public attitude towards crime, is absent. This is not the result of Garland's neglect or oversight. Quite simply questions of crime fear were unaskable at that historical moment and would, I'd suggest, even have been construed as unscientific. While crime was being increasingly problematised as an issue *for* government, this problematisation did not extend to a reflexive notion of the public anxieties or fears that helped motivate these enquiries – to enumerate 'fear', to split anxiety from the question of crime's prevalence, reduction and governance, was simply unthinkable.

Governing a new world of industrial disorder?

In the nineteenth century industrialisation and modernisation accelerated apace and European cities of unprecedented size arose – and along with them anxieties about the new urban condition. Moreover, the nineteenth century was, as Zehr (1976: 12) puts it in the context of cities of France and Germany, 'punctuated with economic crises' which brought 'danger and actual starvation to some of the population' and meant uncertainty for others. Hundreds of thousands were affected by the changes where the threat of 'change itself caused fear and discontent'.

Colquhoun's call for a general social enquiry 'into the unregulated persons of vulgar life' was answered by a growing number of legal, social and moral reformers. For example Wade (1829) produced an enquiry into the crimes and their causes in *A Treatise on the Police and Crimes of the Metropolis*. This was subheaded *An Inquiry into the causes of the Increase of Crime*. Wade's treatise examined the final stages of the 'parochial police' or night-watchmen, as Peel's centralised force gradually took over the policing of metropolitan London; a result of the Metropolitan Police Act of 1829. Indeed, Tobias (1972) argues[4] that Wade may have played some part in securing passage of the Act. Wade's text is full of both colourful accounts of the anxieties of the early nineteenth century, and also how crime might 'sensibly' or rationally be governed:

> ... the robberies committed in a crowded street, only last November, amply show that the ancient leaven of violence and ferocity is not extirpated; and so long as these traits are observable in the character of the populace, every considerate mind must be sensible of the necessity of a powerful police to the safety of the community. (Wade 1972/1829: 27)

By this point the broad programme of science of police is largely redefined by a policing model that is much more familiar to us today; a 'powerful' police required to keep the 'safety of the community'. Periods of panic in Britain during the nineteenth century can be identified in relation to a number of more specific spectacular crimes: the Ratcliffe Highway Murders of 1811 where two families were gashed and bludgeoned to death; the metropolitan 'garrottings' of the mid 1850s and then again in 1862; and the Jack the Ripper murders of autumn 1888. However, perhaps the most obvious fear, at least for the propertied classes in the early nineteenth century, emanated from forms of political resistance evident in the working classes which were still seen as a demonstrable threat to the established social order.

Indeed, the three decades following the Battle of Waterloo saw social unrest in both England and France. Political dissent triggered riots and demonstrations and accompanying demands for a variety of reforms. All these intensified fears amongst the ruling classes despite the major part of this dissent being expressed in peaceful form (Emsley 1987). These fears were clearly reflected in responses to demands for social reform, such as the following news editorial opposing reformers pushing for universal suffrage published in *Bell's Weekly Messenger* (number 1819, Sunday, 6 February 1831):

> Property being a great temptation, acting most violently upon the bad passions of men who have NONE, requires it to be invariably guarded by the possession of political power ... To say that Universal Suffrage would overturn the balance of the Constitution, or to say that it would destroy the Crown, the Church, and the Aristocracy, is not to express one-tenth part of the evils which would flow from it. It would render all kinds of possession insecure; it would unfetter every evil passion, and demoralise the whole population. A more fearful and flagitious revolution could not take place than by introducing such a principle ...

In late-1830s to early-1840s London there was a notable peak in anxiety about crime and social disorder. One response, influenced by the Malthusian inclination for poor law abolitionism first championed in the 1820s, was to deny able-bodied workers poor relief so as to enable them to overcome the proclivity to *indigence* (Dean 1991). The British Poor Law Amendment Act of 1934 legislated a clear delineation between the deserving and undeserving poor (through the principle of less-eligibility) resulting in both the abolition of relief to able-bodied males and a responsibilising of these same males for the support of their women and children as 'natural' economic dependents. Idle hands were to be put to work in 'respectable' workhouses ideally based on models of containment and supervision envisaged by Bentham's panopticon. Indeed, Bentham himself imagined workhouses with governors who would have powers of apprehension and control over all aspects of paupers' daily lives. Subject to this liberal ethos of government the individualised worker devoid of the possibility of collective action

– which was also legislated against – would be responsibilised into a labouring subject. The law of the free market would apply to the free individual, inciting self-regulation for fear that the need for relief would result in the abrogation of freedom (Poovey 1995). The result was an intensification of the exercise of pastoral power with delineated forms of subjectivity being even more clearly articulated. Concern about crime, poverty, economy, freedom, and the appropriate role of government in all of these were interweaving concerns and projects. Bentham's influence in all these spheres seems to clearly confirm this.

The early nineteenth century saw years of acute economic depression as well as radical and industrial agitation, culminating in 1842 with a second Chartist petition. It was at about this point that the term *'les classes dangereuses'* – used by the French public official Honore-Antoine Frégier[5] to describe a growing 'criminal class' in France – was anglicised and taken on by the British landed gentry as a way of defining their 'fears'. This term, first appearing during the period of the French Restoration (1814–1830) was popularised by Frégier's 1840 study of urban criminality, *Des classes dangereuses de la population dans les grandes villes, et des moyens de les rendre meilleures* (see Beirne 1993: 98). Certainly from the 1830s to the 1850s there was a sense of foreboding that social order would disintegrate in both London and Paris. Engels (1844 cited in Philips 1977: 13) understood the situation in London as follows:

> The clearest indication of the unbounded contempt of the workers for the existing social order is the wholesale manner in which they break its laws. If the demoralisation of the worker passes beyond a certain point then it is just as natural that he will turn into a criminal … Consequently the incidence of crime has increased with the growth of the working class population … The criminal statistics prove that this social war is being waged more vigorously … every year.

Engels' words also remind us that some writers at least conceived crime as an expression of class relations and exploitation rather than moral depravity or a lack of self-discipline, causally related to the growth of unfettered capital expansion and liberal principles of the open market.

Anxiety about class and crime would endure. However, there would be a change in the way this anxiety was rationalised as the 'dangerous classes' were gradually subjected to new strategies of classification, differentiation and individualisation and subsequently new regimes of discipline and normalisation. In 1840, the Tory Sheriff of Lanarkshire, Sir Archibald Alison, was able to suggest alarmingly that 'destitution, profligacy, sensuality and crime [were advancing] with unheard of rapidity in the manufacturing districts'. Moreover, this advance was identified with the massed 'dangerous classes' who he suggests 'combine every three of four years in some general strike or alarming insurrection, which while it lasts, excite[s] universal terror' (cited in Phillips 1977: 14).

Louis Chevalier (1973) describes a similar situation in 1840s Paris, a pathological or 'sick' city where dangerous classes threatened an increasingly frightened bourgeoisie. While in France the 'process' of industrialisation lagged behind the British experience, so too the work of moral reformers followed their British counterparts and many social descriptors and models were borrowed haphazardly:

> in many cases the description of poverty and crime in Paris originated in a knowledge of a state of affairs that was probably worse in London than in Paris, or at any rate had been more fully studied, measured and known. The poverty of other towns was elevated with reference to the science and statistics of poverty in London. (Chevalier 1973: 133)

This developing preoccupation with the 'dangerous classes' towards the mid nineteenth century, and the apparent failure to normalise or regulate them, is instructive. It locates the pre-criminological concerns about crime with an identified social group or groups; the dangerous classes became identifiable. As Frégier had noted:

> The poor and the vicious classes have been and will always be the most productive breeding ground of evil-doers of all sorts; it is they whom we shall designate as the dangerous classes. For even when vice is not accompanied by perversity, by the very fact that it allies itself with poverty in the same person, he is an object of fear to society, he is dangerous. (cited in Chevalier 1973: 141)

Crime and poverty constituted fear and dangerousness. The population of Paris had doubled between 1801 and 1851 leading Chevalier (1973) to note that the growth in this mass alone must inevitably lead to intractable problems. Beirne, drawing from Chevalier's observations of Restoration France, suggests:

> The new prominence of crime in the description of urban life in France can be attributed to the fear of the criminality of the so called dangerous classes that endured, at all levels of French society, throughout the nineteenth century ... Paris [w]as a city in which the citizenry was engrossed in reports of crime as one

of their normal daily worries; in certain winters of cold and destitution the fear of crime reached heights of panic and terror. Reports of crime were ubiquitously conveyed in newspapers and eagerly devoured by their readers; in some cases ... fear was transformed into morbid fascination ... The widespread fear of crime was exacerbated by working-class insurrections ... That the carceral institutions had failed to normalize the dangerous classes was therefore confirmed, at least for a fearful and fascinated public, by the rising rates of crime and recidivism during the first years of the Restoration. This failure is an essential condition for the appearance of a vast corpus of studies, instigated by both state bureaux and private researchers, which sought to uncover the vital statistics of the dangerous classes. (Beirne 1993: 69–70)

Beirne, writing in 1993, is able to use the language of fear of crime, precisely because by then it is now a common criminological concept. In nineteenth-century France there is little evidence that it was despite Frégier's use of the term *fear*[6] in relation to dangerous classes. Nonetheless, Beirne's characterisation alerts us to the period's heightened anxieties of crime, and the way in which these were specifically pushing the calls for an expanded social scientific enquiry by 'state bureaux and for private researchers' and for new ways to know and govern the problem of the 'dangerous classes' along with the newly problematised notion of recidivism. Thus, the drive for new ways to understand crime and its punishment in nineteenth-century France was being accelerated by anxiety about crime and about various forms of offending which were in turn being understood as being linked to the so-called 'dangerous classes'. Indeed, Baron Haussmann's rebuilding of Paris in the mid nineteenth century was partially driven by a desire to displace the 'dangerous classes' in order to reduce the threat to the dominant social order (Ellin 1997; McLaughlin and Muncie 2000). This was to be achieved in a number of ways. The new boulevards would signify bourgeois order and rationality while the new houses would signify class; the process would result in the clearing of working-class districts and the dispersion of communities, decreasing the possibility of coordinated public dissent; and finally the construction would provide thousands of jobs for the 'dangerous classes', ensuring that the capacity and proclivity for dissent were reduced (Ellin 1997).

So what of the fledgling body of thought we have come to call criminological? The so-called eighteenth-century classicists, with their focus on *homo penalis*,[7] had applied a plethora of new legal strategies to the general operation of criminal justice systems under which they would operate: new legal codes, new policing models, new prison programmes; new measured punishments. However, the goal of reducing offending seemed illusive. Fear of the dangerous classes was growing in the popular imagination and this required the further attention of both government and the emergent tools of the social sciences. Indeed, the application of this new social scientific knowledge also had the effect of identifying and problematising an increasing number of objects to be governed. With a more centralised apparatus for the administration of criminal justice and its growing bureaucracy came the possibility of enumerating crime in hitherto unimagined ways. This is exemplified by the 'new' threat posed by recidivists as something requiring attention.

The concerns of governing crime and regulating and/or reforming the lives of the dangerous classes led to other pre-criminological work that would have a profound effect on the emergence of the concept of fear of crime some 130 years later, and should be thought of as continuities of this genealogy. In the seminal work of early social statisticians like the Belgian mathematician and astronomer Adolph Quetelet (1984: originally published 1827), French lawyer Andre-Michel Guerry (1833), W. R. Greg in the Netherlands,[8] and R. W. Rawson (1839),[9] Joseph Fletcher (1850)[10] and John Glyde[11] in the UK, and the emergence of Statistical Societies in Europe in the nineteenth century, we see a new enumeration of crime and the emergence of a geo-spatial demography of offending. New statistical techniques focused more specifically on both the general prevalence and the spatial distribution of crime. Offending is 'mapped' by Quetelet in 1827 and increasingly these mapped rates of offending are linked to other social indices. Quetelet's work is cited by numerous authors across Europe and the UK (Levin and Lindesmith 1939), including those early statisticians cited above. This work, conducted at the time largely by amateur social scientists and for largely philanthropic reasons, pre-empted later surveying and statistical collection and calculation – the enumeration of criminology's objects of study. As 'moral statistics', or the 'science of state' (statistics), became recognised as a fundamental component of governmental calculation this new political rationality rendered the production of a new range of (pre) criminological objects possible. In short, nations were being inscribed and described in terms of aggregated statistics and regular fluctuations; hitherto invisible processes and phenomena were made calculable and knowable (Rose 1999: 321) and new modes of government rendered possible. The work of doctors, teachers, philanthropists and police and their new forms of collecting data fed this new thirst for enumeration and urban space was mapped and refigured.

Quetelet's work can largely be seen as a 'scientific' response to new public and governmental concerns of the late eighteenth century identified above – to govern through knowledge of the population. There is little doubt that the genealogy of the fear of crime as a concept is intimately entwined with the development and deployment of crime statistics more generally – statistics we might say are a broad but vital continuity and condition of its emergence. The enumeration of offence rates, of crime itself, has a complex genealogy upon which I can only touch (see Hacking 1990), but without this development it would be unthinkable that fear of crime would be enumerated as it was to be in the 1960s, and without enumeration fear of crime, the concept, would not be rendered thinkable.

In many ways it should be self-evident that concern about crime would influence the development of criminology, a discipline born of identifying the aetiology of crime and prescribing ways to govern it. However, we should not forget that the development of criminology is also intimately related to the technical advances of social scientific methods and an attendant will to knowledge. We might recognise these two conditions of emergence as a nexus of knowledge and power. The power to define dangerous classes was to coincide with new statistical knowledges aimed at calculating recidivism and offending more generally.

As Piers Beirne (1993: 68) has eloquently argued:

Positivist criminology really emerged from the intersection of two hitherto unrelated domains of state activity. From the domain of penalty, criminology garnered an institution position, a measure of financial support and considerable popular interest in its pronouncements. From the domain of the statistical movement, criminology acquired its intellectual orientation and recognition by the scientific community of its major discursive techniques. The many sites of these two domains were entirely separate until, during the Bourbon Restoration (1814–30), they coincided in a common issue – the apparent failure to normalize the conduct of the 'dangerous classes'.

Concerns about the so-called dangerous classes and how they should be governed, or indeed how their conditions could be ameliorated, drove reforms in criminal law (Radzinowicz 1948), punishment (Pratt 1997), welfare policy (Dean 1991), urban planning (Ellin 1997) and they drove the development of what would become criminological knowledge more generally. Fear of crime may not have been conceptualised or problematised in the nineteenth century. It did nonetheless possess productive capacities.

Topinard's baby

While the term dangerous classes became general parlance in Britain, anxiety about crime subsided, or at least shifted, for most of the second half of the nineteenth century, punctuated by the particular specific episodes of moral panic I have already outlined, in particular, anxiety about garrotting. By way of example, Tobias (1979: 70–71) quotes a popular magazine of the day, which highlighted the anxiety of a garrotting[12] outbreak in 1862 in London: 'once more the streets of London are unsafe by day or night … the public dread has almost become a panic'.[13] Garrotting also became general parlance from the 1850s onwards, as this report from *The Times* (9 September 1856: 9) illustrates:

> From information derived from the police it appears that garrotting offences are on the increase, that there are a gang of the worst characters, upwards of 40 in number, most of whom are believed to be ticket-of-leave men whose location is the neighbourhood of Duck-lane and Pye-street, Westminster, who may be seen nightly arranging themselves into bands of four or six, and then spreading themselves over various parts of the metropolis. It is from this gang that the majority of offences originate.

So although there was concern about crime, its articulation had changed. It was now identifiable offenders and very specific offences that were an affront rather than the more general concern about dangerous classes. The following letter to the editor appearing in *The Times* neatly encapsulates the situation in London:

> Sir,—As I was walking this evening (Thursday) at 6-o'clock through Temple-bar two young fellows, respectably attired, passed by quickly, and in passing one of them aimed a blow at my hat with a view to knock it off. Immediately after another gentleman was struck, and his hat dashed to the ground. Thinking this was a little too bad, and it being moreover very like a thieves' dodge, I rushed back and seized one of our assailants by the collar. After a desperate resistance and several attempts to hustle and throw me down, by the friendly aid of two working men, one

of whom lost his hat in the affray, I succeeded in detaining one of these 'gentlemen' for some five minutes, until the arrival of two policemen, by whom he was marched off to the Bow–street station. On the way thither I was treated to the foulest language, and threats of personal violence as soon as he should get free again.

When, however, the fellow saw that I was resolved to charge him with the assault, he altered his tone, and made an humble apology. I, therefore, consented, in a moment of weakness, to forgo the charge. I beg, however, to give notice to 'gentlemen' of this description that I do not mean to be so foolishly lenient again. In these days of garrotting, and personal violence, every outrage of the above nature is calculated to excite great alarm. Had I a lady with me she would have undoubtedly been much terrified, and probably the ruffian would have got off scot-free. Or else, as is more probable, I might have inflicted immediate and severe injury upon him with a heavy umbrella stick which I always carry. I beg to offer my thanks through the medium of your columns, to the bystanders who assisted in the capture. I trust that every attempt at insult or personal injury will be instantly avenged by the persons on the spot. The public have their safety to a large degree in their own hands. If the police are not able to protect us we must and will shift for ourselves.

A CLERGYMAN, London, Nov. 20. (*The Times*, 22 November 1862: 5)

Here the more general discourse of dangerous classes is noticeably absent. Both the threat and the offenders are individualised despite the fact that these are 'days of garrotting and personal violence'. Indeed, here the offenders are 'respectably attired' and the heroic bystanders 'working men'. Moreover, the concern about garrotting is rationalised through the discourse of inactive or insufficient (preventative) policing; police who are 'not able to protect us'. The protective function of police has become normalised. This is illustrative of the invention of new social scientific and popular types of personage, most important amongst these the 'respectable poor'. Offenders cannot simply be identified by the classification of social class. This accompanied the development of the proto-sciences of sociology, criminology and anthropology (Joyce 2003), and more broadly, the invention of the 'social' as a site of governance (Donzelot 1979; Rose 1996).

In the later part of the nineteenth century Britain and other European states witnessed the introduction of a range of acts aimed at both prescribing freedoms and limiting their forms. From restrictions on child labour to the construction of regulated prisons and workhouses to measures of compulsory education, liberal rationalities were transforming the art and practice of government. Similar transformations were under way in the United States where new categories of dependent, dangerous and delinquent persons were being distinguished (Rose 1999: 112).

Emsley argues: '[w]hile there may have been periodic concerns about the dangerous classes during the second half of the nineteenth century, the anxieties never appear to be as acute as in the preceding half century' (1987: 41). This optimism is easily traced in writing of the time. Pike (1873/1968), whose teleological *A History of Crime in England* is a pertinent example, argued:

> The sense of security is almost everywhere diffused, in town and country alike, and it is in marked contrast to the sense of insecurity that prevailed at the beginning of the present century. [A]ny man of average stature and strength may wander about on foot and alone, at any hour of the day or night, through the greatest of all cities and its suburbs, along the high roads, and through unfrequented country lanes, and never have so much as the thought of danger thrust upon him, unless he goes out of his way to court it. (Pike 1968: 481)

Likewise David Philips (1977: 83) argues that by the late 1850s, the 'fear of public disorder' had become less of a pressing issue in England as the memories of the 'Hungry Forties' receded. However, he also notes that this was being replaced by a more general concern about more 'normal crime' (property offences and interpersonal violence) and particularly juvenile crime. Although these had been matters of concern prior to the 1840s, 'normal' crime had always been seen as linked to general disorder. However, concern about the dangerous classes did not die away altogether and was still readily articulated in popular discussion about crime policy. As *The Times* reported in 1863 in terms which seem so familiar to us now:

> The dangerous classes seem to be getting the better of society … Under the influence of philanthropic sentiments and a hopeful policy, we have deprived the law of its terrors and justice of its arms. (*The Times*, 2 January 1863, cited in Pearson 1983: 118)

So along with what appear to be periods of relative security, we still see episodes of anxiety about both criminals (the dangerous classes) and crimes (garrotting). A subtle change of focus no doubt, but anxieties all the same. One reason for this change in attitude might be the decrease in overt political dissent in the second half of the century and the pacification of the working-class population with respect to a new range of governmental interventions. A second and no doubt related reason would be the rejuvenated economy of London and a resultant expansion of suburban development mirroring something of the French programme identified above. Another, however, might be the development of the new science of crime focusing on the criminal and the aetiology of offending. That is, as Pasquino (1991a) put it, the focus on the new personage of *homo criminalis* in which criminal offending could be located – a focus that began with Quetelet's later work but which found its most explicit expression with the classificatory and individualising gaze of Lombrosian criminal anthropology. Population as a problem had become highly atomised.

However, the Lombrosian criminal anthropology of the Italian School was only one embodiment of the emerging field of positive criminology and it would be wrong to discount the work of other figures in the process of knowing the offender[14] which have far closer resonance with this genealogy. Social researchers were at the forefront of pushing this shift in the way offenders and offending were rationalised and problematised in the mid nineteenth century. By the late nineteenth century Charles Booth was producing socio-spatial maps of London depicting the classes of residents street by street with a concern to locate the dangerous and demeaned (see Rose 1999). Henry Mayhew amongst others[15] argued strenuously for the need to classify offenders in order to have any thorough understanding of the causes of crime, suggesting that 'habituals' should be identified in record keeping separately from 'casual' criminals:

It is impossible to arrive at any accurate knowledge of the subject of crime and criminals generally without first making this analysis of several species of offences according to their causes; or in other words, without arranging them into distinct groups or classes, according as they arise, either from an habitual indisposition to labour on the part of some offenders, or from the temporary pressure of circumstances upon others. (Mayhew cited in Levin and Lindesmith 1939: 808)

Mayhew's position is also exemplified in the quotation that opens this chapter. The detail in this early ecological work was paramount in shifting governmental discourse and intervention in regard to offending. It also rendered the problem of the criminal knowable in a manner that went beyond the enumeration of offenders and offending. In Britain this new focus on the *habitual* individual criminal and his/her lifestyle also had its articulation in the passing of the Habitual Criminals Act 1869, reflecting the importance of the discovery of this new personage. By 1870 Lord Derby, addressing the annual meeting of the Discharged Prisoners Aid Society at Manchester, was able to suggest:

> We have taken a great step in the last year or two in the passing of the Habitual Criminals Act. We have begun to recognise the fact that, although with our utmost vigilance and utmost care, the prevention of individual and isolated offences is impossible, it is still possible, and it is our duty, to protect society against the existence of the class who live by making war upon property. (*The Times*, 18 January 1870: 10)

Pratt (1997) identifies this shift in changing rationalities of government. The focus on the recidivist, or habitual, criminal began to overshadow that on the dangerous classes – although as we have seen the two could not be completely dissociated. In short, new forms of liberal government began a process of pacification or at least fragmentation of the working-class population.

> The introduction of such measures as state policing, growing educational provision, the internalisation of industrial work habits and routines, and the securing of territorial boundaries all helped to pacify and fragment those forces which at the beginning of the modern era had the capacity to challenge state power and authority itself. (Pratt 1997: 15)

So the dangerous classes began to fragment in both the popular and governmental imagination, positivist criminological enquiry allowed dangerousness to be identified as separate, individual. The criminal could even be articulated as a different species. This was in line with a strong epistemological shift that followed the publication of Darwin's *Origin of the species* (1902: originally published 1859). While this might not of itself make the spectre of the dangerous classes any less of a threat, it at least identified the threat through new systems of categorisation, rendering it knowable and offering a variety of spurious hopes for a cure for criminality or at least for the prevention of crime. Indeed, we see in accounts of criminality in the later nineteenth century the gradual identification of a smaller criminal recidivist class – as opposed to the more numerous dangerous classes which could never in any case be separated from the general labouring classes (Chevalier 1973). The criminal class, as one commentator of the time argued, 'is in very fact a recognised section, and a well known section too, in all towns of great magnitude … It constitutes a new estate, in utter estrangement from the rest' (*Eclectic Review*, vol. vii (1854) cited in Tobias 1979: 57).

Arguably the term 'criminology' first came into use in 1879 when the French anthropologist Topinard used it to describe 'the science for explaining the causes of criminal behaviour' (Garland 1985; Walters 2003). I say arguably because Piers Beirne (1993) has assembled a compelling case suggesting that Raffaele Garofalo first used the term *Criminologia* in 1887 and that prior to this Topinard's use was actually of the term *criminalogie*. Whatever the case, criminology, in its infancy, now offered a science of determining factors, a positivist scientific method, for the study of the criminal, *homo criminalis*, a newly identified personage. This marked a disjunction, but not a complete discontinuity, as we have seen, from earlier enquiry informed by enlightenment philosophy (Walters 2003), whose imagined target was *homo penalis* (Pasquino 1991); that is, the shift of focus from the subject of penalty, premised on the free will actor, to the subject of criminal or offender, increasingly premised on the predetermined – socially or biologically – actor.[16] Indeed, it was at this point of history, this shift, when criminology began to constitute a discrete disciplinary body of knowledge.

By the late nineteenth century this was explicitly and clearly articulated in the increasing plethora of positivistic criminological work. Morrison in 1891 (cited in Tobias 1979: 57) is able to write:

> There is a population of habitual criminals which forms a class by itself. Habitual criminals are not to be confounded with the working or any other class; they are a set of persons who make crime the object and business of their lives; to commit crime is their trade; they deliberately scoff at honest ways of earning a living, and must accordingly be looked upon as a class of separate and distinct character from the rest of the community.[17]

The reasons for the outbreaks of crime fear in the later nineteenth century are not completely clear. They do not necessarily coincide with jumps in recorded levels of crime – although the criminal statistics of the time must be treated with some scepticism. Indeed, some officials used much the same discourse in order to placate concerns then as they do now. In October 1875, in addressing the inaugural Social Science Congress at Brighton, Lord Aberdare suggested:

> You may consider yourself fortunate if you escape being suspected of a secret sympathy for burglars. As little success attends your efforts to administer consolation or to calm fear, by reminding your

excited friends, when some well known person has been robbed in the streets and the usual assertions are made of the increased daring and number of the robbers, and of the sad degeneracy of the police, that robberies were twice as numerous in London ten years ago as they are now. (cited in *The Times*, 'The Social Science Congress, 8 October 1875: 6)

Pearson (1983: 283) has argued that public fear and various outbreaks of moral panic seem to coincide with periods of political and social instability. There is some merit in the argument, as we have seen, and this theory may well account for the 'respectable fears' he identifies. However, Emsley (1987) contests Pearson's account on the grounds that in the late nineteenth century there was relative social and political stability in England. He points to news reportage and the repetition of notions like dangerous classes as also having a role to play in particular outbreaks of anxiety about crime. Zehr (1976) notes also the decreasing emphasis on the sanctity of private property towards the end of the century and suggests that panic about property crime began to dissipate with this change in public mind. Whatever the case it is not of central interest to this genealogy. Rather, what is of concern is the relationship of this anxiety about crime to the development of social scientific knowledge and the rationalities, technologies and techniques of governing crime: the relationship between knowledge, power and fear, as it were.

All this raises very interesting questions of continuity and discontinuity. It can be said, with all certainty, that the study of, or concept of, fear of crime did not exist in early nineteenth-century France, or the UK, or anywhere else for that matter. On the other hand, however, it can be persuasively argued that crime fear, or its nineteenth-century equivalent, was a significant driving force in the development of pre-criminological objects of research; indeed, a condition of emergence of the fledgling discipline of criminology more generally. That is, if it were not for a growing concern for the normalisation of the 'dangerous classes', driven by new knowledge such as that provided by the 'moral statisticians', policing organisations, social surveyors and the like of the time, it is unlikely that criminology would have developed in the way that it has and around the concepts it has. As Beirne put it, two unrelated domains of state activity were unified by this preoccupation. So while fear of crime was not an object or concept of the fledgling discipline, it was certainly a force driving its development.

Garland's (2002) *History of British Criminology* offers an insight into the criminological enterprise which is worth repeating in full here. He explores how, once the criminological enterprise begins, the many threads of what could be considered pre-criminological work become resources for the new discipline.

> None of these discourses was struggling to create a distinctive criminological enterprise, though once such a subject was created each formed a resource to be drawn upon, usually in a way that wrenched its insights about crime apart from the framework which originally produced them. (Garland 2002: 23)

There are some striking similarities here between the development of a new discipline in the nineteenth century, and what has been referred to as the later 'big bang' period of criminological expansion in the late 1960s (Rock 1994). In both periods there was a popular, and subsequently political, preoccupation with crime. In both periods the fear of political insurrection was intertwined with – and in some cases indistinguishable from – a fear of, or concern about, crime. In both cases marginalised groups became the focus of public fears, the so-called poor and dangerous classes in nineteenth-century France and the UK, Afro-Americans in 1960s USA. Finally, in both periods, technological advances partly driven by popular discourse made possible new objects of analysis.

So while there is no doubt a continuity in public concerns, or panics, about crime which can be traced back at least as far as crime rates could be rudimentarily collated, there is also a rupture or discontinuity which can be identified in the 1960s and on which I will expand below. The 'discovery' of crime fear in the 1960s did not occur simply as a result of the increase in its prevalence, as the various accounts of nineteenth-century concerns above make clear. Rather, it occurred as a result of the alignment of a number of historical conditions of emergence, some of which were absent from earlier periods. One notable omission from eighteenth-century and nineteenth-century criminological thought was any interest in the concept of victimage. There was no such thing as a victim survey in the nineteenth century.

Twentieth-century agendas

By the early twentieth century, criminological and sociological interest in the link between news reporting and crime increased. Interestingly, however, it was not suggested that reportage necessarily increased anxiety or fear about crime. Rather, the thesis was that news reportage increased criminal offending through the high level of imitation or 'copy-cat' as it might now be termed. This contagion thesis was not new. Indeed, proponents of this position drew on criminology's founders Lombroso, Garofalo and Tarde amongst others. Lombroso had long argued that the imitation of crime as recited in the media was a major concern. In 1899 (54–55) he went as far as suggesting that:

> Civilisation, by favouring the creation and dissemination of newspapers, which are always a chronicle of vices and crimes, and often are nothing else, has furnished a new cause of crime by inciting criminals to emulation and imitation.

In the early twentieth century this thesis was taken up by a number of authors. In the US Fenton (1911) suggested that the publication of crime stories incited crime, drawing on an analysis of six papers over a nine-day period. In 1929 Holmes expanded on Fenton's thesis. He noted that '[s]ince the rise of criminology in the middle of the past century there is no writer of note on the subject who has failed to comment on the evil influence of the media' (Holmes 1929: 6). So while Holmes notes criminology's preoccupation with the media, it is, once again, not in relation to any fear, panic or anxiety it may disseminate. He goes on:

> Writers on hypnotism which is but an extreme form of suggestion, agree that one cannot be induced to commit an act by suggestion that is contrary to his moral standards. The hypnotist is releasing tendencies which his subject already has or he develops only the most superficial tendencies. The reader who doubts that men can be led to kill by suggestion, and many of those men of the highest moral type, is reminded of the potency of wartime propaganda carried on in no small part through the agency of the press. (Holmes 1929: 56)

There are a couple of points to be made here. One, that an interest in media reportage was well established from the late nineteenth century onwards, making it a staple criminological concern and one taken up with enthusiasm in the twentieth century. Two, with this underlying criminological assumption that the media can shape opinion and even influence human action in the form of criminal activity, it is not so surprising that, when crime fear did become an object of enquiry in the 1960s, the media was seen as a significant causal factor from very early on. Indeed, I would suggest that criminology's increasing focus on the media from the early to mid twentieth century was a discursive surface on to which fear of crime enquiry could emerge; a condition of emergence, although perhaps less important than some others explored in this chapter.

Like other criminological problematisations, the level of reportage of crime itself was to be increasingly enumerated. In 1938 L. Wilson was able to analyse the tenor of news opinion. Again he enumerated and categorised news content about crime. Fear of crime is of course not one of his categories. However, he does note that in editorials 'while indignation ran high for a time, it was usually short lived and satisfied by superficial efforts rather than any real attempts to eliminate basic causes of criminality' (Wilson 1938: 215). By 1952 Davis (1952: 330) was able to suggest that 'there is no consistent relationship between the amount of crime in newspapers and the local crime rates'. Here the discourse shifted from the content argument of Holmes to a focus on sheer volume – reportage apparently outstripping the reality. Drawing on Wisehart's (cited in Davis 1952) hypothesis, Davis (1952: 325) suggests 'newspapers may increase their crime coverage out of all proportion to increases in crime', thereby implying that a 'crime wave' is under way. The analysis championed by Davis is a precursor to both the moral panic literature and indeed the fear of crime field in its problematisation of the gap between objective crime rates and levels of crime reportage.

However, the emergence of these lines of enquiry did not occur in an institutional vacuum. Indeed, this expansion of criminological problematisations was part of a general expansion of the field of criminology among an ever-increasing range of institutions. Between 1930 and 1960 the criminological enterprise gradually cemented itself into both governmental agencies such as the Home Office and into some universities as an academic discipline (Radzinowicz 1999; Walters 2003). In the UK the Home Office Research Unit was opened in 1957 as a policy-led site of criminological research while the Home Office also set up the Cambridge Institute of Criminology for undertaking scientific research and training recruits for the newly founded discipline of criminology (Garland 2002). The United States saw the opening of the National Institute of Justice in Washington DC in 1968 – a significant historical moment in the development of crime fear as a criminological concept. However, the push for criminological research into new sites did not emanate only from a national level. Indeed, there was a more global push for the expansion of criminological enquiry which had its genesis in the rights agenda of the United Nations and the need for global post-war reconstruction. This reconstruction, and the aid monies earmarked for such a task, was often dependent on social stability. Indeed, Walters (2003) draws our attention to the rhetoric of social defence which drove the development of much government-sponsored criminology in the post-war period. While the war had ended, a new threat to stability was identified within. As Walters (2003: 33) notes, 'criminological research was an element of reconstruction, as crime became an internal threat to safety and prosperity.'

One of the most pressing targets of research, both for the United Nations and for the growing number of national research bodies, was juvenile delinquency. Indeed, the panic about the perceived growing problem of delinquency, and the teenager more generally, began to drive the research agendas of these growing academic and bureaucratic bodies. Concern about juvenile delinquency appeared as a major issue once public opinion research began to take off in the 1950s. For the UN, and particularly the UN Social Commission, crime prevention became a progressively important issue. It was crime prevention that was to provide a social defence and this was all to be tied to broader issues of socio-economic development (see Lopez-Rey 1974 cited in Walters 2003: 30). Elements of the UN criminological platform of the 1950s, a platform which informed the development of the criminological social scientific enterprise more generally, were juvenile delinquency, police-driven crime prevention and, significantly, the compiling of criminal statistics. In order to take this agenda forward the UN Social Commission forged links with national organisations and recognised experts, further pushing international criminological research and helping strengthen and develop the new research sites.

While this institutional activity continued apace, the drive for an expansion of public opinion surveys also gained momentum. In 1949 the first conference on *Attitude and Opinion Research* was held in Iowa. While the conference took election polling as its starting point it flagged public opinion polling in an increasing number of public domains. The conference was attended by pollsters and social scientists. It was reported in *The New York Times* (Blair 11 February 1949: 15) that pollsters George Gallup and Archibald Crossley agreed 'that there was much more to public opinion research than political polls'. Gallup added that he had set up a new department to 'try out every new idea in polling'. Samuel Stouffer, of Harvard University Division of Social Relations, went on to describe polling as an 'instrument of democracy'. All up, the delegates agreed that polling had a 'brilliant future' in areas such as 'public health, government, economics, *crime*, labor relations, education, *law* and other fields' (Blair 11 February 1949: 15, my emphasis). Citizens would have a contribution to make in discussion about crime and its governance and their *attitude* would count, and be counted.

Simmering away behind the expansion of the social scientific enterprise and the equally expanding domains of the pollsters was the increasing use of the term fear of crime in news reportage. While, as

I have suggested above, the term was not used in the eighteenth or nineteenth century in any systematic way at all, it begins to appear in odd news reports by the 1930s. However, it is well worth noting that the term is often attributed to 'experts' as this quote from *The New York Times* (22 January 1934: 9) under the headline 'Lynching Spirit Laid To A Fear Of Crime' indicates: 'The growing trend toward mob violence in this country is born of fear springing from the increase of crime, Dr. John Elliot, senior leader of the New York Ethical Culture Society, said yesterday …'

This would no doubt be one of the earliest articulations of the term fear of crime. Importantly, it is deployed here in much the same context and with much the same meaning as we might use it today. We could argue about whether the term here actually came from the newspaper sub-editor or from Dr Elliot himself, and we might well trace its use even further back – although I've not yet seen an older usage which is in context. What is important though is that by 1934 in the US it was possible to speak of a fear of crime much as we do today, although it was certainly not a term in general usage, nor was it yet a criminological concept. By 1950 another 'expert' is reported in *The New York Times* using crime fear in a similar context, under the headline 'Parents Advised On Sex Crime Fear Are Told to Avoid Hysteria and Teach Danger to Children in Matter-of-Fact Manner' (Barclay 1950: 33). The expert in this case, Mrs Irma Hewlett, was a former member of the professional staff studying the problem of sex offenders at Sing Sing prison.[18] She is quoted as suggesting that 'burdening children with an adult's fear about what "might happen" can result in making them look upon every stranger as dangerous'. It is important to note that this early usage in the US was not mirrored in the UK or Europe.[19]

As we move into the 1960s a change in discourse becomes apparent. By 1961 one newspaper is able to speak of a 'Park – Crime Fear Held Unjustified' (Talese 1961: 17). The article then goes on to quote a police captain who suggests that the public are overestimating the levels of crime in the park and that their fears are actually a 'fear of darkness'. Here we see a notion of the irrationality of crime fear raised. Whatever the case, within three years of this article fear of crime would make much more regular appearances in the news media. Indeed, in searching news media archives in the US, as I have done in researching this book, the explosion of fear of crime stories can be easily traced to around 1965. By as early as 1964 it was reported that Manhattan's Upper West Side had become a 'fortress of fear', or so a local survey had reported (Robinson 1964: 1). By 1966 the *Washington Post* is able to report that 'the No.1 worry in Washington is crime' (2 October 1966: 1). These articles were both front page.

Yet juvenile delinquency continued as *the* problematisation of the time for governments in Western democracies. This moral panic was interwoven with general issues of morality and what was seen as the rise of a 'permissive' society. As recorded crime rates reportedly rose throughout the late 1950s and then into the 1960s, concern for the social fabric of the West heightened even further. However, while these moral panics have historically recurred, as is evident from the discussions above, the new modes of social enquiry that were emerging would allow these panics to be measured in innovative new ways. There were now designated sites of criminological knowledge and these were expected to be productive in addressing any number of pre-existing and emerging problematisations. Moreover, they were hungry for objects to study.

Simultaneously, this period also saw the expansion of the mass media – including the democratisation of a new technological medium, television. With this the population were able to see themselves, and reflect on these new images in ways that had hitherto been unimaginable. In regard to crime they did not like what they saw. The spectre of rising recorded crime rates was easily interchangeable with more general civil unrest, as images of protesters of various hues made their way into the Western democratic living room. The panic of the time is also evident in new genres of cinema which appeared in the period. The juvenile delinquent was writ large in films such as *Rebel Without A Cause* where the viewers – and director – attempt to struggle with the causes of juvenile discontent. Indeed, the title itself connotes that the search for causes is futile, again raising questions of more general morality and permissiveness, despite the empathy that might be conjured for James Dean's character's plight as he drifts into delinquency.

Conclusion

From the late eighteenth century it is possible to trace how concern about crime drove the problematisation of pre-criminological objects of enquiry. Yet, fear of crime itself was not one of these. In the nineteenth century the enumeration and mapping of offending provided the platform or model for the later enumeration of criminological concepts like fear of crime and offered a basis on which risk calculation could later be developed. The discovery of recidivism and its identification with particular classes and, later, types of personage provided the possibility for the projection of one's fears on to identified threats. The development of pre-criminological domains of enquiry and subsequently criminology as a discipline provided a discrete nexus of knowledge and power and with it a new will to understand and problematise an increasing range of issues. Once the discipline developed an institutional base its hunger for objects of enquiry increased dramatically. Over this period crime came to be treated probabilistically. It was no longer random but predictable and calculable.

In the late nineteenth century one such issue became the relationship between crime and the media. Although this relationship was first articulated by criminology's founding figures as one of criminal contagion, by the early twentieth century the discussion around the media had become increasingly sophisticated. Here the gap between media coverage and 'actual' levels of offending came into the spotlight for the first time and rudimentary attempts were made to enumerate this in line with positivistic social scientific thinking. Contemporaneously, by 1938 other 'experts' began to use the term fear of crime as a way of explaining the public reaction to criminal offending in the United States. At about the same time pollsters and social scientists were inventing new ways to represent public opinion and to 'democratise' knowledge about the population. These new reflexive possibilities were complemented by the new technological innovation of television which allowed for a different type of reflection. Crime could enter the middle-class living room in hitherto unimagined ways.

These conditions of possibility are not part of a history waiting to unfold, some infinite teleology. That the study of crime should even be separated from the study of other social phenomena was not a given. That cycles of criminal offending should be enumerated was connected to broader governmental rationalities that were themselves contingent on socio-demographic processes related to industrialisation and modernisation. That public opinion data should become thought of as a democratising tool was a result of a particular form of liberal governance and so on.

This chapter has attempted to delineate a brief prehistory of fear of crime. In doing so it has identified a number of conditions of possibility that would later make fear of crime a thinkable object of social scientific enquiry. It has outlined how it was possible for fear of crime to come into discourse on both a general and criminological level. Chapter 3 explores how fear of crime emerged from these conditions of possibility.

Notes

1 The first quotation is from Nicholas Barbon (1690), the second from Quaker John Bellers (undated), both cited in Dean (1991: 28).

2   See McMullan (1998) for an alternative view.
3   Foucault argues that the development of the modern state constituted not just a new political form but a new form of individualising power; it integrated in a new political shape, 'an old power technique which originated in Christian institutions' (1982: 783). This power, refigured in a new guise, sought to ensure worldly (rather than spiritual) individual 'moral salvation' and to know the minds or 'souls' of those it subjectified; it could not be exercised without this knowledge.
4   Writing in the forward to the 1972 reprint of Wade's text.
5   An official of the city of Paris and author of a number of works on the history of public security and welfare.
6   As an aside it is used in Chevalier's (1973/1958) text from which Beirne draws. What is striking about this is that it is used in a similar context to the one in which we now use it. This would make Chevalier a very early 'user' of the concept.
7   On, as Beirne (1993: 5) puts it, the application to crime and penal strategies of a 'science of man'.
8   Levin and Lindesmith (1939) note that Greg, in his *Social Statistics of the Netherlands* (1835) mapped crime in much the same way as Guerry and Quetelet before him, producing five maps in his publication.
9   Rawson was an early champion of statistics in Britain and advocated strongly for their take-up as a strategy of government in his role of Honorary Secretary of the Statistical Society of London (see Johnson 2000). His own work – broad as his objects of inquiry were – was instrumental in early understandings of the differences between rates of offending in the cities and regional areas (Morris 1957).
10 Levin and Lindsmith (1939) note that Fletcher 'read three papers before the British Association for the Advancement of Sciences of London' which were later incorporated as *Summary of the Moral Statistics of England and Wales* (1850). Fletcher, Rawson's successor as Honorary Secretary of the Statistical Society of London, used Rawson's statistical divisions of England and Wales to explore the relationship between education and crime in much the same way Guerry had done so earlier (Morris 1957).
11 Glyde's work demonstrated how county or country aggregates of persons committed for trial masked considerable differences between smaller geographical units (Morris 1957).
12 Highway robbery in which a victim is throttled.
13 Cornhill Magazine, November 1862, vol. VI: 646–7.
14 Criminology's positivist turn, driven in part by the debates around Cesare Lombroso's *L'Uomo Delinquente* (1876), tends to shadow the earlier enquiries of Quetelet, Guerry and other moral statisticians. However, as Garland (2002) tells us, although the emergence of a 'positive science of the criminal' made Lombroso almost a household name, his original formulations about the nature of *criminal man* were quite heavily reworked to be included under the new umbrella term *criminology*. While the new science of crime was positive, however, causality was understood in a variety of ways, some more determinist than others.

15 'The importance of a direct personal study of criminals outside of institutions to gain understanding of their attitudes and motives and techniques was emphasised by many writers' at this point (Levin and Lindesmith 1939: 807).

16 The 'birth' of criminological positivism was anything but the sudden 'scientific' turn that many textbook accounts of criminological history recite. As Garland's (2002) and Beirne's (1993) detailed and thorough accounts of the development of British criminology and positivist criminology respectively identify, the continuities and discontinuities in the prehistory of criminological thought are not as straightforward as is usually assumed in commonly rehearsed potted histories; in particular the pre-criminological domains identified by Garland (2002), and the subsequent continuities and discontinuities in rationalities which inform the shift from what Pasquino (1991a) and Beirne (1993) characterise as the figure of *homo penalis,* to that of *homo criminalis* as the object of pre-criminological enquiry.

17 In Morrison, W.D., *Crime and its Causes* (1891): 141–142.

18 A notorious US prison in Ossining on the banks of the Hudson River, constructed in 1828.

19 My inability to speak multiple European languages places limits on my authority to claim this point emphatically. However, it seems clear to me that it was in the US that 'fear of crime' as we know it today first emerged into discourse.

Chapter 3

Anxieties in the knowledgeable society: the birth of a new criminological object

> [T]here is a quite unintended effect of enumerating, and I call this subversive. Enumeration demands kinds of things or people to count. Counting is hungry for categories. Many of the categories we now use to describe people are by-products of the needs of enumeration. (Hacking 1982: 280)

The United States of America had been described by Robert Lane (1966) as the 'knowledgeable society'. Others such as Melanson (1973) suggest that the term 'knowledge society' better describes the ideological and political manoeuvring that such a concept should encompass. What did these authors mean by a knowledge or knowledgeable society? And, more importantly, what does this have to do with the production of fear of crime as an object of enquiry? In this chapter the emergent methods of enquiry such as the victim survey, the statisticalisation of criminal offences and new technological advances will be explored in order to illustrate the developing enumeration of crime fear in the 1960s and 1970s; a distinct discursive shift. The chapter will also explore the shifting US political terrain under Johnson, and then under Nixon, in order to trace the emergence of crime fear on a political and popular level. It will argue *inter alia* that concerns about 'black' riots, the growing social scientific interest in victim surveys, and the politicisation of the Omnibus Crime Control and Safe Streets Act (1968) passing through US congress provided the context for a 'fear of crime feedback loop' the likes of which still operates today (Harris 1969). That is to say that the coming together of anxieties, politics and the social scientific knowledge of disciplines like criminology gave the notion or concept of fear of crime a foothold. Moreover, when fear of crime was named, thus also becoming a quantifiable and observable object, it was transformed into something that began to have strong political purchase and subsequently a criminological or disciplinary purchase as well.

The will to be a knowledgeable society

Gradually in the US, as in most Western nations, specialised statistical and social scientific knowledge has become an essential commodity in industry, politics, social policy, crime and even sports (Melanson 1973). Historically, the first US national census was carried out in 1790 and was the forerunner to the current body of statistical information collected by numerous government and private bodies; the US was no stranger to the 'science of state'. During the 1930s the emerging social sciences received a great boost in prominence and support as they developed an ever-increasing appetite for social indicators, a further expansion of enumerating technologies. Socially significant statistically descriptive data about the national well-being of American society was increasingly gathered in time series to show social trends. Between the work of the pollsters and the social scientists, a major shift in the way America both viewed and governed itself was under way.

This will for the United States to be a 'knowledgeable society' accelerated substantially in the decade of the 1960s with a huge increase in the scope and types of surveys and studies conducted. This acceleration owed much to the growing sophistication of statistical collection and evaluation, and indeed to the massive advances in computing technology and computing networks, but, equally, it was a result of a growing political will for the state to ameliorate, by intervening in, the lives of its citizens. As many scholars have argued (Jones *et al.* 1986; Phipps 1986), the US Democrat-led government at this time had become social democratic in all but name. In short, the great social movements of the 1960s had begun to have their influence on political will and by the mid 1960s this was helping drive a new thirst for information about the population. However, it must be stressed that this new interest in social indicators was also taking place at municipal level and in the private sector. Thus, it was not purely led via government policy – although it may well have been governmentally led, to borrow and stress Foucault's nuanced usage of the term. 'Data on labour relations, labour productivity, manpower resources, educational achievement, crime statistics, health and welfare data, consumer purchasing plans – to name but just a few' were increasingly proving valuable in the planning and management of organisations and businesses (Report of the Special Commission on the Social Sciences to the National Science Board 1973).

However, the 1960s heralded more than just an increase in the production of new statistical objects of knowledge and a proliferation in particular modes of enquiry. It also witnessed new democratisation of this knowledge. This democratisation occurred on a scale that had hitherto been thought both impossible to undertake and socially damaging. Previously the belief had been that the general public was better off without access to such information. Habits of secrecy, which had taken hold of American government departments during World War II and the administrative mythology regarding the 'secret' of the atomic bomb, were partly responsible for a hide-and-seek political atmosphere which prevailed throughout the cold war period (Longaker 1973). This had ensured that much of the socio-demographic knowledge produced in the US was withheld from the public under fear of it falling into the wrong hands. While there is no doubt that a secretive atmosphere continued through the 1960s, particularly with regard to foreign policy,[1] there is evidence that the emergence of new rationalities of governance in terms of domestic policy were sparking a need for not only more social scientific knowledge but also its almost universal availability. Indeed Lane (1966: 61), perhaps rather optimistically, suggested that:

> [I]f one thinks of a domain of 'pure politics' where decisions are determined by calculations of influence, power or electoral advantage, and a domain of 'pure knowledge' where decisions are by calculations of how to implement agreed upon values with rationality and efficiency, it appears to me that the political domain is shrinking and the knowledge domain is growing ...

Lane's dichotomy of the political and knowledge domains are no doubt overly reductive. However, they do at least alert us to a change in governmental rationalities at this time. As far back as 1962 the President's Science Advisory Committee made recommendations that social scientific organisations make an effort to produce descriptive statistics on behaviour in American society. Another three reports were presented between 1965 and 1968 which concerned the problem of centralised data management and indeed the proposal for a National Data Centre. Such a centre had been proposed by a committee of the Social Science Research Council and had been given endorsement by a government task force (Report of the Special Commission on the Social Sciences to the National Science Board 1973: 92). The President also made a directive to the Department of Health, Education, and Welfare that they produce a report on the social state of the nation. Policy-makers were hungry for social scientific data.

Simultaneously, the body of data on public opinion continued to grow and this was pushing both the political and social scientific agendas. The Gallup Poll, for example, asking Americans what they thought was the 'most important problem' facing the country, had been continuously conducted since 1935. It was widely reported, with continuous references to public opinion polls, that crime was a growing concern in the US leading up to the November 1964 US presidential election. Conventional wisdom has assumed that anxiety over civil rights and 'Negro riots', as well as over the growing 'crime problem', were symbiotically connected in the public mind and that these anxieties combined to make crime the number one problem for the American public. Much has been made of the opinion polls of this period suggesting that such recorded anxieties pushed the political agenda. Indeed, it was in 1964 that crime became politicised in the US in a way that it had never been before. The opinion polls were without a doubt a vital ingredient in this politicisation and certainly in the emergence of the concept of fear of crime. A defining moment of this politicisation of crime, and where crime was explicitly connected to other forms of public disorder, is an acceptance speech by 1964 Republican Party presidential candidate Barry Goldwater on 16 July 1964:

> The growing menace in our country tonight, to personal safety, to life, to limb and property, in homes, in churches, on the playgrounds, and places of business, particularly in our great cities, is the mounting concern, or should be, of every thoughtful citizen in the United States ... Security from domestic violence,[2] no less than from foreign aggression, is the most elementary and fundamental purpose of any government, and a government that cannot fulfil that purpose is one that cannot long command the loyalty of its citizens. History shows us – demonstrates that nothing – nothing prepares the way for tyranny more than the failure of public officials to keep the streets from bullies and marauders (cited in the *Washington Post*).

However, as Loo and Grimes (2004) illustrate, this discourse of 'crime on the streets' was actually borrowed from a newspaper editorial. On 29 June 1964, the *U.S. News and World Report* editorial suggested that the US was in the midst of 'a crime wave of unprecedented proportions' (Lawrence cited in Loo and Grimes 2004: 55). The editorial went on to link crime to the street demonstrations and actions of certain civil rights leaders.

Loo and Grimes (2004) recently conducted a reanalysis of 1960s public opinion polling in the United States and what they found was revealing.

They suggest that the opinion poll data, cited at the time (and since) as indicating a heightened anxiety about crime and as being the catalyst for mass media and political discourse on crime and insurrection, actually shows nothing of the sort once the data is disaggregated. Rather, media organisations, politicians, scholars and often the polling companies themselves had systematically misrepresented or misinterpreted the data, probably a bit of both, in a way that elevated anxiety about crime. Loo and Grimes argue that there were a number of forms of misrepresentation. First, the conflation of disparate variables into one overarching category. They suggest, for example, that categories such as 'social control' have been used unproblematically as aggregate categories representing responses to questions encapsulating a diverse range of issues. In fact, the aggregate category 'social control' encompassed such disparate items as 'violence', 'riots', 'crime', 'juvenile delinquency', 'drugs', 'moral decay' and even 'lack of religion'. They argue that once such categories are disaggregated many of the polls which purport to show increasing concern about crime in fact indicate very little change. Secondly, they suggest that the numbers of respondents actually citing 'crime and juvenile delinquency' as a problem were overstated. Gallup reported a 17 per cent figure for the category in January 1969 when in fact the raw data suggested the figure was 6 per cent – other categories had in fact once again been problematically aggregated. Third, some polls purporting to show increases in crime had particularly leading questions. The Harris poll of September 1968 is a prime example here. This poll was reported in major newspapers such as the *New York Post* under the headline 'Law and order top issue next to the war: Harris' (cited in Loo and Grimes 2004: 60). The newspaper reported that 81 per cent of respondents agreed that 'law and order had broken down'. But what questions were the 1,481 respondents asked? Here they are. The opening question asked:

I want to ask you about some things which some people think have been causes of the breakdown of law and order in this country. For each, tell me if you feel it is a major cause of a breakdown of law and order, a minor cause, or hardly a cause at all.

The question thus assumes a breakdown in law and order has occurred. 'Organized crime' came in as the top choice for the respondents at 61 per cent, then 'Negroes who start riots' at 59 per cent, 'Communists' at 51 per cent, the 'Courts' at 51 per cent, 'Anti-Vietnam demonstrators' at 38 per cent, 'National leadership' at 37 per cent, 'Hippies and student protestors' at 29 per cent, 'Right wing demagogues' at 20 per cent, and 'Police brutality' at 13 per cent (Loo and Grimes 2004).

There was then a follow-up question: 'Now I want to read you some statements about law and order in this country. For each, tell me if you agree or disagree.' Again I paraphrase from Loo and Grimes: 'Law and order would improve if more people backed up their local police' (87 per cent agreed); 'A strong President can make a big difference in directly preserving law and order' (84 per cent); 'Law and order has broken down in this country' (81 per cent); 'Keeping law and order is much more a local than a federal government problem' (78 per cent); 'The rights of many people can be endangered in the name of law and order' (73 per cent); 'Violation of law and order has been encouraged by the courts' (69 per cent); 'Until there is justice for minorities there will not be law and order' (63 per cent); 'Demands for law and order are made by politicians who are against progress for Negroes' (22 per cent). Thus, the Harris poll first asked respondents a series of questions structured as 'Many people say X has happened. Which of the following reasons would you say are responsible for causing X to happen?' Then, a series of questions, one of which was 'Do you think that X has happened?' The first series of questions assume or prompt the answer to a question asked later. It is not surprising then, given this structure and sequence of questions, that 81 per cent of respondents should then agree that 'X has happened'.

But there is even more to this than Loo and Grimes indicate. That is, give the possible list of causal variables available as responses to the first question and the percentage responses attributed to each of these, the 81 per cent who agreed that law and order had broken down (in the follow-up) might well have done so for reasons as disparate as organised crime, police brutality and right-wing demagogues. Whatever the case, the poll was flawed to such an extent that it was highly misrepresentative.

In many ways Loo and Grimes' (2004) analysis, or reanalysis, of this data is only of peripheral concern to this genealogy of crime fear. I am not particularly interested in either the levels of concern nor the reality or otherwise of fear of crime. Nor do I wish to engage in a debate about objective levels of crime in the period. Nonetheless, their research offers another form of analysis that indicates that crime fear wasn't out in the community waiting to be discovered. Rather, it required a high degree of construction or formation, a particular assemblage of the knowledge to categorise and conceptualise and the power to communicate. It also indicates that the truths through which social scientific enquiry, and particularly criminological enquiry, came to regard the issue of fear of crime as an object were constitutive, contingent and ultimately contestable.

LBJ and the problematisation of crime in the 1960s

> Every citizen has the right to feel secure in his home and on the streets of his community. To help control crime, we will recommend programs: to train local law enforcement officers; to put the best techniques of modern science at their disposal; to discover the causes of crime and better ways to prevent it. I will soon assemble a panel of outstanding experts of this Nation to search out answers to the national problem of crime and delinquency, and I welcome the recommendations and the constructive efforts of the Congress. (Lyndon B. Johnson, State of the Union Address, 4 January 1965)

This excerpt from President Johnson's State of the Union Address that has come to be known as the 'Great Society proposal' heralded a new approach in the US in the 'fight' against poverty, and indeed the fight against the crime that was by then regarded by many policy-makers as a by-product of poverty. The political will to ameliorate the conditions of poverty coincided with technical advances and the push to democratise knowledge in ways that produced new government and political agendas and indeed new objects of political discussion and discourse. The Great Society agenda was in many aspects anti-welfarist, yet it involved the greatest expansion of the American State in the post-war period: increased aid to public education, an area hitherto off limits to federal involvement; an attack on disease via the expansion of medical knowledge and increased Medicare; programmes of urban renewal; beautification; conservation; the redevelopment of depressed regions; a widescale 'fight' or 'war' against poverty; control and prevention of crime and delinquency; and the removal of obstacles to the right to vote. Johnson regarded these aims as of utmost importance and they were to be simultaneously driven by the new reams of social scientific data. It was in this context that the 'Great Society Program' became President Johnson's agenda for Congress in January 1965. He was determined to institute the reforms first flagged, but never implemented, under the Kennedy presidency. Congress at times augmented or amended but generally rapidly enacted Johnson's recommendations in the early period of the reforms.

One of the aims of the programme, as illustrated clearly in the above excerpt from Johnson, was the development of new ways to tackle crime. Thus was born The President's Commission on Law Enforcement and Administration of Justice. Indeed, this became the reporting mechanism for the 'panel of outstanding experts' referred to in the Address. Among other things the work of this Commission resulted in a number of reports and recommendations that would have not only a profound effect on the criminological landscape of the United States and the forms of enquiry commissioned under government sanction but also a profound effect on the quantification of crime fear.

At around the same time that Johnson announced his 'Great Society' programme, momentum was also gathering in other quarters for the development and introduction of new methods of collecting crime statistics. Traditional methods of calculating crime rates, police reports, had been attracting growing criticism from criminologists and others. Phipps (1986) rightly notes that a number of criminological papers began to appear between 1960 and 1965 in the US arguing strongly for such a re-evaluation.[3] Concern about the accuracy and utility of crime statistics was being revived within mainstream sociology and criminology from voices both internal and external to the disciplines. This revival also coincided with an emerging interest in studies into victims of crime. All this resulted in the formulation of new methods of data collection that did not rely on police reporting and could, it was hoped, give researchers an insight into the 'dark figure' of crime. It is here that we see the beginnings of crime and victim surveys and self-report studies. Many of these were to operate in a similar fashion to, and on the model of, the modern census and were also obviously influenced by the methods of the opinion pollsters. Such a change came at an opportune time for, and was consequently pushed by, an Administration hungry for new angles on the crime problem.

This paradigm shift in the way crime rates were to be collected, correlated and calculated deserves emphasis. For not only does it indicate the strong governmental (and disciplinary) will to refine the instruments of research in ways that were designed to produce increasingly detailed representations of social indicators; more importantly it situates the citizenry more directly within the apparatus of knowledge, thus subjectifying them in ways that had hitherto been thought antithetical to the accurate production of social scientific knowledge. That is, the population were not only to contribute to the collection of data and calculation of social indices, they were also to be able to use the data in ways that might improve their own lives. They were able to bring knowledge to bear in their calculations of the every day. This illustrates a shift in the discourses of knowing that places increasing emphasis and importance on the 'truth' of experiences provided by individuals; indeed it constituted a new regime of truth. Moreover, it is based on the premise that this knowledge of population, once it has been subject to statistical analysis, will be of benefit to the individual subject; that the citizenry would have the capacity to be cognisant of these new representations of knowledge and thus be able to employ them in ways that would inform their everyday lives. Therefore, these new calculations would enable citizens to become the objects of their own knowledge and regulate themselves accordingly. So the rolling back of the habits of secrecy that had inhibited the flow of government information to the American public constituted not so much a retreat in government intervention; rather, it constituted part of the increasing governmentalisation of the individual and the state; this new version of liberal governance might encourage the self-responsibilisation of subjects. Indeed, this constituted a proliferation and intensification of government into ever more mundane and minute activities of the everyday – liberal subjects were being implored to govern themselves.

The birth of the victim survey

In the USA in the mid 1960s several organisations were commissioned to conduct research and produce reports for The President's Commission on Law Enforcement and Administration of Justice. These organisations began to interview citizens individually about their personal experiences of crime victimisation with the aim of obtaining more accurate data on levels of unreported crime. And, responding to concerns apparently expressed in polls and in political circles, they were to study public perceptions about crime. The Bureau of Social Science Research in Washington (Biderman *et al.* 1967), The National Opinion Research Center (Ennis 1967), and The University of Michigan (Reiss 1967) began their work in 1965 and reported in 1967. The reports were titled respectively *Report on a Pilot Study In the District of Columbia On Victimization and Attitudes Toward Law Enforcement – Field Surveys I, Criminal Victimisation in the United States: A Report of a National Survey – Field Surveys II*, and *Studies in Crime and Law Enforcement in major Metropolitan Areas – Field Surveys III*. These pilot surveys and their subsequent reports led to the emergence of National Crime Surveys which were subsequently conducted regularly along with the US census by the Bureau of Justice Statistics (Gordon and Riger 1989; Zedner 2002).

One observation is immediately apparent when we look at the character of the three organisations carrying out the research; that is that the organisations themselves constitute a nexus of opinion (NORC), government (BoSSR) and the academy (UoM) in the production of knowledge about fear of crime. While none of these studies focused exclusively on fear of crime all contain a lengthy discussion on the topic and all employed surveys asking respondents about their perceptions of crime and discussing community fears. The tone of each of these reports is quite different, as is the research instrument deployed. The NORC survey perhaps most closely resembles the larger scale surveying that was to follow – at least in regard to fear of crime. Interestingly the preface of the Ennis report (1967: iii) notes that 'ideas for the present study were initially discussed in 1962 by the staff of the National Opinion Research Center'. Importantly the preface also notes that 'neither would it have been undertaken had it not been for the *President's Commission on Law Enforcement and Administration of Justice'*, which 'imaginatively defined its mission to include the exploration of new methods of measuring the amount of crime' (Ennis 1967: iii). The interface between social scientific knowledge and political power here could not be more apparent. As we shall see the power/knowledge effect of the coming together of the social scientific and the political has major ramifications for both the administration of justice in the US and the growth of fear of crime as a discourse (both social scientific and popular). I would argue that, given the context and aim of Johnson's Great Society programme, the consequent politicisation of crime fear was quite unintended.

All three reports note the 'far from perfect relationship between perceptions and attitudes persons hold' (Reiss 1967: 22) about their risk of victimisation. Reiss (1967) also notes the clear inclination of respondents to advocate 'repressive' or 'protective' responses to crime (42 per cent said they would only advocate these measures) over measures aimed at 'ameliorating social conditions' (7 per cent) that lead to crime (Reiss 1967: 91). While Reiss (1967) is quite circumspect in his discussion about crime fear – rarely using the term fear of crime – and Ennis (1967) concerned about the potential politicisation of crime fear, Biderman *et al.* (1967: 119) could almost be described as alarmist:

> The respondents believed that the crime problem in Washington is a serious problem, that it is growing worse and that it is of immediate concern to themselves. They are concerned about crime both on a general community level and as a problem of safety for themselves, their families and their possessions. The fear that harm might come to them or their families has a very considerable impact on the daily lives of the people we interviewed.

Looking at the results now, conducted as they were with no time series data, it is difficult to see how such a clear-cut conclusion could be drawn. For example, respondents suggesting that they chose their place of residence by neighbourhood as opposed to the particular house is represented as being due to concern about criminal victimisation. Indeed, of those who did choose neighbourhood over house as their selection criteria only 56 per cent suggested that this was due to 'crime or moral characteristic' (Biderman *et al*. 1967: 121). The only other option was 'convenience or aesthetic characteristics'. On any objective criteria here, fear of crime was being constructed. If there is a ground zero, an epicentre to fear of crime as a social scientific concept, these surveys constitute it. They did not invent the discourse of fear of crime, but they did give it form as an object.

However, before I move on, the NORC report itself requires further analysis. In its pages are contained, for the first time, direct survey questions about fear of crime. Indeed, the 'scenario'-style question, later a much debated element of fear of crime survey work and a question which endures in surveys today, is to be found here. The example in the NORC report is 'How safe do you feel walking alone in your neighbourhood after dark?' Respondents were given four possible responses to this question: 'very safe; somewhat safe; somewhat unsafe; very unsafe'. It is worth quoting the introduction to this section of the report in full as it outlines, in simple terms, many of the features of fear of crime research which have both endured, and been at times heavily criticised.

> A sense of personal safety in one's own neighbourhood and a sense of security about one's own home is a major American value, one that appears to be particularly fragile in recent years. It is not entirely clear where the burden for securing that sense of security falls; certainly the police have important responsibilities, but so does the citizen himself, through his own efforts and his concerted activities in these communities. In this section the attitude data on how American people feel about these problems, the extent of their concerns, and the steps they take to protect themselves against personal violence and property loss will be briefly discussed.
>
> It has already been shown that crime was the second most important domestic issue currently. That concern was on a national level. But how much concern is there with crime on the local level, and what is its relation to thinking it an important national issue? The respondents to the attitude questionnaire were asked how they felt about going out alone at night in their neighbourhood, about how worried they were about having their houses broken into, and related topics. The answers to these questions are presented below, separately for whites and negroes and for males and females. Where there are significant differences

in attitude and behaviour by income, they will be noted. (Ennis 1967: 72)

The issues of governance, both of self and state, the relationship between the local and national, the scenarios and variables that have endured in fear of crime research are all here. There is a nod to the political power of fear of crime and an insightful recognition that fear can operate as a technique of self-regulation. In short Ennis recognised, to slip into a Foucaultian register, that fear of crime could constitute a technology or tactic of governance. Ennis goes on later in the report to outline that other ongoing tension of fear of crime research. That is, the splitting of fear of crime and perceived or actual risk of victimisation.[4]

It is important to distinguish *fear* of crime from a more objective estimate of actual risk of crime. These may, and as will be seen, do not necessarily, agree (sic). (Ennis 1967: 74)

And

What is the relationship between fear of crime and its perceived risk? While analytically these are quite different notions, it is not clear whether fear (for whatever reasons) breeds a belief in the presence of danger or whether an accurate perception of the risk of crime engenders an appropriate level of concern. If the two notions are not strongly related, there may be good reason for such a discontinuity. (Ennis 1967: 76)

I am not suggesting the Ennis survey somehow constituted a complete break with the past. As we have seen already, and as Rose (1991) and Hacking (1990) have so eloquently illustrated elsewhere, social science is hungry for objects or things to count and it is not so surprising that something like crime fear might become one of these. Rather, the NORC research and report constitute part of a set of conditions – political, social and social scientific – which produced the criminological concept fear of crime. This is fear of crime coming into discourse, becoming a thing, a knowable object of enquiry. While there is an epistemological discontinuity here, there are also multiple continuities.

Are we fearful yet?

Even as the NORC survey – and the other President's Commission-related projects – were in the data collection/analysis stage, the political discourse was changing as a result of the growing anxiety being 'recorded' by the opinion polls. President Johnson himself had begun to draw on the emerging discourse of crime fear. By March 1966 he was reported to have borrowed his former opponent Barry Goldwater's 'point' about crime fear. Johnson (*The Times*, London, 10 March 1966: 8) stated:

> Forcible rape every 26 minutes, a robbery every five minutes, a car theft every minute, and a burglary every 28 seconds. We know its cost in dollars … we know the still more widespread cost it exacts in millions in fear; fear that can turn us into a nation of captives imprisoned nightly behind chained doors, double locks, barred windows … Fear can make us afraid to walk the streets by night or public parks by day. These are costs a truly free society cannot tolerate.

So while the political rhetoric began to respond to the questionable opinion poll reports, the *President's Commission* research teams were positioned to give the discourse a respectable social scientific face.

It was not just this research which exemplified the bringing into discourse of fear of crime. As I noted, this research then provided the expert evidence for the government report, *The Challenge of Crime in a Free Society: A Report by the President's Commission on Law Enforcement and Administration of Justice* (1967). It is obvious, and spelt out quite plainly in the text of that report, that it was as much about addressing fear of crime as crime itself. Indeed, while it assumed that the two were causally related it also assumed that fear of crime could be addressed as a problem in and of itself. Again it is worth quoting and interrogating this document at length. The document begins with another assumption which has had longevity in the fear of crime literature. That is that the fear of crime erodes quality of life. How was this assumption possible? Precisely because of the survey research which attempted to quantify this erosion: 'The existence of crime, the talk about crime, the reports of crime, and the fear of crime have eroded the basic quality of life of many Americans' (1967: v).

In the document 'anxiety' and 'fear' operate almost interchangeably. The commission itself, it is suggested, was a result of public anxiety about crime. Yet the commission was as much about understanding anxiety as it was addressing crime, as is clear from the following passage. Moreover, we see even at this early stage of fear of crime literature the central question of whether the population expresses an appropriate level of fear given the actual threat or risk.

A chief reason that this Commission was set up was that there is a widespread public anxiety about crime. In one sense this entire report is an effort to focus that anxiety on the central problems of crime and criminal justice. A necessary part of that effort has been to study as carefully as possible the anxiety itself. The Commission has tried to find out precisely what aspects of crime Americans are anxious about, whether their anxiety is a realistic response to actual danger, how anxiety affects the daily lives of Americans, what actions against crime by the criminal justice system and the government as a whole might best allay public anxiety. (1967: 49)

The commission document goes on to call for calm. It also delivers a broadside to those who might seek to elevate 'fear of crime' for personal or political gain;

... the Commission must make one general comment. There is reason to be alarmed about crime. In fact, just because crime is alarming, those discussing it – and many people must discuss it often if it is ever to be controlled – have an obligation to be cool, factual and precise. Thoughtless, emotional or self-serving discussion of crime, especially by those who have the public's attention and can influence the public's thinking, is an immense disservice. (1967: 49)

Again though, we see the influence of the questionable polls in driving the social scientific and political programmes:

Public concern about crime is mounting. National polls by Harris and Gallup show that the majority of people think the situation in their own communities is getting worse, that a substantial minority think the situation is staying the same, and that almost no one thinks the situation is improving ... In July 1966, Harris surveys reported that in each recent year there has been an increase over the year before in the per cent of persons worried about their personal safety on the streets. (1967: 50)

These surveys were also able to identify crimes that might be the most fear inducing:

Recently studies have been undertaken to develop an index of delinquency based on the seriousness of different offences. They have shown that there is a widespread public consensus on the relative seriousness of different types of crimes. (1967: 50)

Indeed, for the first time we also see the shadowy stranger appear as the object of our fears. Such a conclusion is somehow reinforced by the results of the scenario question:

> Perhaps the most intense concern about crime is the fear of being attacked by a stranger when out alone. One-third of Americans feel unsafe about walking alone at night in their neighbourhoods, according to the NORC survey. (1967: 51)

Yet despite what must, when compared to whatever measure of 'actual risk', be an exaggerated or misinterpreted fear of being victimised by a stranger, the Commission is at pains to point out that they are not simply suggesting that people's fear is exaggerated. Indeed, we are to respect peoples' fear:

> The Commission cannot say that the public's fear of crime is exaggerated. It is not prepared to tell people how fearful they should be; that is something each person must decide for himself. People's fears must be respected; certainly they cannot be legislated. Some people are willing to run risks that terrify others. (1967: 51)

And the Commission also acknowledged that a fear of strangers was likely to magnify a range of social problems. Indeed, security itself was under threat:

> When fear of crime becomes fear of the stranger the social order is further damaged. As the level of sociability and mutual trust is reduced, streets and public places can indeed become more dangerous ... However, the more dangerous effect of a fear of strangers is its implication that the moral and social order are of doubtful trustworthiness and stability ... the security that comes from living in an orderly and trustworthy society is undermined. (1967: 51)

Moreover, the mass media were for the first time specifically targeted as a source of crime fear – as opposed to a source of crime – via this social scientific data, or at least they were seen as an instrument of its magnification. The report flags much of the media focused fear of crime work that would follow:

> The mass media and overly zealous or opportunistic crime fighters may play a role in raising fears of crime by associating the idea of

'crime' with a few sensational and terrifying acts ... Little attention has thus far been given to ... the creation of distorted perceptions of the risk of crime and exaggerated fears of victimisation. (167: 52)

And the commission was at pains to end the discussion on a positive note – the idea that the report could translate public fears into positive action:

Every American can translate his concern about crime, or fear of crime, into positive action. Every American should ... this report will endeavour to show how. (167: 52)

If the *President's Commission* reports were central to the quantification and objectification of fear of crime, it did not take long for other researchers to follow suit. The concept could hardly have been better suited to the political agenda and the social scientific landscape of the US in the late 1960s. The other important point about the surveys was that their interest in fear of crime was in the context of new ways of counting offending. Victimage and fear would be forever related concepts and the power of the victim survey gave the fear of crime component an increased truth value – opening up little space for an analysis of the fear concept itself.

These surveys were also integral to the growth of the sub-discipline of victimology. Indeed, victim surveys were an important topic of discussion at The First International Symposium of Victimology held in Jerusalem in 1973. While fear of crime was of peripheral interest to the delegates, as the four-volume published collection of papers attests (Drapkin and Viano 1975), mention was made of the expansion of follow-up interview surveys conducted as part of the National Crime Panel in the US. As Marie Argana (1975: 177) noted:

Periodically, supplemental inquiries may be added to the National Crime Panel. One such enquiry is a series of questions designed to collect data on a general attitude toward crime, the fear of crime, the effect of this fear on activity patterns such as choice of shopping area and places of entertainment, and the public's view of the police.

Significantly, Argana was a delegate representing the US Bureau of Census in Washington. Argana's championing of the new area of study and the new techniques of data collecting flags the increasing significance the study of fear of crime was to have in victim surveys in the coming years. The President's Commission had suggested that there was a need for a 'scientific and technological revolution' in criminal justice. Phipps (1986) argues that this Commission heralded a turning point in the reorientation of mainstream criminology towards the collection of knowledge about victims of crime. Indeed, as we saw above, the Commission instigated a number of large-scale samples of crime victims – the first proper social scientific fear of crime work.

A month after the release of the President's Commission report President Johnson was again speaking publicly about crime fear. This time, however, he had the social scientific evidence to draw on (quoted in Wigg 1967: 8):

> Fear assails us all, no matter where we live, no matter how little we own ... America cannot tolerate enduringly this climate of fear. Our streets, our parks, our businesses and our homes ought to and must be made safe.

The politics that were to play out in the name of this safety and security would be extraordinary.

The growing (con)sensus

While Johnson pushed ahead with the Great Society Program a popular and political discourse had taken root from an opposing ideological position. This was a politics of law and order that based itself, like the social democratic discourse, on a perceived growing lawlessness in the US, and indeed on a perception that the public was becoming anxious about the steadily climbing crime rate. However, the methods proposed for dealing with the 'crime problem' could not have been more different. Even more ironically, if the will to become a more 'knowable' society developed in part from the civil rights movement of the 1960s, so too did the new politics of law and order. For despite the new anti-poverty and anti-discrimination programmes, which had had little time to run their course, the unrest and rioting in black ghettos troubled the nation and its politicians. President Johnson steadily exerted his influence against segregation and on behalf of moderation in law and order, but not always with the desired outcomes. Thus, calls for tougher action in terms of policing, disciplining and punishing criminals began to grow.

The emergence of this discourse is well traced by Richard Harris in his extraordinarily insightful book *The Fear of Crime*, published in 1969. As well as being the first publication that actually takes the fear of crime as a title – which is of course symbolically and discursively important to the broader genealogy of fear of crime – it also eloquently places public fears in the context of political manoeuvring. Harris traces the progression of a piece of legislation, The Omnibus Crime Control and Safe Streets Act 1968, through Congress. This process begins in early 1967 and is finalised in Congress on 6 June 1968, the day of Robert Kennedy's death.[5] Indeed, Harris (1969) suggests that Kennedy's death helped hasten the Bill through its final hurdle.

The story of the passing of this Bill is a story of political vengeance, populism, payback, and Machiavellian allegiances of the highest order. Let me offer the following summary.

Without delving too deeply into the complexities and specificities of the Bill itself,[6] it is sufficient to outline that it sought to do the following:

- Give police increased or at least less restricted powers in holding and arresting suspects, in tapping communications networks, in taking confessions;
- Put in place a minimal level of gun control measures;
- Reverse two US supreme court decisions which had resulted in suspects being freed due to legal 'technicalities' concerned with the way police had obtained confessions. (Harris 1969)

In short it sought to wind back the rights of individuals in dealings with the police on a number of levels. The Bill, in the form that it was finally passed, had been the brainchild of Senator John L. McClellan, a Democrat from Arkansas, who was chairman of the Subcommittee on Criminal Laws and Procedures.

However, the history of the Bill went back even further and this history is vital to understanding the emergence of crime fear as a concept. As I have outlined above, in 1965 President Johnson had set up the Commission on Law Enforcement and Administration of Justice in a move which was supposed to produce solutions to the crime problem in a non-political, non-partisan environment. In early 1967 the Commission submitted its report, *The Challenge of Crime in a Free Society*, as discussed above, to the White House (Harris 1969: 15). The Omnibus Bill was meant to act on the findings of the President's Commission report. This report, as we have seen, contained no law and order rhetoric, rather, it suggested that lasting solutions to crime would require comprehensive programmes involving increased education, the elimination of poverty and inadequate housing, new family counselling services, new Civil Rights laws and the improvement of 'inner cities'. Indeed, it went on to suggest very specifically that 'to speak of controlling crime only in terms of the work of the police, the courts, and the correctional apparatus is to refuse to face the fact that widespread crime implies a widespread failure by society as a whole'.

Thus, the Commission set out, principally, a blueprint that sought to continue and refine Johnson's 'great social program'. It provided social democratic images of crime and social structure. It authoritatively suggested that Johnson continue on with his programme and his 'war on poverty'. However, when Johnson, with the intention of having Congress pass legislation on many of the provisions the Commission had suggested, passed his Bill over to McClellan's Subcommittee a train of unexpected events began which would see the Bill altered beyond recognition (see Harris 1969).

To understand these we need some insight into Senator McClellan as a political actor. He was, to quote Harris (1969: 20),

[a] Puritan patriarch who has just led his band ashore and must get down to the real task of saving them from themselves, McClellan has scoffed at the notion that social unrest has social causes; he has sought not more laws but more freedom for police and prosecutors to use the laws they have – and more or less as they please. Those inside Congress and out who hoped that it would not approach the task of insuring domestic tranquillity by simply locking everybody up had little reason to believe that McClellan would provide the leadership they had in mind.

McClellan's convening of the Subcommittee gave him the opportunity to hold hearings on the state of crime in which he could selectively offer up his own solutions. Moreover, he also had an opportunity to argue for the overturning of the two landmark Supreme Court decisions he found so distasteful – *Mallory v. United States* (1957) and *Miranda v. Arizona* (1966). However, Harris (1969: 30) goes further, suggesting that McClellan's persistent attempts to punish the Supreme Court had more to do with him 'getting even' for its seemingly pro-civil rights decisions of the 1950s and early 1960s. Indeed, McClellan was an avid segregationist. For him Dr Martin Luther King's peaceful 'sit-ins' were crimes rather than political acts against unconstitutional forms of law enforcement; as Robert Kennedy's successful attempts to take the cases through the supreme court finally proved. Thus, Harris convincingly argues that, as least as far back as the formation of this Subcommittee, the fear of crime had become a political issue of monumental proportions; and it had racist overtones.

Throughout the course of stacked Senate hearings, McClellan, who, Harris contests, was 'the most adroit committee chairman on the Hill when it comes to generating publicity for something he ...[ ] wants to appear to be concerned about', stuck to repeating the point that 'decisions of the Supreme Court endangered the nation's stability' (Harris 1969: 33). Not one of those he invited to speak at the Senate hearings was a 'criminologist, a leading professor of law, or an expert on the constitution. Instead most of them were police officers and prosecutors, with a few judges who agreed with McClellan thrown in' (Harris 1969: 34). Growing popular discourses of law and order and of the fear of crime that began to have currency around this time can be traced in part to the political strategies used in these Senate hearings. Harris argues that:

> To keep his viewpoint sharply in focus, McClellan relied on repeated use of several currently popular phrases – chiefly, that members of the Supreme Court and others in high places, by 'coddling criminals' and 'handcuffing the police' had dispatched 'the depraved to roam the streets at will' and 'prey on the innocent'. No one seems to know for sure where these phrases originated, but it would appear that they gained currency through constant reiteration by police officials and prosecutors … In time the clichés began to appear in newspapers and on television … and were taken up by and pushed by right wing spokesmen as part of their general attack on the 'Warren Court'. With increasing frequency, the phrases began to pop up in letters written to members of Congress, until today a perusal of the mail that any of them receives reveals that nine-tenths of voters who complain about 'crime on the streets' complain in these terms … In any event, it is increasingly clear that such clichés can have a monumental effect on the political life of a nation. Their repetition thousands of times a day has brought a great many people to the point where they seriously doubt that the Government's interest is the same as their own. (1969: 34–35)

Thus, what Harris and others opposed to the Bill contend – and many Senators did oppose the Bill, in particular Senator Philip A. Hart, a Democrat from Michigan, who led a sustained but ultimately fruitless opposition to the measures – was that it contravened civil rights, that it was unconstitutional and discriminatory. Yet the sustained fear campaign kept it moving steadily through congressional channels with most congressmen feeling powerless to vote against it for fear of their political futures. McClellan of course found welcomed support from the Republican side of politics. Indeed, the then soon to be President Richard Nixon released his first policy position paper titled *Toward Freedom From Fear*. Fear of crime had found its way into the language of policy, its power effects as a discourse were multiplying. Nixon argued that 'If the conviction rate were doubled in this country, it would do more to eliminate crime in the future than a quadrupling of the funds for any governmental war on poverty' (cited in Harris 1969: 74). Throughout the process of the Bill voting from the Senators was split, but not along party lines. Harris contends that many who supported the Bill knew that this was 'bad' law but that their political situation necessitated a 'yes' vote. When President Johnson delayed signing the Bill for some seven days – if it is not stamped within 10 days the President can no longer sign it – there was concern that he would veto the Bill or let it pass into law without his signature. Such was his distaste of the result of events he had put in train. Indeed, Harris (1969: 109) argues that the President was extremely unhappy with the Bill but would not risk discrediting members of his government by failing to sign it. Interestingly he was prompted by the then Congressman Gerald Ford with a demand, 'What is he waiting for?' Thus, the stage was set for a form of populist fearmongering to continue through the Presidencies of both Nixon and Ford. For example, throughout the 1972 election campaign, Nixon constantly repeated the rhetoric that 'welfarism' and 'social Keynesianism' have fuelled inflation and failed to prevent higher levels of crime, and have fuelled black insurrection. Phipps (1986: 104) has convincingly argued that this position was made possible by the new attention given to the victim in social scientific and criminological discourse. If this is the case, the very will to be a 'knowledgeable society' led both by a social democratic politics, a liberal governmentality and social scientific rationale, and a liberal-minded criminology, may have unwittingly contributed to a conservative and populist discourse on crime which would scuttle the former's brief hold on mainstream criminal justice policy.

The fear of crime feedback loop

Thus, in the USA, two almost ideologically competing, yet governmentally complementary discourses helped place the fear of crime in the political, disciplinary and public realm. The growth and sophistication of the statistical domain in the 'knowledge society' and the new political focus on law and order, first reluctantly under President Johnson, but then more expressly under Presidents Nixon and Ford, set victim surveys, and their resultant studies into fear, in motion in the US and constituted a change in the rationality in relation to how crime would be understood – a new regime of truth. In essence, all the sites of knowledge/power and discursive arrangements required to set in train a self-sustaining *fear of crime feedback loop* fell into place in the US at about this point in its history.

By *fear of crime feedback loop* I mean the following: that research into fear of crime – through crime and victim surveys – produces the criminological object fear of crime statistically and, discursively, a concept is constituted. This information then operates to inform the citizenry that they are indeed fearful, information the *fearing subject* can reflect upon. The law and order lobby and politicians use fear to justify a tougher approach on crime (they have to, the citizenry are fearful apparently), a point on which they grandstand and in doing so breed more fear. The concept feeds the discourse and the discourse in turn justifies the concept. All the while the expanding fields of criminology can use their new concept to measure and assess. If 'nothing works' in reducing crime perhaps we can reduce crime fear? The *feedback loop* is inclusive of the productive power of disciplines such as criminology that seek to know and define fear of crime. As a model it provides a way of conceptualising the intensification of discourse without locating a fixed central source in any one of the institutions through which it operates or is exercised.

By 1972, one could even joke about the supposed extent of crime fear and the way the data was collected and compiled, as this foreign correspondent report in *The Times* indicated:

> I may perhaps have disrupted the calm workings of the Census Bureau's computers, though on reflection I must confess this is unlikely. At least I can flatter myself with the hope that I may have shaken a few of the prevailing sociological preconceptions about the nature of suburban life … My revolt came the other evening when a charming woman from the bureau announced we had been selected to take part in a survey on crime … that the dinner steak was sizzling merrily on the grill was politely brushed aside as irrelevant. So, I was compelled to take my revenge in the only way open to me, by telling the unpalatable truth. The fear of crime, I insisted, though I could sense the interviewer found this hard to believe, was not the dominant consideration in our lives. We walked the dog after dark, enjoyed going in town to the theatre … and were not reluctant to meet friends for dinner. I did not add that there had even been a few nights when we had failed to double lock the doors. (McDonald 1972: 7)

It was now possible to feel guilty for not taking the correct precautions, for not minimising one's own risk.

Conclusion

This chapter has explored a number of critical moments in the 1960s which, in different ways, made the objectification of fear of crime possible and which constitute an epistemological or discursive shift in the way crime was to be understood. It explored crime fear's 'discovery' as a criminological concept and illustrated how and why this came about. The increased interest in opinion polling, the intensification of the social scientific enterprise to governmental ends, and the subsequent politicisation of crime and its fear interacted in complex ways in the 1960s. This interaction made possible a discourse about crime fear that continues to hold our interest today. Throughout this period knowledge was increasingly 'democratised'. Ultimately we are now able to reflect on our own survey results, reflect on our own fearfulness – the survey set up a process whereby the object of the study, us, can be subjectified. All this has led to crime fear being both a party political tool and a governmental strategy. The next chapter discusses some of the consequences of this discovery and traces the further dissemination of this new form of knowledge/power.

Notes

1 For example the Nixon administration kept secret the nature of peace proposals which were presented to the North Vietnamese and Viet Cong over a number of years, 1968 to 1971, releasing the information later for political gain (Melanson 1973: 8).
2 'Domestic' meaning here of the homeland, not of the home.
3 See for example Bell (1962), Wheeler (1967) and Wilkins (1964), all cited in Phipps (1986).
4 There is slippage between objective and perceived risk in the report.
5 The day following Kennedy's shooting.
6 See Harris (1969) for all the particularities of the Bill and the many amendments made to it on its passage through Congress.

Chapter 4

Surveying the fearful: the international expansion of the victim survey

> Generally speaking, researchers and policy-makers alike characterise fear as a destructive force, interfering with full participation in everyday life in civilised society. Many people for example avoid certain sections of the city or a neighbourhood, hesitating to frequent shops, theatres, pubs or sports events because they are anxious about their personal safety. Moreover, worrying about being attacked or having their homes invaded by burglars causes an exceptional amount of stress for certain groups, especially the elderly and women. These people have had crime prevention and fear reduction techniques specially designed for them. (Stanko 1990)

This chapter will consider the growing criminological and political interest in both fear of crime and the victim surveys that rendered it quantifiable. I begin by examining a number of early 1970s US-based academic journal articles that take fear of crime as their topic. The chapter then moves on to exploring the migration of the term fear of crime into the British popular, political and social scientific vocabulary. First, I use news extracts to identify this initial migration and shift in vocabulary. Second, I trace the lineage of survey work noting the links between the development of victim surveys in the US and the UK. Third, I explore the conditions of the development of a new conceptual language around fear of crime in a discussion of criminological work of the period from 1970 to 1985; I explore this in some depth, drawing not just on the British experience but also that of the US and Australia. The aim here is to explore some of the unintended consequences of various forms of critical, realist and feminist criminological work and explain how some of that work intensified interest in crime fear and offered up opportunities for fear of crime to be politicised. This politicisation is then discussed in relation to both neo-conservative politics and the emergence of right realist criminology.

The chapter will also traverse the debates over the rationality/ irrationality of crime fear and suggest that such debates ask the wrong set of questions and set up a false dichotomy between fear and risk (see also Sparks 1992: 35–43). Such a dichotomy was reproduced in realist work (of both Left and Right), in much early feminist work and in administrative enquiry. This dichotomy was also illustrative of the split in left criminology in this period exemplified in the development of left realism. The chapter concludes with a discussion of what I call the discovery of the *fearing subject*. That is, once it becomes possible to enumerate crime fear and thus identify populations of fearing individuals, it also becomes possible to tailor policy to suit this new identity. In short, I will argue that by the 1980s the *fearing subject* became the object for a new set of governmental practices and techniques.

Studying a new concept

Throughout the 1970s the number of articles about fear of crime appearing in international learned journals increased, slowly at first, but surely. US-based research articles discussing fear of crime began appearing in criminology journals in the early 1970s. Here there is a distinct shift from the pre-President's Commission discourse. Where once articles might mention 'public opinion', this new research saw fear of crime as a topic in and of itself. As well as this we see an increasing number of papers on neighbourhood disorganisation, victimisation and other concepts related to the President's Commission report. Poveda's (1972) journal article *The Fear of Crime in a Small Town* in *Crime and Delinquency* is illustrative of the shift. Poveda, five years after the President's Commission report, was able to speak confidently about crime fear in the following terms:

> The concern expressed about it reflects not a simple worry about why there is crime in America but rather a *very profound fear* about life in America. The President's Commission on Law Enforcement and Administration of Justice noted that the fear of crime or violence is not simply a fear of injury or death but ultimately a 'fear of strangers' ... The implications of this fear of crime are far-reaching. All too often our solutions to social problems are based

on fears and popular myths rather than on a systematic analysis of the problem in question. The fear of crime is itself a largely unexamined area of investigation. It obscures and shifts attention away from the issues raised by the problem of crime in America. If we are to sort out these issues rationally, *we must depict the fear of crime in some useful perspective*. (1972: 147)

There are some noteworthy points made here by Poveda about the nascent study of crime fear. He specifically notes that the genesis of his own usage of the term fear of crime dates from the President's Commission on Law Enforcement (1967). However, after later asking 'What if fear of crime is anchored in accurate images of crime and criminals?' (Poveda 1972: 153), he also mentions a survey report by a *New York Times* reporter who had polled citizens of Webster City, Iowa and conducted some follow-up investigative journalism. Thus, Poveda has come to the study of crime fear through an assemblage of discourses, governmental, popular and social scientific. Even more striking however is Poveda's analysis. He is wholly uninterested in the quantification or measurement of fear of crime, despite much of the earlier work he cites attempting to do so. The social scientific task he sets himself is to 'sort out the sources of fear' (1972: 157). He does this through a thorough analysis of myth and representation of youth and drug use in his Delta City locality. Moreover, he is not particularly interested in a detailed conceptual definition of what fear of crime is. The later conceptual arguments about this are, unlike the initial steps towards a conceptual framework in the President's Commission work, completely absent from his article. What one finds striking in reading this article now is how, one might say, it eschewed the normative fear of crime framework. Poveda essentially presents a sketch of a moral panic and its very real results. Yet, at the same time, he is at pains to take fear of crime seriously, stressing that 'fear of crime is real and should not be ridiculed' (Poveda 1972: 153). Indeed, his argument is that policy is driven more by fear than by a thorough understanding about crime itself.

Two years later, in the *Journal of Research in Crime and Delinquency*, Michael Hindelang (1974), in a very different type of article, was able to recite statistical data back to 1965 in his article *Public Opinion Regarding Crime, Criminal Justice and related Topics*. Interestingly, Hindelang, while including a section on fear of crime, actually writes the term in inverted commas. For him, in 1974 at least, fear of crime is not yet a thing, an object, despite the quantitative research he draws on. Indeed, specifically noting the political purchase of crime fear, he suggested that:

> In recent years – especially, it seems, during political campaigns – there has been a great deal of popular and professional attention devoted to Americans' fear of walking on the streets at night. (Hindelang 1974: 103)

Nonetheless, Hindelang's argument for the increased application of public opinion data is ominous. Indeed, his concluding discussion is almost a micro illustration of my argument here on the expansion of fear of crime research.

> At this time ... this wealth of data remains essentially untapped. Given the generally inferior quality of criminal justice data which has traditionally been available from official sources, it seems ironic that public opinion data has not been more fully mined. On many issues the data provide a running historical record of changes in the stance of the public regarding matters central to criminal justice. For the empiricist, the theorist, the practitioner, the planner, and those interested in 'social Indicators', the potential of public opinion data is far too great to continue to be ignored. (Hindelang 1974: 117)

If by 1974 one could suggest that this data was still being 'ignored', it would not be for very much longer. Indeed, as we have seen, it was already being mined in the media. As I noted in the previous chapter the emergence of this wealth of 'public opinion' data illustrates a separate surface of emergence for fear of crime to the discourse on victims. Hindelang's call for the expansion of this work also builds on a general call for an expansion in the collection of data on social indicators. It seems Ian Hacking's (1990) notion of an 'avalanche of printed numbers' has its equivalent in the period of 1960–1975.[1] As Rose (1991) has noted, we have developed a hunger for numbers. The social world would become increasingly enumerated and the elementary fear of crime data of the President's Commission, recited by Hindelang, would soon be replaced by increasingly sophisticated – and sometimes not so sophisticated – forms of enumeration which attempt to delineate specific categories and levels of fear.

Indeed, Hindelang, along with Michael Gottfredson and James Garofalo (Hindelang *et al.* 1978), were instrumental in moving this line of enquiry forward in unexpected ways. In their book *Victims of Personal Crime* they use victim surveys to analyse 'participation' in victimisation. Stanko (2000) has noted how this work had the effect of defining new categories of risk along the lines of the deserving and undeserving victims. Their analysis of what would come to be known as 'routine activities' brought the risks of lifestyle to bear on a literature that had hitherto conceptualised victimisation risk as relatively random. In a matter of four years the call for the use of public opinion data had shifted to a new emphasis about risk of victimisation. But I am getting ahead of myself. These developments in the US also had effects on the other side of the Atlantic and it is to these I now turn.

In the same year that Poveda published *Fear of Crime in a Small Town*, Stan Cohen, on the other side of the Atlantic, produced his ground-breaking *Folk Devils and Moral Panics* (1972); same year, similar theme, different terminology. Cohen's analysis differed in that fear of crime as a concept had been little used in the UK, and had certainly not entered the criminological lexicon. You won't find it specifically mentioned in Cohen's book. Indeed, the concept of fear of crime would make moral panic analyses such as those of Cohen much more difficult to articulate when it did make its Atlantic crossing into British criminological discourse some years later. For with fear of crime (the concept) came the simultaneous imperative to treat it seriously. Implicit in the moral panic and other theoretical approaches drawn from interactionism was the notion that fears were 'amplified', overstated. This was at odds with a new realism and the rationalities associated with, and emerging from, the victim survey. Yet the question of amplification in the work of Cohen and others is important and requires closer inspection here. I would suggest that the conceptual space left by 'overstated' anxieties, as argued in the moral panic literature, provided a convenient conceptual space for fear of crime to fill. That is, in later work fear of crime becomes a concept that, among other things, explains away 'amplified' panic.

A new language for a new concept

In Britain in the 1960s fear of crime, for all intents and purposes, did not exist as a criminological concept. Nor did it appear in popular and political discourse. Rather, the British press could report discussion about rising recorded crime rates through the almost two-century-old lens of the Gordon Riots. *The Times* of London, drawing on the words of the Chief Constable of Surrey, could head a report '"Gordon Riots" Fear as Crime Rate Keeps Rising' (30 May 1963: 9). The novel aspect of this particular headline was that crime and fear could appear in the same phrase and yet bear a completely different meaning than they might only two years later in the US.

Yet, by the late 1960s fear of crime begins to receive a smattering of references in the British press. However, it is not fear of crime *in* Britain that is of initial concern. Rather, the reporting of crime fear comes from foreign correspondents in the US. For example, *The Times* reported in 1969, 'at present the fear of crime – an American this year is almost twenty times as likely to be murdered as an Englishman – is the worst practical threat to "life, liberty and the pursuit of happiness"' (27 May 1969: 9). Later that same year, Louis Heren, *The Times* US correspondent, noted that 'in the more populated area, the fear of crime and violence has reduced civility in public behaviour. It is often foolhardy to give a man a lift, when he really wants your wallet' (Heren 1969: 8). By January 1970 Heren, a resident of Washington, is able to commit an entire column of *The Times* to a discussion of America's fear of crime. He notes that Britons are no longer considering comfortable positions at the Washington-based World Bank because of concern about crime:

> The fear of crime and violence in Washington has blocked at least one brain drain ... Many white Washingtonians feel a twinge of apprehension when they meet a black at night even in a secure neighbourhood ... the frightened can, and do, buy guns. (Heren 1970: 8)

By May 1970 there is a major shift when, for the first time, the British Conservative Party makes fear of crime part of their election manifesto. 'A better tomorrow with greater freedom: freedom to earn and to save, freedom from government interference, freedom of choice, freedom from fear of crime and violence' (cited in *The Times*, 27 May 1970: 8). With that reference fear of crime was essentially politicised in the UK. While the uptake of the initial political discourse was slow, this signalled the beginning of a new fascination with the fear of crime in Britain which turned out to surpass even that of the US. By the 1980s fear of crime had become a regular discourse of the British press.

The birth of the British Crime Survey and new administrative criminology

By the early 1970s the large-scale victim surveys in the US had ushered in a new or competing regime of truth about levels of victimisation and fear of crime itself. Like the US, from the late 1960s in particular (the 'big bang' period for criminology), other Western democracies began to develop agencies or capacities that could more effectively and systematically enumerate crime. In Australia, for example, the NSW Bureau of Crime Statistics and Research was set up in 1969. The

Australian Institute of Criminology (AIC), a Commonwealth statutory authority, was established in 1973. In the UK this task effectively fell to the UK Home Office – although it also had active ties to other criminological research centres in the UK, predominant among which was the Institute of Criminology at Cambridge University (Radzinowicz 1999). The growth in these government agencies, their capacities and governmental interest in criminology would not be without influence on the concept of fear of crime. As we have seen in early research in North America, the approach adopted by the early large-scale surveys was first to estimate 'the dark figure' of crime, thereby rendering possible the estimation of 'objective' levels of risk. Over this measure was superimposed estimated levels of fear through the deployment of various survey data. If fear of crime were 'irrational', government criminologists would have to provide statistical support for this through the acquisition of statistical knowledge about the fearful and the reasons for their fears; only then could fear of crime be addressed as a legitimate policy problem.

Broadly, this 'administrative' criminology should be conceptualised as a shifting set of practices aimed at the normative administration of criminal justice. Its genesis lay in technologies and techniques that are historically enmeshed in and, as Garland (2002) has noted, elemental to the formation of the discipline of criminology. These practices continually operate in chorus with, but at varying distances and degrees from, criminology's theoretical or more academic concerns. For example, the NSW Bureau of Crime Statistics and Research, the Home Office and other state and national sites of government criminology often theorise the results of their quantitative findings, and academic or theoretical criminologists are not strangers to descriptive and evaluative work (Walters 2003: 218).

However, from the late 1970s the Home Office in the UK in particular has been described as taking a 'new administrative' (Young 1994) or 'managerialist' turn and increasingly dispensing with research agendas concerned with causality, correction and rehabilitation. This coincided with the development of the British Home Office Research and Planning Unit under the management of Ronald Clarke (Clarke 1980). One should not be surprised by this turn given the pervasive influence of the conservative political rationalities of the first Thatcher Government and subsequent conservative governments through the 1980s and 1990s. Brake and Hale (1992: 9) note that with Thatcher 'the law and order issue thus has been removed from the political economy into the realm of individual morality and pathology'. In terms of new administrative criminology the 'problem' of the fear of crime had to be measured empirically and reduced pragmatically, specifically via the penchant for short-term micro-level preventative strategies (Hayward 2004).

Ronald Clarke and his associates commissioned The British Crime Survey (BCS), the first of which was conducted in 1982. It has largely been this survey that has driven research into fear of crime in the UK. The BCS provided a vast new data set for the Home Office and levels of fear of crime were prominent amongst policy issues drawn from the first sweep. However, this new criminology also involved a new set of rationalities about crime aimed at going beyond what was termed the 'nothing works' (Martinson 1974) rationality which many argued had undermined Home Office research. In this sense it was a stark departure from the earlier radical influence. As Maguire (1997: 147) suggests:

> Facing the apparent failure of the police, courts and prisons to stem rising crime rates, the Home Office Research Unit, under the headship of Ronald Clarke, began a clear policy shift from the late 1970s towards research initiatives in the area of crime prevention, in the sense of attempting to alter the physical environment, rather than the offender. This led to the formation of a separate research unit, the Home Office Crime Prevention Unit.

Hayward (2004) also argues that this move was a pragmatic response to the critique of 'correctionism' constantly echoed by radical criminologists. That is, the move away from the 'pathologisation of the offender' side-stepped the contentious issue of motivation in favour of the seemingly apolitical notion of situation. However, let me backtrack for a moment because all this has a prehistory that is important to this genealogical account. This involves the Home Office's testing some of the US methodologies on a slightly smaller scale and it involves some direct links between key actors involved in the US victim surveys, leading British academic criminologists and the Home Office.

Indeed, the first major victim survey in Britain, published as *Surveying Victims*, pre-dated the BCS and was carried out by Sparks, Genn and Dodd in London in 1977. But the seeds for this project can be traced further back. Indeed, Spark's aspirations to conduct 'more sophisticated' forms of crime survey were noted in his 1970 co-publication with Roger Hood, *Key Issues in Criminology* (1970). Here the authors commit a full two chapters – the first two – to discussions which involve the new US forms of victim survey which they see as offering new knowledge about the 'dark figure' of crime. They suggest:

> ... the real value of hidden delinquency and victimisation studies is not to warn us of the evils lurking beneath the surface, or even

help us get into perspective our concern over published statistics of crime, but rather to provide data to aid our understanding of the way in which deviance is perceived in varying social contexts. (Hood and Sparks 1970: 45)

So while they don't discuss fear of crime *per se* in *Key Issues* they do hint at its importance in understating perceptions as an aspect of victim surveys. It is not surprising then that they imported the Ennis (1967) fear of crime survey model with only minor amendments in their *Surveying Victims* (Sparks *et al.* 1977) research and subsequent publication.

Sparks *et al.*'s research provides a strong direct link to the earlier North American surveys of the President's Commission. Indeed, the three US reports are regularly cited in the pages of *Surveying Victims*. The preface of *Surveying Victims* also allows us to refine the date on which the initial research was conceived and carried out: conceived in 1972, conducted in 1973 (Sparks *et al.* 1977). Moreover, the list of 'academic colleagues' who offered 'advice and criticism' is also instructive: it includes Albert Biderman and Albert J. Reiss, authors of the President's Commission *Field Surveys 1* and *3* respectively. The list also includes Michael Hindelang among others. Thus the conduit for the importation of the concept of fear of crime into the UK has quite a clear lineage. The project, funded by the British Home Office and conducted by researchers then posted at the Institute of Criminology at Cambridge University, also provides a direct link to the subsequent work conducted under the auspices of the BCS. *Surveying Victims* was, for all intents and purposes, a pilot study for the BCS, conducted in order to test some methodological issues. The publication reports on a large-scale victim survey of areas of London.

Instructively though, *Surveying Victims* suggests that:

The use of the survey of 'gallup poll' methods in the measurement and study of crime is fairly recent. The first major surveys of this kind were actually carried out in the United States, for the President's Commission ... in 1966 ... For the first time real progress had been made toward overcoming the problem of the 'dark figure' of crime. (Sparks *et al.* 1977: 2)

And in an equally instructive footnote to this statement Sparks *et al.* (1977: 2) add that in regard to the large-scale surveying of victims, 'it seems to have been first suggested in print, in modern times, by a Finnish criminologist, Inkeri Antilla' (see also Antilla 1964).[2] That aside, the authors go on to cite, as I did in Chapter 3, that Ennis discussed with staff of NORC in 1962 the idea of victim surveys. Sparks *et al.* go on to suggest:

> A belief that crime is prevalent in one's neighbourhood, around the fabric of one's house – can result in fear or concern about a victim which in turn can lead to the reorganisation of one's customary way of life and one's way of looking at the world. It may be that, as several American surveys had suggested, that these fears are not closely related to *actual* risk of becoming a victim of crime. Even so, they still have important consequences for social life. (Sparks *et al.* 1977: 10)

Sparks *et al.* ask four questions related to crime fear.[3] Interestingly, of the fourth, which asks about level of concern about crime in London as a whole, Sparks *et al.* state:

> To be frank, the question about concern was included because other researchers have also asked it; in retrospect we must admit we are not at all clear just what it means, since it is not obvious what 'concern' about crime would boil down to in real life, apart from being a ground for expressing concern to an interviewer. (Sparks *et al.* 1977)

And Sparks *et al.*'s search for fear of crime finds, well, fear of crime. Forty per cent of respondents thought it unsafe to be on the streets after dark; 80 per cent said they were not safe in their homes; and higher levels of these were found in less safe neighbourhoods such as Brixton than in the sample as a whole (Sparks *et al.* 1977). The Home Office would continue the search from the early 1980s onwards.

Ronald Clarke states in the foreword to Michael Maxfield's Home Office Research and Planning Unit Report on the first BCS that 'despite what has been learned from the 1982 British Crime Survey … [about the fear of crime] there are still gaps in the knowledge and understanding. For this reason, *the topic of fear* will be covered again in the second British Crime Survey (Maxfield 1984: iii, my emphasis). And from here the concept of fear of crime became a mainstay of the BCS.

It is important to remind oneself of the change in rationalities which was driving research out of the Home Office at this point. Clarke's decision to eschew any interest in what he called 'dispositional factors' in order to pursue a research programme aimed at promoting 'situational crime prevention' (Maguire 1997) set out a blueprint for the alteration of the physical environment which made the commission of crime more difficult. Thus, from the early to mid 1970s there begins, slowly at first, a flow of 'administrative' governmentally driven research – certainly from agencies such as the Home Office in Britain, but also the ABS[4] in Australia. Again, it all borrowed from the initial US-based research. All of these agencies began, or further developed, their inquiries into the fear of crime around this period or shortly thereafter and many, even in the US, borrowed many of the micro-level policy responses drawn from the Home Office work (Hayward 2004). So despite being roughly 10 years behind the Americans, when the victim survey with its attendant fear of crime component was 'imported' to the UK, it was embraced with zeal. Indeed, the 'technical report' to the inaugural sweep of the British Crime Survey in 1982, as if more evidence was required, makes clear that crime fear is a central concern of the survey:

> The main aims of the survey were to estimate how many of the public are victims of selected types of crime over a year, describing the circumstances under which people become victims and the consequences of crime for victims and providing background information on *fear of crime* among the public and public contact with the police. (Wood 1984: 194, my emphasis)

The author of the report, Douglas Wood, goes on to give details of the genesis of the British Crime Survey, as well as outlining some of the limitations it encountered:

> The design of the survey drew heavily on experience in previous victim surveys – particularly on the US National Crime Survey and on victim surveys in Canada and the Netherlands. The design of this survey had, however, some individual features arising from its particular objectives and the circumstances and constraints under which it was carried out. (Wood 1984: 194)

And in listing the topics covered in the BCS, one can see the intimate relationship being forged by its authors, like those of the US studies, between victimisation and crime fear:

> The central aim of the survey was to assess the incidence of victimisation of selected types of crime among the public and to look at the circumstances in which people become victims. This, as we have seen, involved asking respondents a series of screening questions to establish whether or not they had been victims of relevant crimes during the reference period and to ask a series of very detailed questions about the incidents they reported. Basic descriptive background information on respondents and their

households was also collected to allow analysis of the sorts of people who do and do not become victims. It was decided that information should also be collected on other areas which were of intrinsic interest and which could usefully be related to experience as a victim. These areas were: crime with the police; *fear of crime*; lifestyle; self-reported offending. (Wood 1984: 194)

It goes without saying that the first BCS in 1982 found fear of crime. Hough and Mayhew (1983: 23) were able to suggest using the results that:

Around a third of women (but only 5% of men) said they sometimes avoided going out on foot after dark in their neighbourhood for fear of crime. This figure rose to 51%, 54% and 58% respectively for young, middle-aged and old women in inner cities. 8% of respondents said that they *never* went out alone on foot at night partly or wholly for fear of crime.

And it was burglary (44 per cent), mugging (34 per cent), sexual attacks (23 per cent) and assault (16 per cent) that not surprisingly topped the fearful crime stakes in response to the question which asked whether respondents were worried about the possibility that they might become a victim of crime (Hough and Mayhew 1983). Why wouldn't one be worried? And so fear of crime became a mainstream concern in Britain with the results quickly being taken up and reported in the media.

The BCS questionnaire also contained a version of the now heavily criticised scenario question and its associated prompts (Farrall and Gadd 2004; Hollway and Jefferson 2000). Similar but not identical to the Sparks *et al.* (1977) question, it was in fact closer to the original Ennis (1967) version. The associated prompts to the question push the respondent to discuss how safe they would feel walking the streets at night even if they never do this:

ASK ALL: How safe do you feel walking alone in this area after dark? Would you say (READ OUT)
• very safe
• fairly safe
• a bit unsafe
• very unsafe
(NOTE: IF RESPONDENT NEVER GOES OUT ALONE AT NIGHT, PROBE … "How safe *would* you feel …"). (Wood 1984: 194, emphasis in original)

With the administrative approach, Garland (2002) argues, criminology began to develop an economic rationality, and a reliance on an analytical language. The criminal subjectivity of new administrative criminology was to have '… nothing but choice and rationality. Disembodied from all social context – deprivation, racism, urban dislocation, unemployment, are airily listed as "background factors"', as Cohen later noted (1996: 1–21). The fear of crime increasingly became a target of this consumer-centred economic rationality. The BCS had set out to provide a 'truth' about crime rates under an assumption that this would also reduce what they thought were exaggerated fears. However, these new crime surveys instead began to further establish that many crimes were unreported and unregistered in police recorded crime figures. Implied notions that the fear of crime was irrational began to fade after the first few sweeps of the BCS.

Originally, the government criminologists involved in the BCS originally had a similar philosophy to critical writers such as Cohen; they had attempted to show how these fears were overstated, amplified, media related – most stopped short of the notion of irrational although it was implied. Some, such as Clarke (in Maxfield 1984: 47) had hoped that in demonstrating 'actual' crime levels, they would be able to 'normalise crime'. They had hoped to illustrate that the chances of victimisation for the average person were relatively low, and that the public, particularly women and the elderly, greatly exaggerated their chances of victimisation. Indeed, one of the most striking empirical findings of this research was that the victim was very like the average criminal: male, young and single. Useful data, one might think, in reducing the fears of the elderly and women. However, the experiences of many groups remained unrepresented by the early explanations of the Home Office. The accounting of experiences of gender, racial and cultural difference, became a major problem. Suggesting that the fear of crime was amplified or irrational was of no consolation to the individuals whose experiences of fear seemed very real. Rather than simply indicating the generally low risk of becoming a victim, the BCS data began to be used to suggest ways in which victims' lifestyles contributed to their very victimage. Here fear of crime began to offer a micro-level policy object that might be deployed in reducing the risks of some social groups. This new regime of truth was offering new possibilities that might be applied in the management of risk.

So began a new approach and a new set of rationalities in dealing with crime risk and fear of crime. New administrative-style criminology subtly advocated measures aimed at 'responsibilising' individuals in various ways. I have already identified the genesis of this in the *President's Report*. This dovetailed nicely with the establishment of police-based schemes such as neighbourhood watch and the like. Thus, there was the suggestion that the public have an important role to play in the minimisation of criminal activity – a tag line appropriated by the Thatcher Government. One should secure one's own environment and, hence, also manage one's fear. Further, the point was emphasised that the role of police in controlling crime was limited (Young 1994: 95). These measures constituted part of 'situational' crime prevention and what Garland has described as 'criminologies of the self'; the notion that to minimise crime, measures have to be taken to 'harden' any possible criminal targets through enhanced surveillance and the like, to reduce the rewards of offending, and to minimise the number of motivated offenders. There was also the hope that such schemes as neighbourhood watch, through mobilising and responsibilising citizens, based on a sense of community as they were, would reduce the fear of crime or at least modify it so as to alleviate its socially debilitating effects. Subjects would consume and practise processes of safety via a free market neo-liberal ideal. The welfarist solution had essentially been outmoded in favour of a more economically palatable technical response.

There is little doubt that new administrative criminology had begun to appreciate that fear of crime might serve as one of a plethora of technologies that could function as modes of social regulation; mentalities of *government through fear*. Michael Maxfield asks 'should public policy seek to modify the behaviour associated with fear of crime, or is it functional in reducing the risk of victimisation?'(1984: 47). Thus, the *fearing subject* of neo-liberal rationality is expected to be both governed by fear and to govern fear. I will return to the paradoxical governmental implications of this in Chapter 6.

All this raises further questions about criminological knowledge and how fear of crime became an accepted concept. Given criminology's relatively broad epistemological base, how for example did criminologies of the left deal with or resist the discourse around the fear of crime concept? As we will see, the conditions under which fear of crime took hold were not confined to administrative criminology; indeed other criminological paradigms can be equally, if less directly, implicated in the invention of fear of crime. What follows is an analysis of how fear of crime found ready acceptance as a concept across the criminological spectrum in the 1970s and 1980s in particular.

Disciplinary knowledge and the place of fear: radical criminologies

In the late 1960s and early 1970s criminology, along with the other political and academic realms, had come under challenge from a significant cohort of new radical thinkers. This radicalism and its influence on the discipline requires some discussion as it has ramifications for the emerging concept of fear of crime. By the 1960s a post-war liberal criminology which did little to challenge legal definitions of crime, and the accompanying conservative socio-cultural climate based loosely around capitalist ideology, were increasingly challenged by these radical voices critical of many hitherto unquestioned societal institutions, including those of the state (see Taylor *et al.* 1973). In terms of British criminology, the National Deviancy Symposium in 1968 perhaps best exemplified the emergence of this challenge but it was embodied more concretely in the pages of publications like Taylor *et al.*'s *The New Criminology* (1973). Related work could also be found in the US, Western Europe and Australia. Positivist notions that centred on the criminal being somehow outside societal norms came under increasing scrutiny, as crime was instead to be radically reconceptualised as being 'structured' through social process. The dominance of a pragmatic, legal-administrative criminology was being challenged by radical critics drawing on disciplines like sociology and history (Hogg 1988). The approach employed by Cohen (1972: 12) in his early 1970s work demonstrates this challenge and it is worth quoting him at length:

> This reorientation [of criminology] is part of what might be called the *sceptical* revolution in criminology and the sociology of deviance. The older tradition was *canonical* in the sense that it saw the concepts it worked with as authoritative ... The new tradition is sceptical in the sense that when it sees terms like 'deviant', it asks 'deviant to whom?' or 'deviant from what?'; when told something is a social problem, it asks 'problematic to whom?'; when certain conditions or behaviour are described as dysfunctional, embarrassing, threatening or dangerous, it asks 'says who?' and 'why?'

The debates between so-called radicals and the criminological establishment have been explored in detail elsewhere (Young 1994). However, for a colourful illustration of the 'establishment' backlash towards the new radicalism, one need look no further than Radzinowicz and King's (1977: 61) challenge to the radicalism in their book *The Growth of Crime*. Here the authors note that the radicals have 'distorted and diminished the impact of their message by their vivid exaggerations'.

93

However, Cohen (1972) did not believe that the tradition of 'libertarian pragmatism', forged under the influence in the UK of figures such as Radzinowicz, Mannheim and Grunhut (Hood 2004) would simply somehow fade away. Criminology is not, and never has been, a homogeneous discourse; nor is it a group of separate paradigms which, placed end to end in historical formation, lead to a final moment of criminological enlightenment or disciplinary perfection. Criminological discourse in the early 1970s, therefore, was certainly not dominated, or colonised, by 'radical criminology', but it was shaken by it and even influenced by it at the governmental level of the Home Office for a while. For radical theorists the causes of crime are seen to be in one way or another embedded into the structures or social organisation of society. Hence, crime is not a pre-given natural phenomenon, rather it is produced by material societal structure and/or social relations, which also produced equally destructive social reactions against it. Consequently, within some radical modes of critique, the offender is constructed, not so much as a criminal (although one's offending behaviour is not necessarily denied), but as the victim or product of a system that favours the interests of capital over the working class (see Taylor *et al.* 1973).

Moreover, Radical criminologists stressed that the extent of crime and the perceived risks of victimisation, particularly as a result of street crime, had been overstated or 'amplified' (Cohen 1972). Many championed the 'moral panic' thesis which constructed public concerns about crime and deviance as media instigated and socially produced events; or additionally, sought to place the blame for fear on to external signs of poverty. This form of analysis was taken to its zenith in Hall *et al.*, *Policing the Crisis* (1978). On reading *Policing the Crisis* one notes that one of the strengths of its analysis is that it *does not* explore fear of crime *per se*. Indeed, *Policing the Crisis* is notable in that, once again, it illustrates how the concept of fear of crime had yet, even by 1978, to make it to the UK as a criminological concept of any note. In a sense fear of crime was the delayed conceptual corollary to 'mugging' in the Hall *et al.* (1978) analysis. If mugging the concept was transported from the US in 1972, then fear of crime was to follow soon after – indeed, as we have seen, the transportation had already begun in administrative circles prior to the publication of *Policing the Crisis*. Nonetheless, if there is one thing *Policing the Crisis* is about, it is what we would now call fear of crime. Indeed, it is illustrative to quote Hall *et al.* (1978) in one of the few passages in which they do use the term 'fear'.

Thus, via the American transplant, Britain adopted not only 'mugging', but the fear and panic *about* 'mugging' and the backlash reaction into which those fears and anxieties issued. (1978: 28)

If mugging became a crisis in 1960s USA and was then transplanted to Britain, the fear of crime crisis did likewise 10 years or so later. We were entering a period on both sides of the Atlantic in which there would be a *crisis* of fear of crime.

The analysis in *Policing the Crisis* acknowledged that broader social anxieties could be projected on to the 'discovered' image of the mugger:

[the mugger's] form and shape accurately reflected the content of the fears and anxieties of those who first imagined, and then actually discovered him ... He was a sort of personification of all the positive social images – only in *reverse*: black on white. (Hall *et al.* 1978: 28)

This passage is very insightful. For the mugger – the positive social image in reverse – is a shadowy creature very similar to the *feared subject* of later crime prevention literature. That is, the unknown and unplaceable stranger who has no specific embodiment, but is the opposite of the responsible law-abiding citizen. The criticism of the Hall *et al.* style of analysis has been that fears about crime are constructed as unjustified or irrational. Yet, on closer inspection this criticism is overstated. Rather, what this style lacked, and as I've suggested was perhaps all the more insightful for, was the specific analytical language and conceptual framework of fear of crime as we (mis)understand it today. Nonetheless, Jock Young (1987) later[5] argued that the radical criminologies of the early 1970s engaged in a 'great denial' of the full impact of crime on communities. This, he suggested, 'facilitated both the abstentionist politics of radical pessimism and a concentration on discourse about crime and deviance, especially in the mass media, to the detriment of any careful attention to crimes as social facts ...'(cited in Sparks 1992: 120).

The fear of crime for radical criminology, and, one might add, some of the work coming out of the Home Office in the early 1970s, was regarded as subsidiary to the main line of enquiry, which was to determine empirically the extent of victimisation and, therefore, the objective measure of risk. To this extent fear was generally treated simply as a function of risk (Sparks 1992). That is, if the risk was low (or lower), high levels of concern would be thought of as exaggerated – a function of moral panic. However, the focus of radical theorists on moral panic and the media did provide fear of crime a further discursive surface within the criminological realm. Young (1987) suggests that, as a consequence of moral panic theory, there was an unwitting collusion between radical criminology and the 'new' administrative criminology of the late 1970s and early 1980s, resulting in the search for 'surplus' fear in the form of broken windows (Wilson and Kelling 1982) or perception of neighbourhood change (Skogan and Maxfield 1981: 280). Certainly the search for surplus fear became an aim of the British Crime Survey (Sparks 1992).

My principal interest here in radical criminologies is related to this: given their emphasis on social construction, social plurality, conflict, and their productive relationship to crime, the philosophical basis of radical criminologies ultimately led to notions that explanations of crime and criminality could be found in the analysis of these various structures; the analysis of class, capitalism and later gender, race and age. What we now know of as fear of crime, although a 'subsidiary' line of enquiry, had increasingly to be accounted for in light of the developing business of crime and victim surveys. Or, it had to be explained away. Whether this was in terms of the fears and anxieties being 'irrational' or 'surplus' now seems of little consequence. The concept fear of crime would gradually fill the conceptual gap between objective risk and measured or expressed concern. In this sense Young has a point in regard to the radical and administrative 'unwitting collusion'. This collusion brought with it unintended consequences of intensifying fear of crime discourse, but then so did the work of the left realists themselves.

Increasingly fear of crime became both an aetiological issue (what causes it?) and an administrative interest (what controls it?). In administrative terms fear of crime had to be explained quantitatively and represented numerically – a contrast to the work of the radicals. Crime fear would ultimately have profound effects on the direction and scope of administrative criminology, creeping as we have seen into the project of the British Crime Survey and finding political fuel with the subsequent 1979 election of the Thatcher Conservative Government, which made law and order a central electoral issue (Brake and Hale 1992).

However, it was not only administrative and radical forms of criminology that would take an interest in the fear of crime. Broader cultural and social movements that encouraged the population from the 1960s onwards – and for the first time the female component of the population – to engage in the pleasurable pursuits of full democratic citizenship brought with them new forms of real and perceived bodily risk (see Pratt 1997). This new freedom was partly a result of second-wave feminism which helped open up new problematisations; concerns and anxieties about the risk of victimisation. Thus, as fear of crime gradually became a more popularised term and concept more opportunities arose to describe experience through its lens. The *fear feedback loop* gradually drew in more sites of popular, political and disciplinary power that would in turn increase interest in the fear of crime.

Women's movements and feminist criminology

Along with the radical critique of criminology new feminist criminologies were emerging. Certainly, by the early 1970s the subordination of women to male violence and the questions of an inherently patriarchal social order had become a major concern. Feminists rightly believed that criminology had slighted the offences most likely to victimise women: domestic violence, incest and sexual assault in particular. Some feminists pointed out that criminology as a discipline had ignored the fact that men were overwhelmingly the perpetrators of crime and some even argued that the reason for men's criminality as a group could be found in their very masculinity (Allen 1988); even labelling theorists and radical criminologists, the self-appointed progressives of the 1960s and 1970s, were seen as ignoring or marginalising the experiences of women (Rafter and Heidensohn 1995). This new and specifically gendered set of discourses about crime victims[6] had its effects on fear of crime as a criminological concept.

Much of the work of feminists in the 1970s and early 1980s produced literature on women for women. By this I mean that women were mostly the subjects of a body of scholarship which was attempting to fill a void concerning women and the effects of crime. As Smart (1995: 4) suggests, women were then uncharted territory; there was an eagerness to traverse, map and know this new terrain. A crucial element of this new knowledge was produced through attention to women's experiences as victims of male crime. It was assumed that women as readers would relate to the experiences of women as subjects and women as scholars.[7] While radical criminology had firmly placed class analysis on the criminological agenda, feminist criminologists were placing equal analytical importance on issues of gender. Accordingly, the emerging research into the fear of crime would have to take gender into account, the *fearing subject* of the fear of crime literature would be a *gendered fearing subject*. Indeed, gender as a variable had been used, once again, as far back as the President's Commission (1967).

The year 1975 was declared International Women's Year, and however tokenistic such a declaration may seem, this period saw some major successes for the women's movement. This included the opening of women's refuges and progressive legislative change in a range of areas (Smart and Smart 1975). In Australia, for example, a rape crisis centre was opened in Sydney (Allen 1990: 226). Women's refuges had already been opened in Britain – the first in Chiswick in 1972 – and the USA – the first in 1973 (Dobash and Dobash 1992). The year 1975 also saw the introduction of 'no-fault divorce' in Australia, making it easier, at least legally, for women to escape violent relationships. Further, in 1978 the NSW government established help centres for sexual assault victims in five Sydney area hospitals. These initiatives, gradually taking hold across Western democracies, dramatically increased public, political and police awareness of crimes against women and resulted in an increase in the reporting of such offences to police, although convictions remained universally low – around 3 per cent in Australia (Allen 1990). Dobash and Dobash (1992: 2) describe how stories of violence against women came into public discourse:

> In the 1970s the stories at once described what were then unfamiliar accounts of abuse and informed a disbelieving public of its widespread nature. Women's accounts revealed the nature of men's violence and the sources of conflict leading to attacks. They also described women's emotions and reactions as well as the inactions of social and legal institutions.

The 'Help Centres', shelters and refuges became sites for the production of knowledge for a new form of feminist research and scholarship. This would both engage in an exercise of public consciousness-raising regarding issues of violence against women, and provide a more detailed and critical social analysis of the problem. As Lisa Leghorn, an American feminist activist, urged, 'any research that is conducted should be conducted hand in hand with women who have been through the abuse' (cited in Dobash and Dobash 1992: 256). So began a body of literature that has taken as its subjects *women* as victims and survivors of male sexual/physical violence in particular. By the early 1980s, in the face of this new body of feminist literature, it was no longer politically palatable for any criminological tradition to successfully sustain the argument that women's greater fear of crime was irrational – the 'excessive' or 'amplified' fears thesis was becoming untenable.

The power effects of this literature, however, were not limited to shifting a male-centered criminological discourse or raising general awareness of gendered forms of violence. It also generated a new discourse stressing the possibility, the very real risk, that male violence could be a reality in the lives of women. While the emergence of the women's refuge and the plethora of new studies that followed provided feminism with the tools to report the hitherto hidden violence via women who had experienced it first hand, the accompanying literature, reports and programmes enabled anxiety about this violence to be inscribed on the bodies of women more generally. This research, and the new forms of research and knowledge it utilised, was illustrative of the emergence of new regimes of truth around both victimage and fear of crime. Suddenly, one in four women would be the victim of sexual assault in their lifetime, one in six the victim of domestic violence, yet women were highly under-represented as offenders. On top of this feminist literature and research women's magazines helped to democratise the information. Pratt (1997: 218) notes that women's magazines actively began to survey women about their experiences of male physical and sexual violence from the late 1970s onwards. Accordingly, he suggests that crime risks were no longer to be calculated on the basis of one set of government-produced crime statistics. These had become only one source of statistical knowledge about crime. And most of the new sources of data – phone interviews, victim surveys, self-report surveys and the media surveys mentioned above – suggested much higher levels of victimisation than had the traditional sources. We can of course trace this discursive surface of democratisation back to the emergence of opinion poll data but this was yet another subtle shift.

The growing body of 'expert' knowledge on crime fear also provoked, indeed required, a governmental response. Thus begins the reams of governmental advice literature aimed at enabling women to reduce their risk of victimisation – which feminists such as Elizabeth Stanko have heavily criticised for its inclination to place responsibility for women's safety on to women (Stanko 1990, 1997, 1998). Stanko (2000) has more recently raised major concerns about the ramifications of the historical link between crime fear, victim lifestyle and victimisation. She argues that crime surveys, as a methodological tool, rather than providing a remedy to reduce fear of crime by addressing problems of civil rights, effectively problematise the lifestyles of many as deserving their plight. This will be addressed further in later chapters; suffice to say here that this new body of knowledge produced a number of unforeseen power effects. The irrational *fearing subject* had become a rational, and often although not exclusively, *gendered fearing subject*. Women's fear of crime became a justifiable response to life in a patriarchal world. All this only had the effect of increasing interest in fear of crime and how to deal with it. That is, one of the perhaps unintended consequences of the development of a feminist discourse about crime was that it had the effect of sensitising women to fear of crime and both provoking research into women's crime fear and, as we will see, establishing new and not always constructive modes of governing it.

The new right and right realism: the political economy of fear

The changes identified in administrative agendas were not purely a result of new research mentalities and methodologies. As previously noted there had also been changes in the political climate more generally and these had been, at least in part, reflected in government criminological agendas. It may seem disconcerting to switch from an analytical register that has concerned itself with criminological practices and knowledges, to one concerned with political manoeuvring and popular representations of crime. However, to negate the influence of these popular and political representations would be to offer a version of events which prioritises the administrative and long-term rationalities of government over the short-term political imperatives, namely, the rise of neo-conservatism, and authoritarian populism. Garland (1997: 202) argues, 'switching between rationalities, or moving from one discursive register (the economic-administrative) to another (the populist-political), is very much a political process'. However, as my reading of Harris (1969) has indicated, the domains are intimately interconnected in this genealogy.

Public fears have, since the 1960s at least, proven fertile ground for the political right; particularly neo-conservative political movements and their often associated populist approaches to the governance of crime.[8] The UK Conservative Party made law and order a central element of their election campaign in 1979 and their election marked the endorsement of what Tierney (1996) terms 'common sense amateurism'. By the early 1980s the policies of Thatcherism in the UK, Reaganism in the USA and a 'tougher' approach to criminal justice by the respective states of Australia, had successfully exploited the public's anxieties about victimisation in order to push a conservative political agenda. Law and order had become a politically charged topic. Braithwaite, Biles and Whitrod (1982) argued tellingly in Australia that:

> While fear of communism might be seen as the most appropriate address to a local RSL [Returned Services League] by an astute conservative politician, law and order might be perceived as an even more appropriate topic for an address to the country women's association.

My emphasis here is that neo-conservative political campaigns, focusing on issues of law and order, had as their currency the public's fear of crime: ironic, given that fear of crime was 'discovered' through the surveys initiated by Johnson's social democratic plan. I would go as far as to argue that were it not for this 'discovery' of crime fear, the populist law and order campaigns of the political right would not have had the political scope of appeal they have had; Harris's (1969) US account hints at this dynamic. At the very least they would have lacked the fear of crime as an object on which to hang the need for political and legislative change. Claims of a fearing population could now be backed up by statistical 'proof'. Further, as an object of investigation, new interest in the fear of crime was generated precisely because it lay at the nexus of neo-liberal new administrative concerns and calculations and a neo-conservative political agenda. With the ascendency of a right realist or new right criminology, particularly in the United States, the political right found a criminology with which it could be aligned, and which would have a profound influence in the governance of both crime and crime fear.

The success of the political right in politicising 'law and order' had disastrous effects on the left in general. The right even found considerable political support within the working class, historically the constituency of the left; the so-called Reagan Democrats, the Thatcherite working class, and more recently in Australia the Howard 'battlers'. The political appeal of the conservative right in its engagement with law and order and a public fearful of crime cannot be understated; its practical effects can be seen in what some authors have termed – rightly or wrongly – a 'new punitiveness' (Pratt *et al.* 2005). The philosophy of the conservative right places the responsibility for crime squarely on the individual, virtually ignoring the structural determinants of crime; additionally, it reasserts the importance of the punishment fitting the crime, 'an eye for an eye'. This has resulted in longer prison sentences for offenders, the building of new prisons, growing prison populations, the expansion of police forces and more powers for police, and attacks on welfare expenditure amongst other things. The right has generally overseen a shift from broadly social democratic or 'welfarist' governance, certainly in the UK and Australia, whereby the state takes some responsibility for its citizens' welfare and their actions, to a neo-liberal individualism whereby the citizen is encouraged (forcefully at times) to take responsibility for her or his own actions and behaviours. These shifts in political rationality have also been accompanied by shifts in the language and rationalities of crime control, often driven or condoned by right-thinking criminological actors.

The work of James Q. Wilson and his form of right realism in the United States has been the most notable criminological example of a form of criminology converging with the politics of the right. Wilson was for a time an adviser to the Reagan administration and had been an outspoken advocate for 'law and order common sense'.

That is not to suggest that Wilson was supportive of all of the punitive measures of neo-conservative politics. Importantly though, Wilson and Kelling (1982) suggest that the reduction of fear of crime should be a major priority in the maintenance of order. Further, they suggest that to reduce fear police should be empowered – particularly at the level of neighbourhood and community – to criminalise 'disreputable' behaviour. They suggest that (Wilson and Kelling 1982: 35):

> Arresting a single drunk or a single vagrant who has harmed no identifiable person might seem unjust, and in a sense it is. But failing to do anything about a score of drunks or a hundred vagrants may destroy an entire community.

And:

> ... one broken window becomes many. The citizen who fears the ill-smelling drunk, the rowdy teenager, or the importuning beggar is not merely expressing his distaste for unseemly behaviour; he [sic] is also giving voice to a bit of folk wisdom that happens to be a correct generalisation – namely, that serious street crime flourishes in an area in which disorderly behaviour goes unchecked. (Wilson and Kelling 1982: 34)

Fear of crime is a central concept of the 'broken windows' theory and much of the new right discourse on crime control. It commands an important discursive position at the nexus of right politics and the project of right realist criminology. As I have suggested, in terms of the politics of the right, fear is a key factor in rationalising and selling its tough law and order policies – thus fears are targeted and perhaps intensified by electioneering aimed at securing votes on law and order credentials. However, for right realist criminology it is the fear of crime that has to be reduced by restoring order to the streets. To reduce the fear of crime, for right realism, will break the cycle of community dislocation that produces crime.

That fear of crime is a legitimate area for investigation for criminology is no longer in question. Here we see again how a discursive paradox has driven the emergence of the fear of crime. In terms of the politics of the right, fear proves a key emotive factor in providing electoral support for its tough law and order policies – the electioneering actually produces and plays on community fears. However, for right realist criminology it is the fear of crime that has to be reduced as part of the restoration of order to the streets. The 'fear of crime paradox' is not that the least likely victims are the most fearful, it is rather that the politics of fear provides governments with the power to attempt to reduce the very fears they helped manufacture.

The criminal and the fearing subject of the right

New administrative criminology – through its attention to the statistical calculation and quantification of criminal acts, its victim surveys, and its development of what could be described as an economy of crime – has produced a language and rationality about crime that has been integrated into some aspects of right political ideology – in particular its neo-liberal variants. That is not to suggest that this notion of the criminal as a self-reflective, independent and rational actor is in any way purely the product of the political right or administrative criminological thought; to the contrary both have invoked one of the main tenets of classical liberalism that emerges in the eighteenth century, precisely the notions of free will embraced by classical proto-criminological thought'.[9] Pasquino (1991a) describes the criminal of classical criminological knowledge as *homo penalis,* and argues that, in classical conceptions of the criminal, *'homo penalis* exists as a potentiality in each of us, but is actualised only through such violations of the law as any person may commit simply as the outcome of an erroneous calculation'. However, with the economic rationality of administrative criminology we see a move towards not only a rationally calculating actor but an active citizen who becomes the subject of their own crime prevention strategies, purchases and practices. They are imagined as *homo economous* and it is of this figure that the *fearing subject* is a subset.

The positive side of constructing the offender as an agent of free will is that it has highlighted individual rights, and in particular, the right to feel safe and secure (White and Haines 1996: 234). However, as a result of this, notions of rational choice have also been applied to the 'irresponsible' or 'inappropriate' actions of victims of crime. Individuals are expected to take responsibility for their property, their valuables and their bodies. Hence, these rationalities dovetail with the emergence of private policing firms and a user pays system of policing and security (O'Malley 1992). Here fear of crime operates as a tool of policing in governing or regulating the self, insuring the self in one way or another against the actions of others. The discourse of victim carelessness removes responsibility from a failing police service, and poor political tactics. It helps produce legitimate and illegitimate victims. Hence, Margaret Thatcher has said, 'We have to be careful that we ourselves don't make it easy for the criminal' (*The Age* cited in O'Malley

1992: 25). This is a line also pursued by insurance companies; take for example the rebates offered for the installation of alarm systems; or the sponsorship – until recently – of the neighbourhood watch scheme in NSW by the NRMA.[10] Insurance operates as a moral technology in this contemporary illustration of classical liberal thought. Fear of crime becomes a governmental tool in the economic management and minimisation of risky behaviour in what might be conceptualised as a shift from dangerousness and the unknown and incalculable actions of others, to risk, the actuarial calculations of the behaviours of the everyday. All *fearing subjects* are expected to manage their bodies and property in terms of risk; calculated by themselves and others. Ewald suggests classical liberal thought postulates that:

> [t]o calculate a risk is to master time, to discipline the future. To conduct one's life in the manner of an enterprise indeed begins in the eighteenth century to be a definition of a morality whose cardinal virtue is providence. To provide for the future does not just mean not living from day to day and arming oneself against ill fortune, but also mathematising one's commitments. Above all, it means no longer arming oneself to the decrees of providence and the blows of fate, but instead transforming one's relationships with nature, the world and god so that, even in misfortune, one retains responsibility for one's affairs by possessing the means to repair its effects. (Ewald 1991: 207)

The fear of crime, through the neo-liberalism invoked in modern administrative practices, brings a particular form of *fearing subject* into the realm of government – the potential victim who like the criminal of classical thought, is an 'everyman'. This subject is constituted by two mutually supportive governmental discourses. Firstly, as a *fearing subject* one is the passive and innocent object of possible criminal wrong-doing; but secondly, a responsible actor who must do her or his utmost to insure against the potentiality of victimisation. I will deal with this aspect further in Chapter 6. As a *fearing subject* one has the right to conduct oneself 'freely' but only to the extent that this freedom is amenable to the rationality of specific modes of neo-liberal government. One's victimage is one's own responsibility. Burchell (1993) argues that liberalism constructs a relationship between government and governed that increasingly depends upon individuals assuming the status of subjects of their lives, upon their fashioning themselves as particular kinds of subjects, upon ways of practising their freedom. It increasingly impinges upon one's very individuality, 'in their practical relationships to themselves in the conduct of their lives; it concerns them at the very heart of themselves by making its rationality the condition of their active freedom' (Burchell 1993: 268).

The ascendancy of law and order debates driven by the New Right, and the imagined *fearing subject* of new administrative criminology, paralleled with the re-emergence or reassertion of or a reworked form of the liberal subject provided as surface on which fear of crime could cement itself. It also provided the impetus for a rethinking by criminologists and others on the Left. The outcome of this is what has come to be known as Left Realist criminology. This, as we shall see, has also had its effects on the growing fear of crime debates.

Left realism: the measurement of fearing subjects

The project of left realism, coming as it did as a response to the perceived political 'failures' of the radical, or what it termed 'idealist', criminology, was to put the focus back on to the criminal, the victim, and the reality of crime; to expose the 'real' levels of crime in society, and to carry out this project in a highly empirical and practical way. The focus of radical criminology on crimes of the powerful and crimes of the state, the realists argued, had missed the point and did not address the lived realities of the working class, who were actually the most likely victims of street crime. Left Realism, as noted, emerged primarily from radical criminology in the UK, and in particular via a number of former 'left idealist' academics centred at Middlesex University during the British Labour Party's unelectable years (Hayward 2004). However, its research methods have been borrowed in various guises in Australia, the US and elsewhere.

The primary technique of data collection for left realism was to be the victim survey. These however were conducted on a more localised and ostensibly more sophisticated basis than larger-scale crime surveys such as the BCS, which the realists suggested were blunt instruments. Left realism, via the local victim survey, took the criminological rediscovery of the victim to new levels. Moreover, with left realism came an engagment with the emotional attributes of victimage, including fear of crime. Surveys such as these, although all might not rightly be characterised as 'realist', multiplied from the mid 1980s onwards with work conducted in Liverpool (Kinsey 1984), London (Crawford *et al.* 1990; Jones *et al.* 1986), Edinburgh (Anderson *et al.* 1990, 1991), and Glasgow (Heartless *et al.* 1995). Left realists argued that:

Criminology must embrace the totality of the criminal process; it must be true to its reality. And this reality must include the offender, the victim, informal social control and the state (for example policing). These are the four dimensions of criminology. Victimisation studies fit into this paradigm to the extent that they indeed represent an audit of people's experiences, anxieties and problems of crime. Further, as victimisation studies [extend] ... themselves from the study of victims to that of the police, to public attitudes to penalty etc. they ... [begin] to provide the sort of empirical basis necessary for a realist criminology. (Jones *et al.* 1986: 3–4)

Out of this new empirical knowledge provided by left realist surveys, and the (minor) 'avalanche' of published material that followed, it becomes apparent – and unavoidable, considering the brief outlined above – that a major object of investigation was once again the fear of crime. With left realism we see a fascination with the fear of crime, and accordingly with a new form of imagined *fearing subject*; a subject of whom it will attempt to (re)present the expressive dimensions – 'anxieties', 'attitudes' and 'experiences' – in order to empower. Most particularly it will attempt to claim the victim (and fear) for the politics of the left. Who is most fearful and why? What produces this fear? Why are the least likely victims the most fearful subjects? These are questions that left realists would attempt to answer in a more politically pragmatic way; they were to do this by addressing the 'real' conditions of criminal victimisation and fear. Certainly the criminology of the left has gradually taken left realist concerns on board. And indeed echoes of left realism can be heard in political statements, for example the Blair Government's 'tough on crime, tough on the causes of crime' rhetoric in Britain.[11]

Left realism imagines the *fearing subject* as rational. Fear is seen as an understandable response to a largely undetected or grey area (the dark figure) of crime. This grey area of crime is hidden due to methodological problems involving the collecting and recording of crime statistics but can be exposed by use of a well-constructed, locally targeted victim survey. The main 'realist' argument has been that the discrepancies between public fear and concerns about crime and actual risk of victimisation are more apparent than real and that they have rational explanations. Jones *et al.* (cited in Sparks 1992: 122) argue that:

to take only the most important and controversial issue in the area, namely women's fear of crime, 'realist' social surveys indicate that a proper account of women's subjection to domestic, work related, and other peripherally visible forms of victimisation, their experience of other harassments and marginally criminal incivilities, their unsatisfactory experience of police protection and the multiplication of each of these problems by factors of race, class and age, entirely dispels the apparent disparity between risk and fear.

Realist criminology refuses to concede that the public could be simply mistaken in their relationship to the social world and believes that public understandings of crime – and therefore their fears – have a rational core. Left realism, moreover, has sought to measure this rational core; to organise a body of knowledge that would make the *fearing subject* understandable and knowable – a project that would, it was hoped, loosen the stranglehold of the political right on the 'law and order' debate.

Alison Young and Peter Rush (1994) have been particularly critical of the realist approach, suggesting that this focus on the 'unbounded subjectivism of the victim' means victimage determines the 'real' in realist. In this sense the average *fearing subject* delineates the terms in which policy and policing might respond to a crime problem – perhaps more likely to be a fear problem as recounted to the left realist researcher. Moreover, the realist focus on the reinscription of citizenship – for the victim – through 'empowerment' promotes the victim to the status of active citizen. Young (1996: 58) eloquently explains how this new 'activity' can simply become a form of neo-liberal self-governance or responsibilisation:

> The self government prescribed for the subject-as-victim has a spatial quality, taking place at nodal points in the city; for example, the entrance door to one's house must be strengthened and the windows locked; the dark street must be avoided for the safety of the well-lit pavement; multi-storey car parks must be avoided after dark. Through self-surveillance and self-policing, the victim asserts himself as a citizen of the city.

With the election of the Blair Government in Britain in 1997 the realist model of the local crime survey became the template for a range of new crime audits conducted at the local government level. These audits, centrally coordinated by the Home Office, but conducted usually through criminological consultancies with local government, provided a new set of knowledges and strategies for the prevention and government of crime. I will discuss these further in Chapter 6. Needless to say, once the realist survey became an instrument of government its social democratic political clout, arguable though it might have been, was somewhat blunted. Such are the dangers or mixing criminology, anxiety and politics.

Some new directions

Over the past decade some researchers have developed more sophisticated conceptual models of investigating crime fear. Yet few, if any, of these have been picked up by government criminologists or in large-scale surveys.[12] As Jackson (2004) has noted, words have run ahead of actions in fear of crime research and too few of the key methodological and theoretical insights have been integrated into practice. While in some respects the steam has come off the fear of crime debate and there is some agreement that 'fear of crime is a complex, diffuse, "catch-all" phrase referring to a range of inter-related but theoretically distinct perceptions and responses to crime and risk of victimisation' (Jackson 2004: 20), many problems still persist. Perception questions still adorn most large-scale surveys and many smaller surveys simply mimic these. Politicians and some criminologists still ask why the public's fears outstrip their risks, and as we will see in the coming chapters fear of crime is now a tangible entity in the public mind.

Nonetheless, critical conceptual development has resulted in growing emphasis on the more multidimensional aspects of fear of crime. Social and economic issues, subjective vulnerability and isolation have gradually been broken down into specific mediating factors that have enabled researchers 'to understand the social context of perceptions of crime and its consequences' (Carach and Mukherjee 1999: 6).

Hollway and Jefferson (1997, 2000), working from a psycho-social perspective, have developed new qualitative methodologies designed to elicit biographical narratives about the experiences of the respondent. This, they argue, allows the researcher to understand how the 'anxious, defended subject' deals with their experiences. The authors suggest that the subject is not simply 'a product of the social environment' but is formed by the often creative and imaginative forms through which the self defends against anxiety. One of these forms of defence may be, for example, that a subject displaces a threat to the integrity of their own subjectivity on to another person or group in order to control their anxiety. Thus, for them a fear of crime discourse is not necessarily a negative force within one's subjectivity, it may in fact offer the subject respite from other more debilitating fears (Hollway and Jefferson 1997).

Other innovative studies were conducted by a group of colleagues working out of the Scottish Centre of Criminology. Jason Ditton, Liz

Gilchrist, John Bannister and Stephen Farrall used survey work in critical and creative ways to interrogate the concept of fear of crime (Ditton *et al*. 1999a, Ditton *et al*. 1999b, Farrall *et al*. 1997). In one study, for example, 1,600 residents of the Strathclyde region were randomly sampled and asked if they were angry about or fearful of crime. They found that more people are angry than are afraid, but also that people who are angry are much more angry than people who are afraid (Ditton *et al*. 1999a). They replicated these findings for every age group and across genders with only minor divergences. Females, for example, were found to be more afraid than males but also reported being angrier. The point here was that if you offer respondents an alternative discourse through which to express themselves, anger rather than fear, it became very unclear as to whether fear of crime was a useful conceptual category at all.

Farrall and Gadd (2004), in more recent work, argue that when questions are introduced about the *frequency* that one feels fearful, overall levels of fear expressed by respondents drop significantly. That is, most fear of crime research has never bothered asking how often respondents experience fearful episodes. In other work Sutton and Farrall (2005) have developed a lie scale that suggests that men underplay their fear of crime for the sake of machismo. This tends to undermine the risk/fear paradox in an altogether new way.

Others have emphasised the need to understand 'crime talk' and 'safety talk' (Stanko 1997). That is, to analyse the broader contexts in which people talk about and situate crime. For example, Girling, Loader and Sparks (Girling *et al*. 2000; Loader *et al*. 2000) rejected the tick-a-box survey for a contextual approach exploring the meanings associated with individuals' perceptions of threat of victimisation. Removing fear as a 'central organising principle' they listened to people make connections to broader cultural signifiers, their larger sense of perspective. They were interested in locality: the place where their respondents lived, their place within it and its place in a bigger national set of stories (Girling *et al*. 2000). In short, they found that talk about crime disclosed concerns and perceptions of their respondents' neighbourhoods, their social make-up and status, and their place in the world. They concluded that talk about crime had the effect of providing individuals with some ontological security through the identification of insiders, outsiders, self and other. Likewise Stanko (1997) has directed us to the various ways in which 'safety talk', directed at and often engaged in by women, operates in ways that govern women's movement in space and time and makes them responsible for their own conduct in particularly gendered ways. Indeed, Stanko explores a framework not dissimilar to that which I employ in the following chapters of this book. She suggests that the 'criminologies of self' which have such purchase in crime prevention and the crime prevention literature have the effects of making women responsible for their own safety.

Overall, the field of fear of crime research is increasingly multi-dimensional and fractured, perhaps reflecting the object it attempts to study. Moreover, it seems that, as more research is conducted and more literature is produced, the concept of fear of crime itself slips further from the grasp of those who wish to measure and define it. And perhaps we are all the better for this. Nonetheless, at a general level it seems that there is still an enduring assumption held by many that conceptual complexities and inconsistencies can be overcome or tamed by producing more accurate research instruments, better definitions, a closer understanding of the variables, larger sample groups, more localised sample groups or more universalised research design. I could go on. But perhaps the ultimate goal of this form of fear of crime research is an unobtainable one.

Conclusion

Throughout the 1970s the concept of fear of crime made its way into mainstream criminological discourse. Following the President's Commission report and the political discourse in the US it could hardly be ignored. In the 1970s the first clue that crime fear would become an issue in the UK is notable with the term's appearance in the Tory Party's election manifesto. However, from the late 1960s onwards reports about America's growing crime fear had been filtering back to the UK via foreign correspondents in the news media. While radical voices in UK criminology largely ignored fear of crime as a concept during the 1970s their work around moral panic and deviance amplification opened up conceptual space that fear of crime might later fill. In this sense radical criminology was unwittingly to collude with an emerging administrative criminology aimed at a new form of crime prevention through responsibilisation. Feminist criminology also played a part in fostering a fear of crime discourse. This new feminist literature raised awareness of the prevalence of men's violence against women, rendering every woman a potential victim.

By 1982 large-scale victim surveys were under way in the UK, driven by a new generation of Home Office researchers. They largely borrowed the US President's Commission model – running a large-scale pilot in 1977 – rendering fear of crime a central concern. With Thatcherism in the UK and Reaganism in the US fear of crime became further politicised. Indeed, it was nicely situated at the nexus of the

US right's cherished political tools of law and order and individual freedoms. Through all this enumeration 'remained hungry for things to count'. While the large-scale victim surveys such as the BCS offered a new regime of truth to traditional criminal statistics other forms of surveys also emerged. The opinion poll model was popularised in women's magazines and the like. By the mid 1980s in the UK a left realist agenda had emerged which lionised the localised crime survey. By the time of the election of the Blair Government in the 1990s this had become the model for crime audits across the UK and part of a New Labour agenda which saw the centre left wrestle back the law and order agenda from the right. This recent obsession with 'fear of crime' should not come as any great surprise. Cohen (1985: 177) has suggested that criminology has approached its disciplinary practices via a process he describes as the 'what works' principle, or – borrowed from Raymond Mack – as a 'Reverse Midas Principle ... whatever turns to gold you touch'.

Through all this, fear of crime has been of central concern. Indeed, by the mid 1980s a range of policies was being developed aimed at its reduction. However, the genie was out of the bottle. And however hard governments and policing agencies seemed to work to reduce crime fear the increasingly sophisticated surveys they commissioned appeared to indicate that it was increasing. However, it was not quite this straightforward. It was also evident that some had recognised fear of crime as a tactic that could be used to regulate citizens' risks – a new technology of government in line with a range of changing political rationalities. Indeed, such a rationality can be drawn from new administrative criminology, left realism and right realism despite their political divergences; another paradox of fear of crime the concept.

Notes

1 Hacking (1983) suggests that shifts in governmentalities in the nineteenth century saw an 'avalanche of printed numbers' between the years 1820 and 1840.

2 See her paper on 'The Criminological Significance of Unregistered Criminality' (1964), *Excerpta Criminologica* no. 4: 441.

3 Respondents could answer the first three questions Yes, No, or KN (don't know). B13: Do you think that people in this neighbourhood are safe inside their houses at night? B14: Do you think it is generally safe to be out on the streets of this neighbourhood after dark? B15: Are there areas in this part of London where you think you would not be safe on the streets after dark? And later, B17: Are you personally concerned about crime in London

as a whole? Would you say you are, 1 Very Concerned, 2 Quite concerned, 3 A little concerned etc. … (Sparks *et al.* 1977: 243).

4 The Australian Bureau of Statistics. Other agencies involved in the production of this knowledge in Australia include the NSW Bureau of Crime Statistics and the Australian Institute of Criminology.

5 Young came to be critical of his past position as an 'idealist' and was an originator of the left realist movement in criminology.

6 I do not wish to imply here that existing discourses concerning crime were not themselves gender specific, i.e. phallocentric. Only that with the emergence of feminist criminology and a feminist discourse on crime more generally gender became explicitly a central concern.

7 I do not want to suggest that there was a single feminist discourse or even one dominant paradigm within feminist criminology. Ideologically, politically, theoretically and philosophically, feminist criminology, like feminism more generally, has historically been a highly diverse and contested field (Carrington 1994). Feminisms have been influenced by, and in turn influenced, other theoretical, political, legal and governmental concerns. Certainly, a considerable amount of the influential feminist literature and rhetoric of the 1970s, particularly in Britain, was influenced by Marxist and socialist agendas (Grosz 1989; Schwendinger and Schwendinger 1975).

8 See Hogg and Brown (1998) for a detailed discussion of this.

9 As noted in Chapter 2, Garland (1994) and others argue that there was no unified Classical Criminology as such.

10 A large Australian insurance company.

11 This recent realist focus on the 'fear of crime' moved Hale (1996) to suggest that as a topic for investigation 'fear of crime' has become a distinct sub-discipline within criminology which may be studied independently of crime itself.

12 Although it must be noted that at the time of writing (2006) Farrall, Jackson and Grey (2006) are about to begin analysing respondents' answers to new frequency questions (4,448 respondents in the 2003–04 British Crime Survey were fielded such questions).

Part 2

Governance

Chapter 5

Fearing subjects: some new questions of (the) discipline

I don't know what it is, but every time I see a white guy walking toward me, I tense up. My heart starts racing, and I immediately begin to look for an escape route and a means to defend myself. I kick myself for even being in this part of town after dark. Didn't I notice the suspicious gangs of white people lurking on every street corner, drinking Starbucks and wearing their gang colours of Gap Turquoise or J. Crew Mauve? What an idiot! Now the white person is coming closer, close – and then – whew! He walks by without hurting me … White people scare the crap out of me. This may be hard for you to understand – considering that I am white … We've been taught since birth that it's people of that other colour we need to fear … Yet, when I look back on my life, a strange but unmistakable pattern seems to emerge. Every person who has ever harmed me in my lifetime … has been white. (Michael Moore 2001)

We have seen in the first four chapters how it is that fear of crime became a social scientific or criminological concept and an object of enquiry. I have argued that a complex assemblage of power/knowledge made fear of crime a recognised part of the criminological canon, political rhetoric and popular discourse. But why has the term fear of crime – as opposed to the concept – remained a legitimate one despite concerted attacks on this legitimacy? One reason, I will argue in this chapter, is because it (fear of crime) proves difference in the social world. We have already seen in the preceding chapters how enumeration is ever hungry for categories to count, and what better categories to count than gender, ethnicity, and age. The fearful cohort are now easily located. They are those who are repeatedly identified in crime surveys, victim surveys and the like as being more fearful of crime; women and the elderly in particular. As *fearing subjects* members of this group hold something of a privileged place and are, as we will see in Chapter 6, the target of a range of governmental interventions aimed at governing both their fear and their actuarial risk. However, I want to extend this argument and add a reflexive element. I want to suggest, in relation to *fearing subjects*, the identification of difference in fear levels between groups actually serves to keep fear of crime on the agenda, to maintain its status as a criminological concept. It serves to intensify interest in fear of crime through providing categories of enumeration and in doing so, as we have seen in previous chapters, intensifies, and itself gains intensity from, the *fear of crime feedback loop*.

As a case study of sorts this chapter will take the issue of the gender variable and identify the mechanisms by which the categories of gender intensify the fear of crime research agenda. Here again I use Hacking's (1982) notion of the enumeration of categories as a backdrop. The supposed gendered nature of fear of crime offered criminology a pot of gold. The notion that women were more fearful of crime than men provoked the generation of an enormous body of research into the gendered differential of fear 'levels'. I will argue here, taking a lead from recent feminist literature, that rather than fear being gendered it was the notion that fear helped articulate gendered difference that made such research so pervasive (Carrington 1994; Young 1996). Moreover, the word fear itself is loaded with meaning. Here I will deconstruct this gendered nature of fear of crime the concept by examining this largely ignored historical and semantic baggage.

Gendering fear

Criminological research into the fear of crime has often unproblematically, and non-reflexively, taken gender as a potent signifier of fear levels. Indeed, gender has been to fear of crime research the most important independent variable. Empirical studies have repeatedly found that women are more fearful of crime than men and yet are less likely to become the victims of most categories of serious crime – excluding of course sexual assault and domestic violence.[1] The apparently gendered aspect of the 'risk/fear paradox' has exercised the minds of criminological scholars who have developed an array of explanations for the phenomenon. As Maxfield (1984: 47) noted, 'the differences in fear by sex and age are so substantial that something other than direct victimisation experience must be involved'. This 'something other' has been of great interest to researchers and has helped drive the research agenda.

Ultimately the question of gender and fear of crime has largely been about women. This recurring theme in the fear of crime literature has resulted in protracted debates as to the rationality or irrationality of these fears (Hough and Mayhew 1983; Mugford 1984; Sparks 1992), the validity of the victimisation statistics used to arrive at this paradox (Young 1988), and the lived reality of women's lives in terms of physical and sexual harassment. Further, these debates eventually began to question the rationality or irrationality of men's lesser fears about crime (Goodey 1997; Walklate 1994) and indeed the constraint of machismo in reporting feelings of unease about crime.

Researchers involved with the early sweeps of the BCS, following the US lead once again, discussed – with some sensitivity, it must be added – whether women's greater fear of crime was irrational given the relatively low risk of victimisation (Hough and Mayhew 1983: 59; Maxfield 1984: 47); however, the possible under-reporting of fear in the male cohort was also discussed. Nonetheless, there was a suggestion that women's fear of crime was irrational, or at least excessive.

Generally however the literature has been made up of two broad accounts of the fear / risk paradox as it applies to women. The first account has it that women have a heightened sense of vulnerability that entails three dimensions (Killias 1990). Risk is one of these, the others being loss of control and the consequences of victimisation. Maxfield (1984) also goes some way to defining what vulnerability might be in regards to fear of crime, suggesting it refers to an individual's capacity to resist attack and the likelihood of suffering injury from a given level of violence. 'In the rather complex calculus of perceived threats to one's safety, the likely *consequences* of victimisation are as important as subjective assessment of risk.' Moreover, Carach and Mukherjee (1999) found women's exclusion from the labour force was a significant factor in women's fear of crime. Grabosky (1995: 8) further suggests that socialisation processes might be such that 'traditional sex roles have been learned in a manner which fosters in females a lesser degree of self-confidence and autonomy than those roles learned by men'. According to these accounts – whether the cause is posed in rational or irrational terms – women's crime fears outstrip the reality of their risk.

The second general set of accounts has been influenced primarily by left realist criminology, radical feminism and feminist criminology. These posit women's tendency to be more fearful as a reflection of actual levels of risk and vulnerability. It is simply the case that official recorded crime statistics, victimisation surveys and questionnaires, and the fear of crime literature more broadly, has failed to capture or to take into account the full extent and broad nature of women's victimisation. Victimisation for women, it is argued, is an ongoing 'sub-legal' (Goodey 1994) process that includes being stared at, harassed at home and in the workplace, and shouted at in the street (Gordon and Riger 1989; Stanko 1990; Young 1988). Advocates of this position also stress the fact that women are much more likely to be the victims of hidden crime such as sexual assault and domestic violence, both of which are highly under-reported in official statistics and victim surveys. Further, it is suggested that women have lower rates of victimisation primarily because they are less likely to place themselves in risky situations than men (Goodey 1997; Sacco 1990). This suggests that women's victimisation rates should be 'adjusted up' to account for the gendered differences in exposure to risks that are not reflected in the statistical data. These accounts attempt to (re)rationalise women's fears (Jones et al. 1986; Stanko 1990; Young 1988).

More recently a new body of critical literature has attempted to question and 'deconstruct' this apparent paradox by undermining the very idea that fear of crime can be a useful conceptual framework through which to explore gendered crime concern (Ditton et al. 1999a, 1999b; Farrall et al. 1999; Hollway and Jefferson 1997a, 1997b, 2000; Lee 1999, 2001; Sparks 1992; Tulloch et al. 1998a, 1998b). Hollway and Jefferson (2000) for example, argue that the British Crime Survey has produced gendered difference in fear of crime. They suggest that BCS survey results showing gendered differences in levels of fear are largely artefacts of the question: 'How safe do you feel walking alone in this area after dark?' This scenario question, and the subsequent coding and quantification of results, strips the context from any responses (Hollway and Jefferson 2000: 166). As we have seen in previous chapters, this question has been a standard and enduring aspect of large-scale fear of crime surveys. Indeed, the fact that the gender risk/fear paradox generally decreases in these surveys when the more general question about 'worry of becoming a victim of a specific crime' is posed (La Grange and Ferraro 1989; Maxfield 1987) seems to bear out the Hollway and Jefferson criticism. Likewise, Gilchrist et al. (1998) convincingly qualitatively examine 'fearful' men and 'fearless' women and in doing so break down the stereotypical images produced through large-scale victimisation surveys and their amateur equivalents. Following the lead of Newburn and Stanko (1994) they argue that '[w]hilst [a] body of work has developed a challenge to the assumed irrationality of the hysterically fearful female, it has not questioned the underlying stereotypes that women are fearful and men are not' (Gilchrist et al. 1998: 285).

Here I want to explore the question of gender stereotyping in fear of crime research from an altogether different perspective while drawing on these later critical traditions. I want to suggest that in proving gendered difference through survey results – producing gendered *fearing subjects*, to use the language I've developed in this book – social scientific research has helped maintain fear of crime as a conceptual framework for exploring attitudes to crime. That is, that the concept fear of crime and its accompanying body of knowledge has been able to endure partly because fear of crime research proves difference, and in particular gendered difference. The very fact that the concept and term fear of crime have endured despite myriad noted shortcomings supports this proposition that other assemblages of power/knowledge are driving the general programme of fear of crime research. Drawing on the work of Jacques Derrida (1977), and a now rich tradition of post-structuralist feminist theory, I want to explore the links of meaning, the discursive relationships between gender and fear of crime, and how these discursive links have been important to this prevalence both of the concept fear of crime and gender as a signifier of fearfulness.

The body of research knowledge produced around fear of crime has involved, and supposedly been driven by, the search for causation; the 'what *causes* fear of crime?' question – the Lombrosian or aetiological project as David Garland (2002) might put it. Equally, there has been the question of how to govern or control fear of crime, the administrative question the likes of which I discuss in Chapter 6. These dual criminological projects have intensified interest in the fear/risk paradox and gender more generally. If one is to understand the causes of fear of crime (the Lombrosian project) one is implored to explore who is most afraid of crime and why? The control or governance of fear of crime (the administrative project) requires answers to the same question, but to different ends, in the search for fear reduction techniques. These lines of questioning have in turn resulted in debate about whether fear of crime was rational or irrational – was there a level of fear of crime that was beyond any rational calculation?

I want to suggest that the two sets of binaries that inform these lines of questioning – actuarial risk of victimisation and fear of crime on the one hand, and rationality and irrationality on the other – are linked in the fear of crime literature; that actuarial risk implies rationality where the term fear itself implies irrationality; that the concepts themselves are already loaded with meaning and that this saturation of meaning has had power effects in the fear of crime debates.

Deconstructive method and crime fear

The argument that follows is informed by a number of 'deconstructionist' concepts initially developed by Jacques Derrida. These ideas have also been explored and expanded upon more by a number of contemporary feminist scholars (Gatens 1991; Grosz 1994; Young 1996). I use Derrida's concepts here in the context of this later feminist work. The deconstructionist method is employed here in order to explore some of the contradictions, hierarchies and binaries submerged in the social scientific concept and discourse of fear of crime (Arrigo 2001). My main aim is to highlight the mutual interdependence of binary concepts like fear of crime and actuarial risk of crime and to explore how their links to gender serve to animate and/or produce a regime of truth around fear of crime research. Before proceeding it will be necessary to outline some of these key Derridian concepts, particularly the notions of *différence, play* and *presence*. I will explore these in relation to the field of fear of crime and my intended problematisation of this field.

Firstly, Derrida's (1991: 625) term *différence,* is used to describe the playing movement of meaning that 'produces' differences. These differences between social groups, and across the terminology used in the field of fear of crime research, are vital to the argument that follows. Arrigo (2001: 80–81) suggests *différence* has three elements: (1) that terms in binary opposition 'differ' from each other to maintain their meaning; (2) that the two terms in opposition 'defer' to one another – they each imply the other term; (3) that the terms in opposition 'defer' to one another to maintain their interdependence. So, for example, fear of crime as a concept cannot exist without its binary opposite concept; this is, I believe, actuarial risk of crime as calculated through victim surveys. Actuarial risk and fear of crime are binary opposites in the social scientific narrative of fear of crime. Fear of crime can only be an empirical concept because it is constructed as different, and excessive, of actual risk of victimisation. If there were no measure of risk fear of crime would be a redundant social scientific concept. Moreover, the measurement and identification of fear of crime drives research into the actuarial risk of victimisation. These categories are interdependent. They differ, one defers to the other and they imply one another. Indeed, we see this in the genealogy of fear of crime I have outlined in this book. Fear of crime as a concept was born of the victimisation survey; the very instrument designed to uncover levels of actual risk. Derrida suggests that the centrality and structure of an *origin* is only brought into being through *différence*. That is, difference is always a product of particular plays of meaning not an essential truth. As I've argued, fear of crime is not an essential truth 'discovered' by social scientific enquiry.

Rather, its very existence is a result of an assemblage of discourse and its relationship to risk and the enumeration of this. However, this is only the first of at least five sets of binaries that help provide fear of crime with its regime of truth. As we will see, the terms risk and fear are loaded with meaning, with historical and cultural baggage.

Secondly, the term *play*. Derrida substitutes the term origin (which, as we have seen, he sees as redundant) with the term *play*. *Play* is the movement between differences – in both the spatial and temporal sense: the deference of difference. It is this *play* of meaning, of *différence*, that produces truth. *Play* is independent of the individual authorship of a text; that is, texts have contextual meaning that is inexhaustible, prior to and beyond authorship. *Play* produces the sign – to use the semiological term. In this sense the sign does not signify something elsewhere, something absent for the social scientist to decode or identify. Indeed, it is precisely this ideal type origin, this *signified*, which Derrida is at pains to dispense with; it is this gap between the signified and signifier within the concept of the sign which Derrida argues is already always a metaphysical leap (Derrida 1991: 625). Rather, through this Derridian framework we might ask with what links of meaning and discourse does this *play* occur? What linkages of meaning (historical, cultural, social, textual) produce the truth effects of difference? So, in the context of fear of crime we might ask, what other submerged meanings produce or animate the *play* of meaning between actuarial risk and fear of crime. My conjecture here is that gender is one of these.

Thirdly, *presence*. Let us look briefly at Derrida's critique of semiology and structuralism as here Derrida clearly explains the notion of *presence*. He suggests (Derrida 1991: 625) that:

> The sign is usually said to be put in the place of the thing itself, the present thing, 'thing' here standing equally for meaning and referent. The sign represents the present in its absence. It takes the place of the present. When we cannot grasp or show the thing, state the present, the being-present, when the present cannot be presented, we signify, we go through the detour of the sign. …The sign in this sense is deferred presence.

Derrida sees structuralism and semiotics – and indeed the entire history of Western philosophy – as an *epistémé* that has been founded upon the *presence* of various origin 'truths'. The origin is understood in semiotics as the signified; it produces the sign through a system of signification. We have already established that this origin, for Derrida, is a fallacy. That it is in fact endlessly deferred; the origin myth is a product of a *play* of difference, of *différence*. For example, Derrida argues that constructs of identity, even woman and man, are conditional (Gatens 1991: 162). Within each of these terms exists that which the term seeks to define itself against – its binary opposite – man/woman, presence/absence, self/other; the constructs cannot exist without their binary opposite. In structuralism, in semiotics, and indeed in the empirical positivism of most fear of crime research, the myth of origin is *presenced*. Fear of crime is said to signify a *thing* or things. However, according to Derrida, it can only be present in the absence of its binary opposite, as a result of the play of *différence* with its opposite. I will now outline five examples of binary oppositions which serve to legitimise both fear of crime as a concept and gender as a signifier of crime fear.

Binary 1: actuarial risk of victimisation/fear of crime

All this might sound conceptually complicated, but in fact we can apply this deconstructive method to fear of crime and particularly its gendered nature quite simply and effectively. I want to suggest that the criminological discourse of fear of crime receives much of its very legitimacy, its claim to signifying some *thing* as it were, through the play of *différence* with actuarial risk of crime and a number of other binary and linked oppositions. In this *play* of difference it is not that risk is necessarily rendered *present* and fear of crime submerged or rendered absent. It is, rather, that fear of crime is *presenced* as an anomaly of actuarial risk. This play of *différence* means that we never really have to address the unanswerable origin question of what fear of crime actually *is* or represents. It is by nature of its production a concept always *other* to actuarial risk. The origin question can be deferred under these conditions. But it is not only its binary opposition to risk that renders fear of crime present. Indeed, this alone might not have been enough to keep the fear of crime concept alive. Rather, fear of crime functions productively with the language of the literature, research and variables that seek to explain and understand it; with the historical baggage implicit in terms like risk and fear themselves; with a linguistic economy. To this extent the discovery of gendered difference in fear levels has power effects; it serves to reinforce the legitimacy of research into fear of crime and the concept fear of crime itself, and as I will explain below, it feeds into the *fear of crime feedback loop*.

Let us return briefly to the question of what fear of crime is – or at least what the term has pretence to signify. In the first British Crime Survey the term fear of crime was 'used to refer to any anxiety or fear about being victim of either violent crime or crimes against property' (Hough and Mayhew 1983: 59). Fear of crime in the first BCS was a sign therefore for an amorphous group of anxieties about the perceived threat of victimisation. Yet, in Michael Maxfield's (1984: 47) *Fear of Crime in England and Wales*, which was in fact a Home Office report on the fear of crime component of the 1982 BCS, the definition is much more broad. He draws from Garofalo (1981), suggesting that empirically fear of crime is more like a 'potential fear of crime'. An 'emotion [ ] experienced by someone who anticipates the possibility of a risky situation' (Maxfield 1984: 47). For Kenneth Ferraro (1995: 179), who argues that fear of crime should be replaced by the concept of perceived risk, fear of crime involves an 'emotional response of dread or anxiety to crime or symbols a person associates with crime' (Ferraro 1995: 179). A recent definition can also be found in the *Sage Dictionary of Criminology* (McLaughlin and Muncie 2001: 118–119). Here Eugene McLaughlin suggests that 'fear of crime is a rational or irrational state of alarm or anxiety engendered by the belief that one is in danger of criminal victimisation'. One commonality between these various definitions is that fear of crime represents an emotion or emotions (fears or anxieties). The metaphysical leap the concept makes though is when it attempts to measure these. That is, the leap is from fear of crime as descriptor to fear of crime as measurable *thing*. Here fear of crime the *thing*, the social scientific object, can only be present in opposition to risk. However, where actuarial risk has a conditional (if always problematisable) measurability, it can be calculated as an object; fear of crime because of its emotional baggage as it were, is always subjective.

Binary 2: subjective/objective

So in this sense, the second linked binary is that of subjectivity and objectivity. Fear of crime can only ever be discussed in relation to the supposed objective value of actuarial risk. And although fear of crime the concept has pretence to be an *objective* measure, it can only ever be *subjective*. In fact it is the subjective nature of crime fear that drives the research agenda. It is an 'almost universal finding', as Maxfield (1984: 47) calls it, that 'those who least often become victims of crime are most often fearful'; this opens the field to problematisation. In all of its definitions the term fear of crime stands for something absent; an emotion or emotions that are always subjective. The empirical question of what fear *is* is always deferred.

Binary 3: emotion/reason

As I have noted, most definitions of that fear of crime emphasise its 'emotional', or 'emotional response', component. Interestingly, McLaughlin has, in the definition quoted above, divested fear of crime of much of its overt emotional content. But on closer inspection, the term emotion may be absent but it is certainly present in terms such as 'state of alarm' and 'anxiety' – these are emotional states. Let us focus on this emotional component for a moment, for the word 'emotional' almost always passes unremarked upon. Tellingly, the Oxford Dictionary defines emotion as a 'disturbance of the mind; mental sensation or state; instinctive feeling as opposed to reason' (Sykes 1976). Thus, reason and emotion are binary opposites, emotion functions in discourse as other to reason. Therefore, given that fear of crime is an emotional response, it is both abnormal (a disturbance) and unreasonable (instinctive) – not by some abstract metaphysical proposition, but simple definition. The term is pre-loaded with this meaning. Thus, to describe a proportion of the population or any particular demographic group as 'fearful' we are also defining them, by extension, as in opposition to reason, unreasonable, irrational. To follow my analysis through to its logical conclusion it is not that fear of crime has a poor conceptual framework or that this framework needs further refining, as most critics of the concept suggest. Quite the opposite. In fact the term fear of crime is so loaded with meaning, so affected by discursive power, that it cannot legitimately stand for anything in any way universal or objective. We have historically had trouble rationalising away fear of crime because the concept itself connotes irrationality; the researcher cannot be free of this textual trace. By contrast actuarial risk is always rational.

Binary 4: irrational/rational

McLaughlin, as we've seen above, in an attempt to go beyond the rational/irrational debate, has a bet each way; fear of crime can be irrational or rational according to his definition. But of course, we only know which of these it is when we situationally compare recorded levels of fear of crime to calculated actuarial risk and then factor in other variables. Gender is one such variable. In order to ascertain whether fears are rational or irrational we analyse divergent levels of fear between different groups in different situations. But let me backtrack to the question of how we make these measures.

The most commonly articulated problem for fear of crime researchers has been the question of how to measure fear of crime (Ferraro 1995; Ferraro and La Grange 1987; Gordon and Riger 1989; Hale 1996; Warr 1984). Kenneth Ferraro (1995), for example, rightly suggests:

> Given that fear involves an emotional, and sometimes physiological, reaction to perceived danger, there exists an inherent difficulty in

measuring fear from questionnaire or interview data collection methods.

Still, the overriding premise of the majority of research in the area is that something like fear of crime *can* be usefully measured empirically; hence it is presumed that the sign fear of crime has a hidden signified (truth/reality/objectivity) to be decoded, and counted. It is assumed that it is only a matter of asking the right questions, constructing the right survey instrument, or articulating a more sophisticated conceptual framework. However, this assumption of measurability itself rests upon another deferred assumption; that there exists something tangible against which to take measure; that there exists some kind of *normative value* (or rational level) of fear of crime.

What is a 'normal' amount of fear of crime and how do we know it is so? Here, it seems, the Bell curve reigns supreme and the very history of fear of crime research accumulates in a manner that excuses us from answering this in any other way than with numbers – or more to the point, the power of numbers. The expanding body of fear of crime research – with all the attendant problems and ambiguities – builds us our normative or rational value. The various large-scale crime surveys discussed in the previous chapters are vivid examples of this. There seems to be general consensus, for example, that because of the now 23 years or so of longitudinal data of the BCS, we can take fluctuations in recorded fear levels as reflecting the public mood in a generally accurate way. This numeric construction obscures the fact that the normative question remains unanswerable; here actuarial risk defers to fear of crime becoming the hidden *other*. Indeed, many of those researchers who rightly suggest that the measure of 'fear' is problematic implicitly take their normative assumptions from the very research results they openly question. I have argued that the term fear of crime already connotes emotion and subjectivity. It is always already excessive of actuarial risk which is its binary opposite. Therefore, generally, the normative level of fear of crime is a low level of fear of crime; that which most closely resembles actuarial risk.

Importantly, to suggest that we can have a *normal* amount of fear of crime is simultaneously to suggest that there exist *abnormal* levels of fear. The research only functions with pretence to objectivity if we leave this normative question unanswered and the normal/abnormal binary deferred. The abnormal is both present and absent in any conceptualisation of a normal amount of fear of crime and vice versa. The important point is that it is the abnormal that becomes of interest to the researcher. The (re)search for fear of crime is by definition a search for the abnormal, the excessive. It must be, otherwise, why try and reduce crime fear; and more particularly, why target those identified as most fearful with fear reduction literature and techniques? Women are, of course, one such target demographic. Despite attempts to rationalise away women's apparent surplus fear of crime they remain, somewhat ironically perhaps, a prime target of fear prevention campaigns.

Binary 5: femininity/masculinity

Let us explore this play of meaning further. Above I have suggested that the rational/irrational dualism could only have established itself on the assumption of a normative measure of fear of crime and that by definition fear of crime is abnormal, irrational, *other* to reason. Let me now suggest that interest in gender differentiation in levels of fear of crime is also intimately connected to the reasonable/unreasonable, rational/irrational binaries; that in fact the concept of fear of crime is an already gendered one. The women of fear of crime discourse are to fear and emotion as men are to risk and reason (men's fear is always less, lower in level). Thus, fear of crime serves the purpose of 'proving' gendered difference.

This difference is produced through fear of crime's discursive links. Thus, the list of interconnected binaries which produce meaning in fear of crime are self-referential and self-sustaining; masculinity/femininity, reason/emotion, object/subject, fearless/fearful, rational/irrational, risk/fear. Contemporary feminist theorists have continually attempted to problematise similar binary distinctions and have shown how these serve to normalise and obscure masculinity by signifying femininity as problematic (Gatens 1991; Mohanram 1999; Thornton 1995; Young 1996). Similarly, in fear of crime research maleness has remained largely unquestioned while volumes have been written about 'women and the fear of crime'. Women have been the abnormal of fear of crime research, the emotional and the irrational. It has been women's fear that has been the problem to explain or reduce.

The inscriptions of fear and the bodies of women

Let me turn now to method in fear of crime research and discuss the ways in which enumeration operates to normalise both fear of crime the concept and gendered difference. Alison Young (1996: 230) argues that statistics – and we might include crime fear surveys here – are often held to provide the evidence that sex roles are realised in the social world in ways that prove the social world's division along gender lines. Gender identities are imposed upon individuals through research methodologies and subsequently in results. The differences between identities as ascribed by research and identities as experienced by individuals are rarely questioned (Young 1996: 230). Thus, the 'discovery' of gender distinction through fear of crime research, a 'discovery' that dates back to the very beginning of this research in the late 1960s (Ennis 1967), serves to prove the worth of the research concept itself. This 'discovery' has led to a whole programme of research activities that have allowed researchers to 'gloss over' many of the inconsistencies and inaccuracies that underlie a good proportion of this work – the ends are held to justify the means. The 'will' to know and enumerate gender difference both obscures and produces the *play* of *différence* that allows such research to function with 'objectivity'.

However, this myth of women's conformity here – women as a fearful and therefore conformist demographic – operates simultaneously as a deviance. Conformity, imposed and inscribed through statistics, marks women as 'fearing', but leaves masculinity as natural. Carrington (1998) is critical of calls from some feminists for the study of women's conformity, maintaining that to do so is to collude with the criminological canon that implicitly accepts women in this way. This process of thinking sexed bodily groups only serves to reinforce a male-centred conception of what sexed difference may be. Young agrees, arguing that:

> The notion of femininity as obscurity can be discerned in the construction of women as objects to be decoded (by the analyst/criminologist/detective). For example women have to be represented as analytic opacity: their nature is not open to be read by the criminologist, who is thus unable to know them. Women have also been represented as hysterical, thus rendering their real natures hidden to themselves as well as the analysing criminologist who is forced to interpret behaviours as symptoms and symptoms as traits. (Young 1996: 230)

The fear of crime researcher then engages in the interrogation of women as a group, the search for 'truth' about their fears. It attempts to peel back the layers of 'femaleness' that must cover the rational core with rational fears. Moreover, as Gilchrist *et al.* (1998) show us, this can occur when even the empirical basis of this exercise is fatally flawed.

Enter risk?

We might then surmise that if fear of crime is not a theoretically useful or empirically accurate object to measure and base our research around, we could frame our research differently. As noted above, Kenneth Ferraro (1995: 179) in his influential publication titled *Fear of Crime: Interpreting Victimisation Risk* suggests that respondents' 'perceived risk' might be a more appropriate object to measure. Such a project sounds hopeful until we see that it operates on exactly the same hidden premises and deferred questions and assumptions that I have outlined above – perceived risk becomes a mediator and fear of crime one possible reaction to this. Women's fear of crime is then rationalised away; 'why women fear non-sexual crime appears to be largely due to the possibility of sexual crime contingent with any blatantly non-sexual crime' (Ferraro 1995: 179). This is a statement most would not have a major problem with, but why reduce a complex set of ontological questions back to the problematic signifier 'fear'? Moreover, the title of Ferraro's book is *'Fear of Crime...'*, not 'perceived risk of crime', and not 'risk assessment'. As I have suggested above, the word fear is historically inscribed with *emotion* and accordingly with gendered meaning. The book includes a chapter on women, *Unraveling Fear of Crime Among Women* (Ferraro 1995), yet there is interestingly no chapter about men.[2]

As I suggested above, the notion of risk has, more generally within fear of crime research, produced our surrogate normative level of fear. Richard Sparks (1992) suggests that left realists, for example, despite their wish to conceptualise women's fear of crime as completely justified, cannot let go of the totalising model of rationality based on an antecedent and 'real' level of objective risk. Thus, the objective risk of crime becomes the rational, the normal, against which levels of fear are systematically justified. The researcher must rationalise away women's fear so that it somehow balances on the ledger with objective risk. Maleness remains unmarked and normal with this search for femininity's hidden lack (measured in this instance in excess fear). So researchers produce a string of factors that are said to account for women's 'surplus fear' – to use Sparks' (1992) terminology.

For left realists, and many feminist researchers, the home – and domestic violence within it – becomes the rationale of women's heightened anxiety of crime (Jones *et al.* 1986; Stanko 1990). Rather than abandoning the search for rationality or irrationality in the gendered specificity of levels of fear, the genesis of women's excessive fear is located in a spatial site obscured from the criminologist's vision, in a space where even the victim survey has failed to penetrate. Alternatively, excess fear is located in a temporal zone again hidden from the criminological gaze. A history of routine sexual harassment throughout women's lives then is said to account for these excess fears.

We might now also include mind/body in our set of binaries. The search for surplus fear almost always concerns itself with the bodies of women. These bodies, precisely because of their femaleness, are at risk. Women are all body, as Margaret Thornton has put it. Sexual assault (Gordon and Riger 1989: 230), vulnerability (Carach and Mukherjee 1999: 6), and domestic violence (Stanko 1990) become the sources of women's surplus fear of crime. Masculinity's discursive association with the mind as opposed to femininity's association with the body obscures it as an object of enquiry.

Let me now explore the implications of these discursive links further. Fear of crime research, conceptualising fear as something to be found in women, as irrational (by definition), feeds into discourses which invite us to exclude women from the social body. The exclusion is hastened via responsibilisation techniques found in the likes of the crime prevention literature which ask women to minimise their risk by curbing certain activities (Stanko 1998). If fear is the antithesis of freedom and freedom the mark of citizenship, women must be non-citizens. As Margaret Thornton (1995: 318) suggests:

> women have never been fully accepted as citizens of the polity. Their indelible association with nature, the body, disorder, and non-rationality has been used to render them less fit for public sphere responsibilities according to both historical and prevailing democratic norms. Thus, while women have been 'let in' it is only as fringe dwellers.

My argument here might seem directly at odds with the commonly held belief within the fear of crime literature that women's fear of masculinised public space, both physical and psychological, and so male-centred public life, renders women unlikely to engage in the public sphere. But in fact, this is the other side of the same coin. Conceptualising women's bodies as (even rationally) fearing – what I have termed *fearing subjects* – in effect continues the historical tradition of seeing women in terms of lack. The characterisation of women as fearful in itself serves to underline the ready-made belief that women are unfit for public life despite attempts to rationalise these fears. To become fit one must engage in the array of responsibilising practices which would, ironically, likely render one less able to engage in public activity, and perhaps even render one fearful.

The deferred antithesis here is: what do men have in relation to 'fear of crime'? The answer is of course, fearlessness and freedom, the ability and acceptability to engage in risk taking activities: maleness is fearlessness, fearlessness is freedom and freedom is citizenship. The next line of enquiry is why are women lacking these qualities? Or, why are women incomplete? Why are women *still* non-citizens? Women have been constructed through research – indeed in criminological discourse – as desiring to be free of fear, as free to experience the social world *as* men. Thus, women are seen as desiring the subjectivities of men. This desire has always been seen in these terms of lacking, of being incomplete. The project, therefore, for criminology has been to *make* women complete, make their experiences equal to men's, to extinguish desire by delivering the tools for equality. However, to make complete, to have to make equal, can only ever have the opposite effect. To *have* to make equal proves difference. The continuance of fear of crime as a descriptor of women's experiences and perceptions can only perpetuate this problem, only prove difference.

A deconstructionist moment?

Some feminist writers (Goodey 1994; Walklate 1995), as I have suggested above, have argued for a reversal of just who are the irrational and rational demographic groups of fear of crime research. They have suggested that it might be young men who are the irrational subjects because of their lack of fear and their dangerous behaviour in the face of evidence which indicates that they are the most likely victims, the most at risk social group. This tactic, while an extremely useful one, merely shifts the object of disciplinary focus while leaving the notion of gendered difference, and indeed the string of signs that inform it, intact. However, it also represents a deconstructionist moment. At this moment fear of crime research is implicated in the inscription of women's bodies with social meaning; a moment also that stresses the role of criminological enquiry in the processes that naturalise men's bodies. It is a moment, therefore, when criminology is implicated in the production of truths that constitute gendered difference. The binary is reversed. Here feminism deconstructs. The textual space in which this subject of criminological enquiry is situated is disrupted. If feminist scholars can flip the rational/irrational and masculine/feminine binaries that give truth-value to research into fear of crime, and indeed inscribe a *gendered fearing subject* within this research, it demonstrates the arbitrary and contingent nature of such division.

Why then is this 'switching' of binaries not enough? The problem is that what it still seeks to establish is a woman's rationality. This means that women who take risks could be considered illegitimate victims if victimised – irrational and so deserving of their fate. It does not break with the totalising model of women's conformity. This highlights the relevance of Sparks' (1992) criticism of totalising models of rationality. Moreover, in attempting to prove women rational it essentially attempts to *make* women 'normal'. Women are thus expected to transcend the female body. Moira Gatens (1991: 162) for one eloquently argues against this strategy. If the escape of Otherness means escaping from the female body surely this doubly emphasises its shortcomings.

Conclusion

Thus, methodology used in the fear of crime research has tended to involve two broadly definable dimensions. This methodology was followed in the earlier influential feminist work of Elizabeth Stanko (1990),[3] and is followed widely – albeit in different forms – by left realism (Jones *et al.* 1986) and in much of the administrative literature (Hough and Mayhew 1983; Hough and Mayhew 1985; Maxfield 1984; Maxfield 1987; Skogan 1986). The first of these dimensions is the collection of some form of statistical quantifiable data (usually a victim survey or recorded crime statistics), whereby the data collected is used to objectify the subject of investigation. The second dimension involves some form of analysis of this object with the intention of explaining or discovering the conditions of its very objectivity. This form of research takes gendered divisions unproblematically. It actually produces the *gendered fearing subjects* it then pertains to know through its will to explain reason or unreason in fear of crime.

Further, I would argue that this imposition of fear of crime on to subjects, as carried out by these researchers, may also turn out to be self-substantiating in terms of future research. Some (Egger 1997; Young 1996) have argued that crime prevention tutelage, in the form of media and governmental strategies, aimed at relieving anxiety about crime, can actually induce fear in individuals. If these strategies can sensitise the public, why not the questions of a researcher? Thus, research may not only produce representations of the fear of crime in research results, but may actually produce fear of crime in the populations it surveys. As Grosz argues, the disciplines have tangible effects on the bodies they study. 'Bodies are not inert, they function interactively and productively' (1994: 250).

Notes

1   A notable exception is recent work by Robbie Sutton and Stephen Farrall (2005). Sutton and Farrall suggest that by including a 'lie scale' men's tendency to downplay their fears can be corrected.
2   I choose this text as an example only because it is one of the few recent texts to be entirely devoted to the question of 'fear of crime' and that it takes this as its title. The reality is that it is one of the more sophisticated analyses in this field.
3   Though much revised in her later work.

Chapter 6

Governing the fearful and inventing the feared

An element of fear can be considered helpful in persuading people to guard against victimisation. (Home Office 1989: 12)

The term prevention does not indicate simply a practice based on the maxim that an ounce of prevention is worth a pound of cure, but also on the assumption that if prevention is necessary it is because danger exists – it exists in a virtual state before being actualised in an offence, injury or accident. It entails the further assumption that the responsible institutions are guilty if they do not detect the presence, or actuality, of a danger before it is realised. (François Ewald 1993: 221–222)

As I have shown in Part 1, historical contingencies and their resultant shifts in disciplinary practices and governmental rationalities have played a considerable role in the formation of the current discursive terrain through which fear of crime is conceptualised or imagined. Indeed, contingent factors have informed the entire conceptualisation of the fear of crime as an object that might be rendered intelligible through empirical enquiry. It is not pre-discursive, self-evident, or a-historical. Indeed, I have suggested fear of crime has emerged at the intersection of a number of late-modern governmental, disciplinary and political discourses. Fear of crime became an object of governance not because its was 'out there', 'waiting to be discovered', but because of a number of accidental or contingent discursive alignments or conditions of emergence. Fear of crime is a concept born of late modernity and nourished by contingency. It has become a self-fulfilling concept fed partly by its own invention through what I've termed a *fear of crime feedback loop*. However, while it has been fostered by a will to knowledge, a will to enumerate and understand crime fear, a *Lombrosian project*, it has also increasingly extended its discursive reach into the domain of governance; it has also become an *administrative project*. Empirical enquiries have produced a set of rationalities, essentially rationalities of crime prevention that suppose particular forms of governable subjectivity or personage, or to put it another way, *fearing subjects*. *Fearing subjects* are the imagined and targeted subjects of particular governmental policies, and in turn of many academic (disciplinary) enquiries – a circularity which I will attempt to make clearer. Particular tactics and technologies of government have attempted to govern and shape the conduct of *fearing subjects* and these tactics are informed by particular governmental rationalities rendered possible only through social enquiry. Governing fear of crime is big business for private enterprise, government institutions and criminology. As we have seen, while research into the causes and cures of this late-modern malady has kept many researchers funded conducting 'fear of crime surveys' and 'community safety audits', and while it has fuelled much academic debate, reducing fear of crime appears a difficult task indeed. For, despite all these varied and ongoing attempts to curtail or govern fear of crime, recent criminological studies suggest that the public are as fearful of crime as ever, despite relatively dramatic falls in some offence categories in many Western countries in recent years (Simmons and Dodd 2003). The same high levels of anxiety are reflected in surveys undertaken by various media organisations.[1] Fear of crime has resulted in a range of programmes and strategies being formulated, presumably to reduce crime fear. But is it quite that simple? Paradoxically, it seems that the more we attempt to govern crime fear, the more tactics and techniques of government we deploy to reduce crime fear, the more fearful we become.

I want to argue that there is something much more complex going on; that if we use an alternative framework the apparent paradox I have identified all but evaporates. Indeed, we need to conceptualise fear of crime the concept as an artefact of disciplinary and governmental knowledge, and one that now has its own productive capacities and effects. Moreover, we need to understand these in the context of increasingly neo-liberal forms of government and crime prevention strategies, the imperative to govern at a distance subjecting the objects of governance to the less direct disciplines of the market economy (Rose and Miller 1992; Stenson 1993b). I want to suggest in this chapter that fear of crime is not only an object or problem of governance, something to be controlled and reduced, but that it also operates as a tactic or technology of governance, a strategy that can be invoked with the aim of encouraging individuals to regulate or minimise their own risks in a variety of ways. That is, fear of crime becomes a tactic or technique which can be deployed with the aim of conducting that conduct. Put simply, the risk of victimisation can be governed at a distance through fear of crime.

However, there is also another side to this analysis: that fear as a tactic of governance, a tactic for the reduction of risk, also presupposes something to be fearful of. An analysis of both sides of this ledger evokes a framework around what David Garland (2001: 137) has termed both the *criminology of the self* and the *criminology of the other*. He suggests:

> There is a *criminology of the self*, that characterises offenders as normal, rational consumers, just like us: and there is a *criminology of the other*, of the threatening outcast, the fearsome stranger, the excluded and embittered. One is invoked to routinise crime, to allay disproportionate fears and to promote preventative action. The other functions to demonise the criminal, to act out our popular fears and resentments, and to promote support for state punishment.

Garland argues that taken as a whole government discourse on crime – not just that of elected officials but also that of administrative agencies – is structured by a barely suppressed set of 'schizoid' characteristics that are illustrative of these two criminologies. They are, he suggests, contradictions that are played out as struggles between different actors, at various levels of organisation, and through different ways of framing problems. In many ways the paradox I am examining here fits Garland's characterisation. The first half of the chapter here focuses on policies of fear management which, as we will see, are schizoid in and of themselves; the second half of the chapter focuses on some of the 'outcasts' evoked in the name of, not only the promotion of state punishment, but also in the promotion of active *fearing subjects* who manage their risks of victimisation. Indeed, the analysis that follows outlines a web of governance even more contradictory and mutually reinforcing than Garland's characterisation implies.

Governmental rationalities of fear reduction

Fear of crime is now not only a 'prominent cultural theme' (Garland 2001), it is part of the normal language of crime prevention. See, for example, this extract from the Wollongong City Council Crime Prevention Plan (Wollongong City Council 2000):

> Fear of crime and apprehension about safety is a matter of extreme concern to residents in the Wollongong area.

In modern crime prevention literature fear of crime is as important an object of governance as crime itself (see Braithwaite *et al.* 1982; Home Office 2001). Indeed, since the early 1980s fear of crime has been the target of a number of different, often overlapping, forms of governmental technologies. Firstly, there are strategies that specifically target and seek to reduce fear through the proliferation of information. This information is largely disseminated from agencies like the British Home Office and the various statistical bureaus and agencies in Australian states. Secondly, there are more broadly based strategies and programmes of crime prevention that seek to reduce both crime and crime fear. I will discuss only briefly examples of the first set of tactics and then develop a more detailed discussion and critique of examples of the second.

Governing fear from above

As noted, one method of governing fear rather specifically has been to attempt to supply the citizenry with knowledge of the relatively low risks of becoming a victim of crime, suggesting instead that one's risk of victimisation is usually overestimated (see Grabosky 1995). To give a specific example, the NSW Bureau of Crime Statistics and Research published a well-publicised article (Weatherburn *et al.* 1996: 6) that suggested just this, that Australians often 'greatly exaggerate their risks ... [of being victimised]'. Their findings were disseminated via press release to many Australian newspapers and given relatively wide publicity. Similar strategies have been attempted in the UK with the Home Office constantly disseminating such information aimed at reducing anxiety about crime. Indeed, such strategies followed the release of the very first BCS when it was envisaged that the new data on victimage might provoke increased concern. At present, the Home Office website is designed as an information system where one can inspect just what is being done about crime in the UK on the one hand, but also get advice on personal aspects of crime prevention and risk on the other. For example:

> The chance that you or a member of your family will be a victim of violent crime is low. Violent crimes are still comparatively rare and account for a very small part of recorded crime. But some people are still frightened that they, or someone close

to them, will be the victim of a violent attack. (Home Office 2001)

Likewise, as I noted in Chapter 3, with the release of the President's Commission report in the US in 1967 we witnessed the strategy of informing the public of their relatively low risk of victimisation.

These modes of governing fear see 'experts' proclaim the 'truth' about victimisation to the citizenry in order to reduce fear of crime. This is emblematic of governance from above, 'seeking as its goal the common good', to paraphrase Foucault (1991). This is also, in part, the reason for the failure of this form of governing crime fear in late modernity. Fear of crime and concern about victimisation, as discourses, have become so embedded in our everyday knowledges and practices that the voices of 'experts' are likely to offer scant comfort. If theorists of late modernity are correct we have become so sceptical about the abilities of central government and 'experts' to speak the truth that they are unlikely to be believed – particularly by those who might feel the most anxious. Indeed, we are inevitably told by a plethora of shock jocks, talk-back hosts, conservative columnists, and (usually) opposition politicians and political parties, that such experts should not be believed. Moreover, we have seen how information about crime, and fear of crime, is now produced via a range of public and private agencies and organisations. That is, there are competing regimes of truth that undermine the single 'expert'. Governing fear of crime it seems requires a much more precisely targeted and tailored set of strategies – although these too might involve the input of 'experts'. Now I want to explore the reasons why many of these strategies also fail even while they succeed.

Governmentality of fear

The second method of governing fear is primarily through locally targeted crime prevention strategies (which have also increasingly become fear reducing strategies). Here, responsibility for government of crime fear is increasingly falling under the auspices of local government and other local agencies. However, central coordination is usually strategically administered by various national, state or commonwealth departments. In NSW, for example, the Attorney General's Department acts as overseer with input from the NSW Police Service and other agencies. Expert knowledge of how to govern fear is supplied by institutions like the NSW Bureau of Crime Statistics and Research or the Australian Institute of Criminology. These agencies' publications are often cited in council crime prevention plans evidencing this expert involvement. Governments and their agencies, in a sense, formulate and/or organise the technologies and techniques of governing fear, but carry out this governance at a distance. They have, for example, responsibilised local government to develop crime prevention by tying the development of such plans to continued crime prevention funding and access to programmes. The Attorney General's Department assists in the development of these plans and provides councils with a clear set of guidelines to facilitate some uniformity in the process, as is evidenced in their literature:

> Crime, disorder and fear of crime have become major concerns for many communities. Traditionally, we have turned to the police and criminal justice agencies to deal with these problems. In the past, this worked reasonably well because crime levels were low. Today, however, crime levels are higher than they were 20 years ago, society has become more complex and demands on the police have increased substantially ... The development of local crime prevention *partnerships* involving organisations such as the police, local councils, government departments (eg Department of Community Services, Area Health Service, Department of School Education), local business and community representatives are therefore seen as the best way of tackling local crime problems. Local government is about more than providing basic services. It is about creating vibrant, lively communities where people can live comfortably and happily. Crime and the fear of crime reduce the quality of life in a community. People enjoy their lives more when they feel safe. (NSW Attorney General's Department 2001)

Likewise, in NSW the State Government's Department of Urban Affairs and Planning now takes an active role in the responsibilisation of local councils in matters of crime prevention. A new set of guidelines released by this department (Department of Urban Affairs and Planning 2001) gives local police and local government the power to require that developers provide low-risk environments. Unsafe areas are to be 'designed out'. Again the governance of this process, although coordinated at the state level, is devolved to local functionaries. In the UK the Home Office fear of crime 'toolboxes' perform a similar function.

Local crime prevention plans and fear reduction strategies

We can see the importance of fear of crime, as an object of these crime prevention strategies, by simply looking in more depth at some examples of NSW local government crime prevention plans. These plans are now also often disseminated on local government websites providing general citizenry access. Hawkesbury City Council suggests that:

> There is a discrepancy between community perceptions of crime and reported incidents of crime … There is a strong … perception that public spaces are unsafe – the fear of crime is most prevalent in public spaces. (2001)

Similarly, Newcastle City Council (2000) argues that there is 'a perception of unease about the CBD'. The crime prevention plan sets out to 'restore confidence in, and encourage people to use, the CBD'.

The crime prevention plan for Wollongong (2000) sets out 'to provide the community with a range of strategies which when implemented will enhance people's feelings of safety and see a reduction in crime in the Wollongong LGA'. In Wollongong 'fear of crime and concern for safety' were the 'key issues' in the crime prevention plan:

> Fear of crime and apprehension about safety is a matter of extreme concern to residents in the Wollongong area. A recent survey by the Bureau of Crime Statistics revealed that 58% of Illawarra residents perceived a crime or public nuisance problem in their neighbourhood in 1995 and 1996. This compares with a NSW average of 53.4% and 57.3% average for the Sydney region. Illawarra residents have the highest concern about their safety than any other region in NSW. This has also been confirmed by research and surveys that SCAT and its partners have recently undertaken. The Seniors Safety Survey, the Police Safety Survey, the Safe Women Project and the Young People in Public Space Forum all revealed extremely high concerns about safety and anti-social behaviour.

It's much the same sad story in the Manly municipality (2001):

> Fear of and incidence of crime stifles the participation of residents in community life and undermines their well being. It can disrupt the effective functioning of the community, damage social harmony

and generate tensions which lead to further crime, major costs and significant human suffering amongst victims, perpetrators and their families.

The policy response to fear of crime issues from most of these councils has been, in one way or another, to 'increase understanding of crime prevention models and facilitate understanding within communities to address fear of crime' (Wollongong City Council 2000). In other words, it is assumed that education about the risk of crime, and more importantly about the strategies being put in place to deal with crime, will result in a drop in fear of crime. Common local fear reduction strategies include CCTV, extra lighting, police/public partnerships, environmental design measures (territoriality, sight-lines etc. ...), hot-spot policing, community policing, security, transit police, safe areas, and the list goes on.

Fear of crime as a tactic of government

All this should seem relatively straightforward and we might be forgiven for thinking that the problem of fear of crime is being well and truly addressed. However, the message being promoted is often not as clear as these examples suggest. Indeed, there is an abundance of evidence to suggest that under some circumstances governments and policy-makers believe that certain levels or 'elements of fear' might actually be desirable in ensuring citizens adequately govern their own safety; fear becomes a governmental tactic or technique employed in pursuit of the reduction of risk. Let's look first at the big picture again. The British Home Office has been explicit about fear of crime being a possible tactic of governance. This is clearly detailed in the following:

> An element of fear can be considered helpful in persuading people to guard against victimisation. Arguably, however, being mentally prepared in this way is better defined as awareness or concern, not fear. Fear itself can slide into hopelessness or terror, either of which can be counter-productive in terms of taking reasonable precautions. (Home Office 1989: 12. *Report of the Working Group on the Fear of Crime* (Chairman M. Grade). Home Office Standing Conference on Crime Prevention)

Without going into the obvious arguments of definition that this passage poses, it neatly encapsulates the dilemma of governing fear of crime and illustrates its productive utility as governmental tactic.

This dilemma is not only faced at this level of 'expert' information, the same problem is also present throughout the entire web of governance when it comes to crime prevention. Thus, governing fear of crime is indeed an *art*, to use Foucaultian parlance. Government must calculate and balance its policy interventions. But it's also an *economy*. That is, government entails incurring the economic costs (in the broadest sense) of responsibilisation of subjects.

Tactics of crime prevention

I have already noted that fear of crime is a major concern of contemporary crime prevention strategies and programmes. However, we do not have to delve too deeply to discover also that fear is often used as a tactic of governance in instructing individuals to take preventative measures, in conducting conduct, in order to reduce the risk of crime and victimisation; a *governance-through-fear*. That is to say, we are to be sensitised, through governmental instruction or advice, and constantly expected to evaluate, police, *govern* and insure our bodies and property against the wrongdoings of others. This is a form of bio-politics aimed at the government of the self (Foucault 1991). The *fearing subject* is a responsibilised active citizen whose civic duty includes keeping one's self and one's belongings safe. This has the effect of minimising active and coercive state intervention in crime prevention but is intervention in itself, albeit of a seemingly much less intrusive kind. There are no curfews in place, no legal restrictions on individuals' movements, yet the *fearing subject* is expected to curfew the self and only venture into areas or situations of low risk. Here no doubt there is slippage between my conceptualisation of *fearing subjects* and personages identified in the work of other governmentality scholars. *Fearing subjects* for example share characteristics with O'Malley's (1992) idealised figure of *homo prudens* and they no doubt embody obvious elements of what Garland calls the criminologies of the self. However, my characterisation of *fearing subjects* seeks to tease out particular elements and governmental potentialities of subject formation that remain submerged in these other characterisations: the potential both to govern one's fear and risk and to be governed through fear.

The governmental literature, in a sense, prescribes forms of prudent action for the everyday in order that we avoid the risky situations of the late-modern social world. Of course there are differing degrees of prescription and differing and contested objects and sites of risk contained within these texts. These differences are largely a result of the particular agencies, functionaries or companies and the programmes and targets of these agencies. Thus, there is little worth in conducting a totalising form of analysis here; the imagined *fearing subjects* of these texts, no doubt, vary quite considerably from text to text. Further, each individual – to turn more to Giddens' (1993: 304) conceptualisation of the subject – has differing degrees of access to the material, differing capacities through which one might take on the advice, and differing ways of dealing with, or perhaps ignoring, the material. Thus, its effects are anything but totalising. However, there is little doubt that each particular form of literature imagines a very particular form of subject. Elizabeth Stanko (1998: 422) concludes, in relation to advice for women for avoiding sexual assault:

> Publicised advice, generated by in-house police publicity ... reinforces the message of our sexual vulnerability ... Our *anxiety may be raised*: By placing the responsibility for avoiding men's violence once again on our shoulders – for it is our behaviour that can minimise the chances of becoming a target of men's violence – we are responsible for sorting safe from unsafe men [my emphasis].

Moreover, in some cases such information imagines the very type of *fearing subject* least likely to require regulation or indeed least able to afford the products required to avoid risk. Hope (2000) has noted for example that the economically disadvantaged, demonstrably more at risk of most forms of violent offending, are in no position, either geographically or financially, to join the security 'club', and thus are excluded from realising much of what safety advice might prescribe. So this literature is imperfect and diverse. My argument is not that the citizenry simply consume and comply with the instruction prescribed. Rather, what I'm suggesting is that this form of instruction adds to a more general and diffuse crime fear discourse, it is part of the *fear of crime feedback loop*.

This material is produced, not as a coherent or organised body of literature by, if you will, a central government, but as a diffuse and seemingly disorganised array of documents that spring from a host of sometimes decentralised, and often relatively autonomous, governmental functionaries and private institutions or businesses: the police, to be sure, but also women's advocacy groups, insurance companies, local government, private policing companies, the security industry, community groups, academics and others. Thus, these are not totalising 'iron cage' forms of governance but multifarious institutions and organisations. The literature discussed below has been selectively sampled as a set of case studies from various police organisations, governmental agencies and private companies around Sydney NSW. However, one can find such texts in any liberal democracy.

Take (my safety) advice

The following are examples of this 'advice' literature and illustrative of how, to varying extents, the literature attempts to *govern through fear*. The NSW Police via their various area commands, like almost any modern police service, produce posters and leaflets on how to avoid becoming a victim of crime. These may focus on any number of offences. There is information about how to avoid sexual assault, how to avoid being burgled or robbed, and how to avoid being assaulted or worse. Much of the literature covers more than one of these offence categories:

> The community needs to be our partner in the fight against crime. We need to be aware of what's happening in your neighbourhood and to contact your local police or Crime Stoppers if you notice anything suspicious [sic]. We also need to make life more difficult for burglars by increasing the security of NSW homes. Only by working together can we make our homes safe from burglars. (NSW Police Service 1995)

The message is clear. 'We' all have a role to play in policing, and policing 'burglars' also means, to some extent, policing ourselves. We are told for example to 'lock all doors and windows', 'don't leave keys sitting in the lock', 'never [put keys] in hiding places', and to 'engrave … your property' (NSW Police Service 1995). And if *governance through fear* is only implicit in this text then the small drawn images that border the police brochure make the point clearly: images of a pot plant being lifted up by a gloved hand to reveal a hidden key; a lock with a key left hanging tantalisingly in it; a slightly opened window with the pitch-black outside, a blackness that could easily hide an intruder. The message is that if you do not self-govern you are likely to be victimised. Fear of becoming a victim will spur one to self-govern. Are you reckless and putting yourself or your family at risk?

A poster produced by the Leichhardt Area Command (Leichhardt Area Command, no date) in conjunction with the local council, the safety committee and the local member of parliament, is headed: 'Leave it about and it will go without a doubt.' Such a slogan is indicative of much of such literature.

> Crimes of opportunity are becoming a major concern to our community. They affect all of us and visitors to the area ... [ ] Remove visible articles from your car when parking and be careful with handbags, luggage, and other valuables when shopping or dining. Advise visitors and guests to do the same. It is better to prevent crime than to replace or repair your belongings.

Making the public aware of the risk of having property stolen through this form of *criminology of the self* may seem quite removed from the at-distance governance of *fearing subjects*. However, such literature illustrates the rather mundane but rigorous techniques of governance designed to alert residents to the dangers posed by poor risk management; the rationale being that these behaviours can be minimised and appropriate behaviours fostered if the appropriate information is available. Moreover, we are instructed to tutor other citizens – 'visitors' – in these precautions along with ourselves. Through this further tuition the field of governance is expanded and normalised.

The more recently updated NSW Police Service website is even more explicit. Indeed, there is advice offered on any number of potentially risky situations. What, for example, to do when visitors call:

> Don't open the door to anyone you don't know and trust. If someone is at the door and you are alone and feel a bit frightened, pretend there is someone else in the house ... If someone wants to use your telephone for an emergency, don't feel rude about not allowing them in. Offer to make the call for them – if they are a genuine caller they will not mind ... Be suspicious of people requesting entry to your home to check appliances or equipment. Ask to see their identity card and take time to look at it carefully before letting them in. If you are still unsure, ring their company to check. *If in doubt, keep them out* [author's emphasis]. (NSW Police Service 2001)

Suddenly, having visitors sounds like a risky, indeed I would suggest *fearful*, enterprise. It entails one taking a number of precautions and being on guard and suspicious. As does going to the bank:

> Vary the days and times each week that you go to the bank or building society. Varying your routine helps prevent theft ... Put your money straight into your purse or wallet before moving away from the teller. (NSW Police Service 2001)

It's lucky that bank branches are closing down, minimising our need to use these rather dangerous facilities.

Keeping your home secure is also an ongoing and important process:

> Many burglaries occur during the day. In a large number entry is unforced because people have not locked up properly. Before you go out, double-check all the windows and doors are locked, especially laundry and bathroom windows … Lock doors where an intruder might enter, particularly if you have the TV or the vacuum cleaner on and are unlikely to hear someone … Never leave keys in 'hiding places' like under the doormat. Leave a spare key with a trusted neighbour or friend. (NSW Police Service 2001)

But to be clear, this instruction is not confined to the work of the NSW Police. Westfield, a company which owns and runs 'enclosed mall'-style shopping centres, produces similar brochures in 'conjunction with the NSW police'. In particular I've focused on a leaflet on 'bag-snatching' (no date). The brochure suggests that 'bag-snatching' has increased in 'recent years' and that this could be due to 'the thief realising every handbag contains money', that 'the handbag is a visible target, usually draped over the shoulder', and that 'women normally do not have the strength to resist such an attack'. It goes on to suggest that:

> There needs to be *strategies* in place where *women* can hopefully *avoid* the 'trauma' of a handbag snatch. The following information has been provided to *give some 'tips'* on *how to keep yourself and your properties safe* when going shopping or *out and about* generally [my emphasis]. (Westfield)

There are a number of inferences that can be drawn from this. Firstly, these points leave little doubt that the shadowy stranger, the bag-snatcher in this instance, is male and rationally acting. The victim, indeed *fearing subject* of this literature is female – not surprising given that the focus is handbags, but worth highlighting just the same. Secondly, there is the danger of 'trauma' or worse used to instil concern in the reader who, it is supposed, positions herself as the potential victim of this crime. The message is again clear, be responsible or risk the consequences. Thirdly, the brochure makes no secret of the fact that these are 'tips', 'tips' that will keep you 'safe' if you follow the tuition. Fourthly, there is no doubt where the danger lies, it's 'out and about generally'. The brochure goes on to suggest that in being out and about you should try to:

> Travel and shop with friends (safety in numbers).
> Be in control of your handbag at all times.
> Be aware of the people around you ... have eye contact ... thereby, you may assess someone's possible actions before anything happens.
> When driving your car, lock all the doors, especially if you have central locking, and place your handbag under the seat or on the floor.
> When withdrawing money from Automatic Teller Machines, ensure no one is directly behind you who may memorise your pin number and can see what amount of cash you're taking out. (Westfield)

There is little doubt that these are actions that most carry out fairly automatically. They are either 'common sense' or we have already been tutored in these procedures – without necessarily being aware of the tuition – on other occasions. However, there is also quite a fear-inducing message being given here. The subtext of the first point is that you are *not* safe alone; there's 'safety in numbers'. The third point tells us that no stranger can be trusted and must be 'assess[ed]', surveilled as a matter of course by the maintenance of 'eye contact'. Moreover, this should be carried out in the name of general risk management 'before anything happens'. The fourth point tells us that even in our cars we are not safe; the responsible citizen will 'lock all the doors' to guard against the unknown outside. And the tuition continues, suggesting that 'most importantly':

> If someone physically attempts to steal your handbag, **DON'T RESIST**, as *no amount of money is worth the risk of serious injury.*
> Bag snatching usually occurs around shopping centres and parking areas. However, this may not always be the case as this could occur on the street or elsewhere. *Consider the 'danger' times and locations and take preventative measures* [my emphasis] (Westfield)

These last two points really sum up the entire tenor here. If someone does 'physically attempt' to victimise you, you are essentially powerless. If you have taken every precaution you are an unfortunate victim, a responsible citizen fallen foul of life's ungovernable risks. However, as a responsible citizen you will keep yourself safe by letting the crime take its course and by reporting to the police after the event – thus you still have some role in managing the event and its accompanying risks. Conversely, if you have not heeded the earlier warnings you are by your very ungovernability implicated in your own misfortune. You become what Shearing and Stenning (1985) suggest is a new form of deviant, the irresponsible subject/victim. The second point here also asks us to 'consider the danger times and locations' before we venture out. Here we are all, as responsible citizens, meant to be our own risk managers. We are expected to know the dangers, know when our fears are justified, and act accordingly. Of course there is also an economic imperative at play here. A *fearing subject* is much more likely to find the Westfield enclosed mall an attractive site of consumption – a point I will expand on in the next chapter. It is worth noting here though that the governmental aims of the public sector often chime in exceptionally well with the economic imperatives of the private sector under these forms of neo-liberal rationality.

The NRMA/police/resident cooperative initiative Neighbourhood Watch produces a number of brochures that instruct us how to conduct our lives in safety. The advice offered here includes tips on how to ward off threats by 'thieves' and other types of criminals. The brochures inform us that 'carelessness accounts for nearly 20 per cent of all house robberies in New South Wales', and exhort us to 'remember, a lock is not a lock unless you use it' (NRMA 1990). The word-play of the second slogan (the interplay between the interchangeable verb and noun, 'lock') is designed to be the memorable tag line – indeed much of this literature is slogan driven. Thus, in the name of being a responsible citizen we are told to:

- Make sure your house number is clearly visible from the street for emergency services.
- Make sure there are good locks on perimeter doors and windows to the home and use them.
- Lock away tools, ladders and other implements which a thief could use to break into your home.
- Never leave notes that a thief could read (to milkman, family, friends, etc.).
- Don't leave keys in 'hiding places' around the house for a thief to find.
- Don't forget to lock up even if it is only for a few minutes.
- Trim trees and shrubs away from around doors and windows.
- If you go on holidays, use timers on lights and radios to give your home that 'lived in' appearance.
- Have your neighbours clear mail and maintain the lawns whilst you are absent.
- Make an effort to know your neighbours and their daily routines.

- Check your neighbourhood for things that might contribute to crime, poor lighting, abandoned cars, vacant land littered with rubbish or abandoned buildings. (NRMA 1990)

And that:

If you take the precautions outlined in this brochure, a would-be thief will quickly see what *he* is up against and probably look for an easier target. Be aware of the need to protect your home and yourself at all times.
Break-ins occur when people are at home asleep, watching television etc.
Assaults do occur in the home [my emphasis]. (NRMA 1990)

There is little doubt that these final two points in particular are aimed squarely at changing or keeping in check one's regulatory regime through instilling a little fear. There is no clarification (statistically or otherwise), nor is there an explanation (criminological or otherwise). These points are presented as objective, unquestionable facts (and of course they are accurate to some extent but constitute a very reductive picture of offending).

Not only do these Neighbourhood Watch brochures instruct us how to look after our property, they also instruct us how to look after ourselves by providing us with 'some very important 'DOs and DON'Ts': These are as follows:

- Never admit you are alone in the house – either to a caller at the door or to someone on the telephone.
- Never allow a stranger to enter your home – check their identification or telephone the organisation they claim to represent. If they are who they say they are they won't mind.
- Never wait at bus stops or railway stations at night any longer than you have to – know the timetables.
- Never take short-cuts at night through parks or vacant lots.
- Never place an advertisement in the newspaper which requires people to call at your home, unless you have someone with you.
- Never walk close to doorways if you are forced to use a poorly lit street.
- If you are forced to wait for public transport at night, stay as close as possible to the lit area (shop front etc), or where there are other people (railway staff office).

- Fit good quality locks to your house (front and back) and have either a security door or peep hole – USE THEM!
- Always carry your handbag clutched in front of you – don't let it dangle from your shoulder or hand.
- If you are walking and a car is following you, go to the nearest place where people are likely to be (a neighbour's house, a shop etc.), taking care to get a description of the vehicle – notify police immediately.

SELF PROTECTION
- First and foremost – don't panic.
- Your best protection is noise
- If you can't escape, scream as loud as you can.
- Yell 'FIRE', rather than 'HELP', as people seem to react more readily.
- Avoid violence if possible – most women escape by talking their way out of trouble.
- Think about carrying personal safety devices, such as a shrill alarm.
- Remember, there are always items in a woman's handbag which can be used to defend yourself, such as a nail file, bunch of keys etc. (NRMA 1990)

The list of personal security measures here is long and relatively detailed. Indeed it reads like an instruction manual for the reduction of risk. Certainly it would leave us with the feeling that the social world is far from a safe place to be – it also leaves little doubt that it is the outside world, the *other*, that is to be feared rather than the familiar, or more to the point, family.[2] It does not necessarily automatically follow, however, that this list of behaviours would not be beneficial in reducing victimisation or risk of victimisation.

The point is that all this 'responsibilising' advice aimed at making us self-governing subjects is potentially fear inducing. We are presented with examples of what might happen if we do not regulate our behaviour effectively and 'appropriately' – and for the most part these images and examples are frightening. Paradoxically, much of this information is provided by police, local government and insurance companies,[3] the same institutions that also attempt to reduce fear of crime, the same institutions and agencies that take part in the development of crime prevention plans in part aimed at reducing fear of crime. Local community becomes an institutional form for communicating risk management (Stenson 1993a); one I would add which may also have the effect of intensifying fear of crime discourse.

We might equate many of the forms of government I have discussed with what has been identified by some scholars (O'Malley 1992; Stenson 1993a; Stenson 1993b) as a broader shift towards neo-liberalism, policies and practices that emphasise individual responsibility and free choice over broader social and state interventions. Some have argued that neo-liberal government takes the focus off the failures of the police force (O'Malley 1992), the continued rolling back of the public sector (Stanko 1998) and structural inequalities, by attempting to produce responsibilised individuals that take on many of the burdens once governed by the centralised state. No doubt this is illustrative of Garland's notion of the retreat of welfarist criminology. Governmental intervention becomes governance through outsourcing, privatisation, through instruction and facilitation rather than direct action. Stanko (1997, 1998) has made repeated and concerted attacks at governmental instruction as it relates to the governing of women's bodies. She argues that it is misguided and that it ignores the realities of women's risk at the hands of men – particularly men they know. Indeed, most of the crime prevention literature and advice available plays down the fact that serious victimisation is most likely to occur at the hands of intimates rather than strangers.

However, I wish to reject the negative hypothesis regarding *governance through fear.* I want to suggest that fear of crime, as a tactic or technology of governance – like all knowledge/power – should not be conceptualised as an inherently negative regulatory force. Rather we should conceptualise it as a productive force, neither inherently negative nor inherently positive but part of the processes that produce modern active liberal subjects. If there is to be some sort of normative evaluation of the effects of *government through fear* it should be focused on the performance of specific strategies of governance and their ability to enhance civic access and a sense of ease and worth within their everyday private and social interactions. However, it should also be focused on the programme's ability to reduce risk, a not altogether unreasonable goal. In particular neo-liberal rationalities of government are likely to heighten fears when they deploy private institutions and business to govern through fear; we should not be surprised at this. This outsourcing to the private sector will be discussed in the next chapter. Couple this with a political rhetoric invoking the *criminology of the other* and we find a recipe for the intensification of fear of crime discourse. A thorough evaluation of alternative strategies is beyond the scope and not the aim of this book. I simply want to emphasise this productive capacity of governmental power rather than painting it as an inherently negative force. By doing this I emphasise the capacities for other possible modes of intervention, other possible governmental strategies.

Fear reduction and triumph

There is another interlinked reason that fear of crime has become such an important object of governmental intervention. Put simply, it has offered another possibility of a policy or administrative triumph for the police, politicians, criminologists, and an array of other specialists. All of these groups or institutions, in one way or another, and often by their own measures, have failed successfully to govern crime (see Braithwaite 1989); crime has not disappeared, nor can it. If policy-makers can be seen as doing something about crime fear, the constant and inevitable failure to govern crime can be somewhat obscured. As Garland (1996: 448) has noted:

> ... better management of risks and resources, reduction of the fear of crime, reduction of criminal justice expenditure and greater support for crime's victims, have become the less heroic policy objectives which increasingly replace the idea of winning a 'war against crime'.

However, recently the reduction of fear of crime has begun to disappear as an explicit policy target for some policing agencies, replaced by new problematisations such as 'anti-social behaviour'. Could it be that the envisaged triumph has proven more difficult than expected? It appears that the task of reducing crime fear has not heralded the success that might have been hoped for.

Fear of crime as an object and concept has had, developing around it, a new group of specialists dedicated to its government. Requests for more police by police unions and politicians are now often based upon fear of crime rather than just crime rates *per se* (see Weatherburn *et al.* 1996). Fear of crime commands the attention of an expanding cohort of criminologists and other researchers who in turn are rewarded with research funding from governments and private industry for their interest. Indeed, entire conferences are held around the problem of crime fear. Fear is increasingly surveyed, calculated and quantified, necessitating the development of more surveys – ever increasing in accuracy and detail.

Another binary? The fearing subject and the feared subject

But there is also a flipside to this constitution of the fearful. That is, those that are, or become, the feared; the binary opposite to *fearing subjects* if you will. If *fearing subjects* are the target of *criminologies of the self*, the target of *the criminology of the other* is the *feared subject*. Usually these are strangers, the unknown *other*; the stranger danger discourse as it relates to children is a classic example of the constitution of this usually – but not always – shadowy figure. Almost by definition strangeness connotes difference. Thus, those that are considered feared groups can also be those who are, or at least appear to be, different. Indeed, a number of scholars have argued that fear of crime is actually fear of black people or fear more generally of difference.[4] I think it is overstating the case to suggest that such feared groups are somehow a universal element of crime fear discourse. However, there seems little doubt that Afro-Americans, Muslims, indigenous groups and others are often the idealised or imagined *feared subject* of fear of crime discourse – at least in Western democratic states like the USA, UK and Australia.

In the final section of this chapter I will discuss how minority groups are constructed as stranger, other, or *feared subjects* of fear of crime discourse. I will also argue that once a discourse like fear of crime becomes available it is possible to construct as *other* particular minority groups of people. That is, difference, strangeness, becomes fearful and such fear can then be reflected back in the form of survey results and the like. I will then move on and discuss the construction of *feared subjects* in the 'war on terror'.

The unplaceable other

One of the symbolic effects of the governmental production of the *fearing subject* over the past decades has been the production of, or at least some clarification, of its *other*; what could be referred to as the *feared subject*. This shadowy figure pervades the subtext – and often the text itself – of the fear of crime literature and is wanting of its own analysis. Often this *other* is featured in drawings or photos, half obscured from our sight, caricatured, hidden in bushes (the ones we should have cut back), lurking in the shadows as we saw above. The notion of feared *others* is of course not new. As we have seen, from the eighteenth century onwards a variety of pariah figures have haunted the imaginations of the respectable classes. The dangerous classes, the recidivist, the homeless, the vagrant, the indolent, the idle, the ex-criminal, the unemployed; at various times all become the embodiment of this *flâneur*-like *other*.

I will use the analogy of the *flâneur* to briefly explore the *other* of the *fearing subject*. The *flâneur* is the man who wanders the city, the man who finds pleasure in being away from home, freedom in being non-locatable. Lechte (1995) describes the *flâneur* in Baudelaire (1972: 460) as 'an ego athirst for the non-ego'. The *flâneur*:

> ... searches out the ephemeral, the transitory and the contingent. The *flâneur*'s trajectory leads nowhere and comes from nowhere. It is a trajectory without fixed spatial coordinates; there is, in short, no reference point from which to make predictions about the *flâneur*'s future. For the *flâneur* is an entity without past or future, without identity: an entity of contingency and indeterminacy. (Lechte 1995: 103)

Like the unidentified spectre-like criminal of the governmental literature, *he* is unknowable, unplaceable. What is the task of managing one's risk through engaging in the practices outlined in the governmental crime prevention literature if it is not guarding against the unknown, the contingent, the hidden danger? There is of course a need not to push this particular analogy – between the *flâneur* and the feared subject – too far. For, according to Baudelaire, the *flâneur* was anything but dangerous. Rather, he was one at play; a player whose playground was the city, the metropolis, his game was to observe – maybe also to be observed – but not to harm. However, Wilson (1995) describes the *flâneur* as a gendered concept or subject. This freedom to wander where one wishes is, she argues, a masculine freedom. He is the embodiment of the 'male gaze' and is the symbol of men's 'visual and voyeuristic mastery over women'. Like the *he* of the instruction literature this unknowability and invisibility are unsettling and gendered male.

So while the *feared subject* that haunts the instruction literature is quite removed from Baudelaire's *flâneur* in terms of intent, they do share a number of traits. Both are only possible through the infinite lens of the contingent: their movements are unknown: they are removed from discourse, from the social body, and indeed from a history. One could never be sure they are not being viewed or observed by either. Their embodiment takes place in only a moment in time and a discrete place in space. Both can come into being only in regard to their opposites and can come into being at any time. The *feared subject* must feed off the *fearing subject*. The floating *flâneur* must have fixed spaces and the citizens that inhabit them in order to play and gaze.

Indeed, it might be that the shadowy *feared subject* has largely replaced the *flâneur* in the public imagination. That is, the continuum between the two is not all so accidental or metaphoric. As Bauman (1993: 255) suggests:

Today's action is, after all, different: it is, mostly, about passing from here to there as fast as one can manage, preferably without stopping, better still without looking around. Beautiful passers-by are no more to be seen; they hide inside cars with tinted windows. Those still on the pavement are waiters and sellers at best, but more often *dangerous people* pure and simple: Layabouts, beggars, homeless conscience-soilers, drug-pushers, pickpockets, muggers, child molesters and rapists waiting for prey. To the innocent who has to leave for a moment the wheeled-up security of cars, or those others (still thinking of themselves as innocent) who cannot afford the security at all, the street is more a jungle than a theatre … A site fraught with risks, not chances; not meant for gentlemen of leisure … The street is the wilderness 'out there' from which one hides, at home or inside the car, behind security locks and burglar alarms [my emphasis].

While Bauman's apocalyptic vision – here taken slightly out of context – might seem an over-exaggeration he eloquently illustrates an important point. The imagined unknown dweller of social space, the *flâneur*, has been replaced by a much more feared entity; the street no longer a *theatre* but a *jungle*. In risk-rich late modernity the unknown is no longer exciting, rather it becomes an anxiety or indeed a fear. That is not to suggest that this fear has an objective reality but that the *fearing subject* would do well – according to the advice literature – to believe that it has. For Baudelaire's subjects the street was a playground, for those of Bauman it is a 'nightmare'.

Overwhelmingly though the menacing *feared subject* of these texts illustrates their gross mistargeting. In communities where the risk of crime, and especially the risk of violent crime, is demonstrably high, that is generally lower socio-economic areas, the risks are well known to residents. Moreover, most residents are unlikely to be able to do very much to reduce their risk levels. Certainly they can't afford to purchase elaborate private security measures. Likewise, much of the literature aimed at reducing the risk of women becoming the victims of sexual assault focuses not on where the highest risk lies, and where women have less control over their own risk management; that is, in familial situations or in the home.

The panoply of feared subjects

Feared subjects are constantly and easily created. The experience of fear makes us hungry for a range of stereotypical *others* through which our anxieties can be justified. As David Sibley (1995: 206) has so eloquently put it:

> Both the self and the world are split into good and bad objects, and the bad self, the self associated with fear and anxiety over the loss of control, is projected onto bad objects. Fear precedes the construction of the bad object, the negative stereotype, but the stereotype – simplified, distorted and at a distance – perpetuates that fear.

In the USA in the late 1960s the stereotypical figure of the Afro-American could easily become the *feared subject* of middle-American sensibilities. While fear of crime as a social scientific concept identified for the population the extent of their own fears, these could be simultaneously projected on to the 'bad object'. Thus a mutually intensifying process could begin where fear would increase the processes of stereotyping while at the same time the stereotypes could increase fear which could faithfully be recorded by the social scientist. One can envisage the development of a panoply of *feared subjects* that might resemble Lombroso's (1876) (in)famous frontispiece. Here however each individual *fearing subject* might construct their individual panoply.

In areas of rural Australia indigenous Aboriginal people would constitute one such feared stereotype for some Anglo-Australians. When one is asked to secure one's property in many small country towns in western NSW there is little doubt against whom they are securing – indeed one piece of fear-inducing crime prevention literature might be read differently in different parts of the country (see Lee 2006); locality, space and time being major factors in one's panoply of *feared subjects*. This is not to suggest that prevention literature and its attendant responsibilisation is somehow causally responsible for the imagining of *others* as stereotypes, only that it provides scenarios on to which these stereotypes can be imagined.

In Sydney in 2006 no doubt young Lebanese men would take pride of place and even Burkah-clad women might be included in one's panoply as they oscillate in the public (and indeed political) imagination between criminal and terrorist. Ten years ago the same position might have been occupied by young Vietnamese men in the reified panic about Vietnamese gangs. The *feared subject* of the crime prevention literature is usually faceless, de-identified. Thus, we are invited to apply to this the face we wish, faces that change through space and time. Needless to say that such stereotypes can be reconfirmed through various forms of authoritarian populism and party political politics. Perhaps the most recent embodiment of the *feared subject* is that of the terrorist. The lack of control over terrorism, the randomness, the ungovernability; terrorism is both a metaphoric and concrete attack on the foundations of modernity and reason. Its very unreason increases its fearfulness.

Fear of terrorism: be alert and alarmed (but not too alarmed)

The distinction between domestic and foreign affairs is diminishing.
(George W. Bush in 2002, cited in McCulloch 2004: 314)

The discourse of crime fear has also provided a more general blueprint for other fears and anxieties, and indeed for the governance and political manipulation of these. That is, new problems of governance are able to slot easily into the governmental, and by now highly politicised, discursive space rendered open by the invention of fear of crime. Perhaps the most pertinent example of this is the emergence of terrorism[5] as a 'new' problem for the Western nation states. This new 'war on terror' can sit alongside the 'war on crime', the 'war on drugs', and even displace other wars like 'cold war' as a legitimation of the military industrial complex of nations like the United States. The 'war on crime' has in many respects morphed into the 'war on terror' – indeed any distinction between the criminal and the terrorist, crime and terror, has become increasingly blurred in official discourse. Accordingly, 'fear of terrorism' and fear of crime are becoming interlinked in the public mind. These war metaphors have consequences, one of which is the blurring of the line between warfare and police work (Steinert 2003). In Australia the recent panic about 'Middle Eastern crime gangs' has been seamlessly linked to the broader threat of fundamentalist Islam and terrorism; so much so that recent racialised riots at Cronulla Beach in Sydney's south, in which a large violent mob of Anglo-Australians terrorised and assaulted anybody in the vicinity who was of Middle Eastern appearance, were constructed by participants – and many commentators and onlookers – as 'reclaiming our beach' from the Muslims who don't 'assimilate'. (The equally repugnant reprisal attacks were however constructed by the same commentators as proof of the dangerous Muslim *other*). Likewise, the Australian Howard Government has successfully mobilised the suggestion that groups of asylum seekers, who face mandatory detention on reaching Australia,[6] might include terrorists. Indeed, such a strategy turned the Howard Government's political fortunes around in the November 2001 federal election (McCulloch 2003; Weber and Bowling 2002). The Government refused a Norwegian container ship, the *Tampa*, permission to land on Australian territory following the ship's rescue of 430 Afghani asylum seekers at sea. When the captain of the vessel disobeyed the refusal order and attempted to dock, armed SAS personnel boarded the ship and took control. While its human cargo was packed off to New Zealand and other South Pacific island states the Government's political fortunes rose (Hogg 2002) with 70 per cent of the Australian public apparently supporting the tough stance. Their 'tough' strategy was then celebrated further following the 11 September 2001 attacks on New York, making Australian national security the number one election issue. While Australian State elections[7] have for many years been fought with law and order a key issue, the federal election had its equivalent with 'new terrorism' and national security.

Beirne and Messerschmidt (2006) argue, drawing on the 2004 US Gallup polls taken following the September 11 attacks on New York, that 'the public has transferred their highest level of fear from the violence of street crime to the violence of terrorism'. McCulloch (2004) comes to a similar conclusion claiming that the war on terrorism and its 'offspring' security are perhaps a new and more dangerous extension of domestic law and order politics and that 'security' is more about getting politicians elected than protecting people from violence or harm. Rothe and Muzzatti (2004), writing of the USA, suggest that terrorism constitutes the moral panic of our time through which the 'polity and the media' have elevated 'societal fear'. Huysmans (cited in Loader 2004: 54) puts it more broadly, noting the symbolic political value of security:

> Security policy is a specific policy of mediating belonging. Discourses of danger and security practices derive their political significance from their capacity to stimulate people to contract into a political community and to ground – or contest – political authority on the basis of reifying dangers.

In this sense we might see the September 11 attacks as a form of 'signal crime' (Innes 2004) which stimulated both political community and political action. The initial mobilisation of particular political rationalities enabled 'security' policy, or the securitisation of policy, to proliferate following this event. However, this was not the genesis of such a move, as Weber and Bowling (2002) argue in relation to the policing of immigration. Rather, it was an acceleration and crystallisation. Moreover, this political stimulation could and would draw on an already-available discourse of fear to intensify 'political community'.

Meanwhile, the pollsters and the like busily enumerate and 'reify' these 'new' fears about terrorism, telling us what we are fearful of, and what we should be if we're not already. In a recent Sydney

Daily Telegraph survey 74 per cent of respondents replied yes to the question 'Should the death penalty be introduced for terrorism?' while 73 per cent responded yes to the question 'Should the death penalty be introduced for murder?' (*The Daily Telegraph*, 12 July 2004b: 4–5). Terrorism is winning the poll race! Blood lust aside, this type of media poll does indicate the success with which terrorism has been mobilised as something to fear. The fact that it registers at all in this 'law and order survey' also indicates how seamlessly the 'fear of terrorism' slides into and becomes part of our catalogue of crimes to fear. *The Telegraph* (12 July 2004c: 4) went on, under the headline 'Terrorist Attack Fears Mounting', explaining that:

> Many people believe a terror attack will occur in Australia in the next twelve months … Almost half the respondents to the Daily Telegraph law and order survey feared a terror attack, compared to 17 per cent who believed it unlikely.

It all sounds so familiar. The article continued with respondents to the survey apparently telling us which Sydney landmarks will attract the ire of 'the terrorists': the bridge, a football stadium, Sydney tower, high-rise buildings and the like. These fears in turn give the political green light to new methods of securing such infrastructure amongst other things. One can sense a new fear of crime scenario question being formulated here, 'Would you feel secure visiting X Sydney landmark without a visible security presence?'. So this 'new' fear of terrorism never had to be invented or discovered. It was there already in the form of crime fear to be mobilised by just the right signal crime.

Like the 'war on crime' the war on terror's attendant fears have had effects in relation both to changes in policy, domestically and internationally, and legislation. The US doctrine of 'pre-emption' against terrorist activity has become entrenched and operates as an omnipresent threat to any government, state or organisation that does not toe the line of the US model of global capitalism and Western-style democracy, supplanting the cold war threat of mutual destruction. Indeed, current US foreign policy dictates that 'peaceful intentions' must be proved, especially if you are part of the 'axis of evil', essentially reversing the burden of proof (McCulloch 2004). Here risk is not to be managed but controlled with the brute might of US sovereign power. Indeed, McCulloch goes on to note that the domestic twin of pre-emption is to be found in a proliferation of legislation that gives policing organisations and other security forces powers to detain individuals believed either to be terrorists, to have links to terrorist organisations, or to have information about terrorist activity. It is here that the line between 'the war on terror' and the 'war on crime', police and military, are at their most blurred. Simultaneously the power and authority of the executive has been expanded, particularly in the USA but also in Britain and Australia, and the separation of powers, legislative, judicial and executive, has been eroded. Hocking (2004) notes the 'astonishing' ease with which political and legal rights, central to the rule of law, have been surrendered in the name of 'countering terrorism', and how these have been welcomed by a fearful 'tremulous' public. In Australia a plethora of new legislation has been pushed through parliament under the auspices of 'national security' – a term barely used 10 years ago. This has been hastened by the fact that the Liberal-National Coalition government has effective control of both houses of parliament, but the discursive power of the terrorism narrative, including symbols of imminent risk and the fear thereof, has made political resistance almost impossible. The Anti-Terrorism Act (no. 2) 2005 for example introduces measures that: broaden the definition of terrorism; expand provisions on the financing of terrorism; institute court-approved control orders that restrict an individual's liberties based on what they *might* do; institute preventative detention allowing for the detainment of individuals for up to 48 hours without charge or questioning; increase stop and search powers of police and introduce new sedition offences that go beyond the incitement to violence. And this is just one of many such post-September 11 2001 acts of parliament. The Australian changes follow similar legislation in the UK (the 2001 British Anti-Terrorism, Crime and Security Act and The Prevention of Terrorism Act 2005 for example) and the USA (the Patriot Act). Of course, we are sold such legislative change under the promise that the honest and law-abiding have nothing to hide. It is only potentially offending others, identified via other techniques of risk management and control, suspect populations who can be classified as risky, who need view these changes with apprehension.

As Hardt and Negri (2000) put it, fear is the ultimate guarantee of new segmentations, it creates struggle and conflict. In the USA immigration took the political spotlight within days of the attacks on the World Trade Center and ethnic profiling became the preferred mode of policing. Within two months the USA had detained 1,200 immigrants under the new Patriot Act (Welch 2003). In Cuba, at the US naval base of Guantánamo Bay, Camp X-Ray and Camp Delta began filling with some 680 'unlawful combatants' following the war in Afghanistan (De Lint 2004), others were held in Afghanistan at Bagram air base. Technically detained 'offshore', these nationals from some 43 different countries, were refused rights under the Geneva Convention and under US and international legal jurisdiction. The measures employed at Guantánamo Bay are continually justified through the discourses of counter-terrorism, national security and fear of an unknowable and unknown enemy. As Colonel Donald Woolfolk, acting commander of Guantánamo Bay, put it on 13 June 2002:

> We are now living in an age where our nation is engaged in international armed conflict against terrorism … we face an enemy that knows no borders and perceives all Americans, wherever they may be, as targets of opportunity. Under such circumstances the need to maintain the tightly controlled environment, which has been established to create dependency and trust by the detainee and his interrogator, is of paramount importance. Disruption of the interrogation environment, such as through access to a detainee by counsel, undermines this interrogation dynamic. Should this occur, a critical instrument may be lost, resulting in a direct threat to national security. (cited in De Lint 2004: 142)

Yet, at the same time as it tears it apart, fear actualises and produces communities and active subjects of governmental discourse; it enables order and domination; the *governance through fear* of communities built on shared victimage to use Alison Young's characterisation. However, while I'm able to identify attempts by government to reduce fear of crime, the same cannot be said of 'fear of terrorism'.

The sometimes uneasy alliance of varying degrees of neo-liberal and neo-conservative governance which currently characterises many Western nation states (O'Malley 2004) is likely to encourage forms of active citizenship while simultaneously pursuing a tough and exclusive stance on those it constructs as non-citizens, or those it constructs as a threat. As responsibilised 'active' citizens we all have a role to play in this 'war on terror'. Yet, at the same time we defer to our governments, many of whom employ neo-conservative and authoritarian responses.

As I've argued above, fear of crime has become a tactic of government; more recently fear of terrorism has likewise become a governmental tactic. Australian federal government adopted the slogan 'Be alert but not alarmed' after September 11. Indeed, they went to extraordinarily great lengths to ensure that responsibilised citizens could and should be active (alert) in the 'fight against terror'. This would extend to the act of alerting authorities should one witness anything that could be construed as terrorist activity or planning. The advertising campaign and the attendant policy gained extra momentum following the London Underground bombing in 2005.

As part of the campaign each Australian household was provided with an information kit aimed at making the provision of information to authorities as easy as possible for the alert citizen. Central to the package was a fridge magnet with contact details of the 'national security 24-hour hotline'. These packages were circulated, at great expense to Australian taxpayers, to every home in Australia. They were derided by many of the government's critics as a political stunt and indeed thousands of the packages were reportedly 'returned to sender'. Nonetheless, the terrorism hotline had received 24,000 calls in the period to August 2005 (*The Age*, 24 August 2005),[8] cementing the potential threat of terror as a political issue writ large on the Australian psyche. And while the fear of terror escalated, it was used to silence opposition to the passage of new legislation aimed at 'pre-emptivity'. Mythen and Walklate (2006) note that this active 'state of alert' is an extension of the capabilities of Neighbourhood Watch, particularly in the USA where this has been formalised and Neighbourhood Watch itself includes the reportage of possible terrorist activity. Citizens become unpaid security guards, spies and informants.

If any slogan best encapsulates the governmental tightrope now almost routinely traversed by Western Governments it is 'Be alert but not alarmed'. It echoes the warnings of the UK Home Office's conceptual balance of fear and terror about crime discussed in earlier chapters but it also operates more generally as a political tool. The Australian Government's 'national security' website contains the daily terror 'alert level'. At the time of writing it was 'MEDIUM'. This is defined as 'terrorist attack could occur'. The British and United States Governments have almost identical alert meters attached to their web pages. And so we live on in uncertainty, waiting for fear to be lifted by the very governments who have used it so effectively. As a recent speech by President Bush announced:

> America is answering new dangers with firm resolve. No matter how long it takes, no matter how difficult the task, we will fight the enemy, and lift the shadow of fear, and lead free nations to victory. (Bush 2005)

Conclusion

If the grid of governance I have outlined here is accurate then attempts to govern and regulate fear of crime seem destined to fail to a greater or lesser extent – that is, of course, if we equate successful governance purely with fear reduction. However, if we also conceptualise fear of crime as a tactic of governance, notions of failure or success become quite clouded and subjective; if success in the governance of fear of crime entails obscuring the failures of government agencies and producing citizens who consume services from the private sector, if success means the exercise of government at a distance and the development of self-governing *fearing subjects* then perhaps the governance of crime fear is indeed a triumph. It seems, however, that governing fear of crime is a kind of governmental balancing act. There is no doubt that governments and other agencies 'conceptualise fear as a negative force'; on the other hand, however, there seems little doubt that many of these same governing bodies also see fear of crime as a tactic to be deployed in the governance of population. Additionally, private-sector involvement complicates this balancing act by feeding fear which in turn often requires additional input from governments who attempt to keep the balance. I will address this private-sector involvement in Chapter 7.

The fear of crime has emerged as a potential instrument or technique of governmental normalisation, or at least self-regulation, whereby the *fearing subject*, sensitised – through instruction or advertising, for example – to the reality of these fears, is constantly expected to evaluate, police, *govern* and insure her or his body and property against the wrongdoings of others. The *fearing subject* is an imagined responsible citizen whose civic duty includes keeping one's self and belongings safe. This has the effect of minimising active and coercive state intervention but is intervention in itself: albeit of a seemingly much less intrusive kind. There are no curfews in place, no legal restrictions on individuals' movements, yet the *fearing subject* is expected to curfew the self and only venture into areas of low risk; to become self-regulating.

We might equate such forms of government and shifts in philosophy with the policies of neo-liberalism, policies that emphasise individual responsibility and free choice over broader social state interventions. And indeed we should not downplay this equation. Neo-liberal governmental intervention often takes the focus off the failures of the police force (O'Malley 1992), the continued rolling back of the public sector (Stanko 1998) and structural inequalities, by attempting to produce these responsible individuals. However, this intervention is not only the result of New Right policy, its beginnings are far more disparate and the rationalities informing it far less sinister or conspiratorial than the 'shift to the right' thesis would imply. Nonetheless the discourse is highly susceptible to the influence of authoritarian populism as is obvious in relation to the war on terror.

The intervention is, in a sense, governance through instruction – it constitutes and makes attempts at the tutelage of the *fearing subject*. In relation to women's risk of victimisation Stanko (1997, 1998) has made repeated and concerted attacks on such intervention, arguing that it is misguided and ignores the realities of women's risk at the hands of men – particularly men they know. While I believe Stanko's point is an important one I also want to suggest that we should not lose sight of the productive libertarian possibilities in terms of personal safety that this intervention may make possible. If such tutelage actually helps some individuals stay safe we can hardly characterise it as wholly coercive or negative – even if it might be misguided or naive. If we take this middle ground and conceptualise these interventions as, for the most part benign, we can see how the fear of crime constitutes a *problem* for the government of population rather than simply a tactic of coercion – although it can of course also be this in some cases. Fear of crime can impinge on individuals' freedom to the extent of contributing to 'social dislocation', 'ill ease', 'anxiety' and 'restrictions to movement', problems which themselves have their effects on politics. Therefore, it is vital – from a governmental policy perspective – that the *fearing subject* is not *made* too fearing but is fearful enough to govern their own risk-taking activities. This inherent contradiction is eloquently illustrated in the statement from the Home Office (1989) with which I opened this chapter. One of the reasons that the fear of crime makes such a problematic object of governance is this nexus between its supposed ability to *make* citizens – or *fearing subjects* – live safer lives, and its propensity to hinder individuals' lives by rendering them too fearful to engage in their normal social and communal activities – and thus actually eroding community and social ties.

Thus, we can see that governing fear of crime is complex, paradoxical and multifaceted. However, the task of governing fear becomes even more complicated when we bring other realms of *economy* into the equation. In particular private enterprise has increasingly played a role in fear of crime's governance. But that is the topic of the final chapter. First, it is important to reiterate that the historical conditions of the emergence of *fearing subjects*, and the contemporary modes of their governance, are not empirically separable; rather, each constitutes part of and reinforces the other; their development has been in a sense parallel, complementary and symbiotic. They are part of a circularity: a *fear of crime feedback loop.*

Notes

1   See Weatherburn *et al.* (1996) for a discussion of a number of these.
2   Even the point quoted above that suggests that 'assaults do happen in the home' seems to indicate that these assaults are as a result of intruders.
3   The NRMA publishes mounds of such literature for example.

4   This proposition was also first raised in The President's Commission report (1967).
5   Black (2004) criminologically defines terrorism as 'unilateral self help by organized civilians who covertly inflict mass violence on other civilians'.
6   Laws introduced under a previous Labour government made detention mandatory for all arrivals. This means incarceration in a detention centre pending the determination of refugee status (Hogg 2002).
7   In Australia policing is a State government responsibility.
8   http://www.theage.com.au/news/national/terror-hotline-hits-24000-calls/2 2005/24008/24023/1124562833847.html accessed 1124562833801/1124562833 803/1124562833806

Chapter 7

Consuming fear: the marketing (of) monsters

Property For Sale: Exclusive and security safe, Overlooking golf course, Good size land. Your own swimming pool, golf course and tennis court in the estate.[1]

This chapter discusses the growth of commercial interest and investment in crime fear and the place of securitisation in the *fear of crime feedback loop*. The private sector, in particular the security and insurance industries, are increasingly finding that fear of crime is a discourse that can be invoked in order to sell particular risk-reducing or security products and services aimed at hardening possible crime targets; insuring prospective targets; policing and securing prospective targets; or all of these. Moreover, many of these commercial security technologies can be interlinked. For example, in many localities it is impossible to purchase home contents insurance without the specified target hardening hardware (and increasingly software). Even real estate is sold specifically on its security credentials[2] as evidenced in the growth of 'gated' communities. Further, media organisations have increasingly discovered that the public fear of crime can sell newspapers, attract listeners, and attract viewers if it is invoked with just the right editorial zeal and is aimed at mobilising deep-seated anxieties in the public. In short, security, and by extension fear of crime, has developed around it a range of service industries, both public and private. Fear of crime is big business and the onus for managing both crime and fear is increasingly in the hands of individual citizens.

In recent decades we have witnessed the proliferation of a range of industries and their related products which, *inter alia,* service our fears about crime: private policing and private security firms, insurance companies; security hardware and software; mobile phones; and 'gated' or lifestyle communities. These private industries have expanded almost in chorus with the apparent growth in anxiety about crime and the general discourse of fear of crime. In particular, the growing governmental discourse of fear of crime and its accompanying responsibilising messages feed directly into our consumption of these fear of crime service industries. As Crawford has argued, 'fear is an incentive for crime prevention, one which commercial interests are willing to exploit' (1998). This chapter discusses why it is that this proliferating list of private security interests has found such a ready market in late-modern consumer societies, and in turn, how this market has made crime fear a target of its service. It also explores examples of many of these fear service industries and discusses how they have constituted part of the *fear of crime feedback loop*. To this end the focus of the chapter is on how fear of crime as a tactic or technology of government can (or indeed can't) be contained in the face of growing private sector involvement that explicitly targets community and individual fears. That is, once the genie is out of the bottle, and crime fear becomes a marketing tool for selling consumer security-orientated products, and increasing profit; once *fearing subjects* become an identified target market to be serviced, how can the discourse of crime fear be controlled and/or contained? Finally, the chapter discusses media interest in crime fear in much the same way as other commercial interests. In treating media organisations in this way I hope to avoid reifying media influence to the neglect of other components of the *fear of crime feedback loop*. International examples of the above are explored and attention is drawn to the links between the social scientific, governmental, commercial and popular discourses of crime fear. That is, I will argue that power invested in every one of these each feeds off other related discourses to produce a self-perpetuating cycle of fear of crime.

The private governance of crime fear

We currently live in a social milieu where our security is sold to us, packaged and commodified. In what once might have seemed like some frightening Orwellian irony, freedom from fear is to be found in the secure 'lifestyle package'; the gated community; biometric recognition systems; the home security monitoring system; CCTV; Global Positioning Systems (GPS); and the ability to track our 'electronic fingerprints' through credit cards and the like. These technologies apparently secure our freedom. Freedom from fear is somehow to be found through an increasingly ubiquitous surveillance society with nation states anxious about the protection of borders (of all kinds) against terrorism and crime. We have increasingly smaller but tougher government promoting active citizenship, but only of very specific kinds. On any objective criteria we are busily reversing many hard-fought freedoms – perhaps the most obvious examples being the reduced freedoms related to the new 'terror' laws discussed in the previous chapter. Barry Glassner (1999) quotes former US president Richard Nixon, a strong advocate of the politics of fear as we have seen in previous chapters, as saying, '[P]eople react to fear not love.' Glassner then suggests that:

> That principle, which guided the late president's political strategy throughout his career, is the *sine qua non* of contemporary political campaigning. Marketers of products and services ranging from car alarms to TV news programs have taken it to heart as well.

In a recent televised interview the Australian Prime Minister John Howard noted that the most important right a citizen could have was the right to 'live safely and securely'[3] and that reaching this goal involves the trading off of some freedoms in a post-'9/11' world. While some argue that this idea of 'trading' rights for security is a smokescreen (McCulloch 2004), this discourse is pervasive. Alison Young (1996) has suggested that we now share our victimage, or that community as we now understand it is often built around the potential of victimage – something like the inverse of Durkheim's collective conscience. The gated community is the privatised securitised embodiment of the more coercive measures taken by the state to secure borders, at least if we accept the more dystopian readings of the changes of later or post-modernity (see Davis 1990; Dear 2000). Community can be artificially produced, moulded and delineated through the proliferation of the gated community, CCTV, private police and security. Yet, with each security purchase, with each new safety device aimed at managing our fear, at securing our security, our anxieties seem to increase. Such is the nature of the *fear of crime feedback loop*. Moreover, our worst fears are continually confirmed by myriad tabloid media sources greedy for the readers and the advertising revenue that follows them. Indeed, we can pick up a newspaper with a survey of our fears and anxieties and look upon it reflexively. All offer discursive surfaces which help frame our *crime* or *safety talk*: surfaces on which we can project either other deeply held anxieties (Hollway and Jefferson 2000: 166), or on which we can share our anxieties about threatening outside others or those *strangers* amongst us (Loader *et al.* 2000). As Caldeira (2000) puts it, drawing from de Certeau, talk of crime is not only expressive, it is productive. Narratives open up the field for social practices. The fear and talk of crime not only produce 'interpretations and explanations', they organise the urban landscape and public space, shaping social interactions which also acquire new meanings.

Secure yourselves!

The private sector has become a major part of the governance of fear and *governance through fear*. Ultimately, with the withdrawal or retreat of elements of state intervention from areas of our lives, including the state provision of various forms of security and public insurances, the private sector has increasingly moved to fill the gap and has, in many cases, been encouraged to do so – even with state-provided economic incentives. As Hope and Trickett (2004) suggest, citizens are being implored to do more in their everyday lives to provide for their private security as responsibility for individual security is devolved from the central state to local and individual levels. This is in line with the shift towards neo-liberal rationalities of government; here our fears of insecurity have increasingly been open to private sector intervention; security is transformed into a commodity.

Zedner (2000) reminds us of the ambiguities surrounding the notion of 'security' – a term she notes, drawing on Freedman (1992), that is best described in its absence; 'when bad things do not happen rather than when they do'. Threats to security can vary from the personal to the global. Interestingly, writing in 2000, prior to the September 11 terror attacks in America, the Bali bombings and the 2005 suicide bombings in London, Zedner notes that '[i]nternational security has largely taken a back seat to domestic concerns with personal and community safety and social order as the primary preoccupation of political life' (2000: 201). How things have changed. Threats to national security are both international (the war on terror) and domestic (the 'home-grown' terrorist within) and threats to personal security are international, national and local. Moreover, security now appears to require not simply the absence of 'bads', but positive reinforcement of a variety of kinds. That is, the 'taming of chance' (Hacking 1990), the mastery of one's future through the reduction of risk, requires the conspicuous consumption of security 'goods'. Security apparently secures our security, and yet we continue to feel insecure the more security we secure. Simultaneously, fear and anxiety become part of an economy of insecurity; needs, or 'bads', to be serviced.

All this means that there is now an economic imperative in sensitising populations to crime fear as there is in regard to terrorism; in other words in representing the world (local or international), in advertisements and other media campaigns, as dangerous, risky, insecure. Put simply, the fearful buy forms of security and insurance. However, the demand for this security, partly brought about by its commodification, can never really be met (Hope 2005), either by private consumption or public provision (Loader 1997). There remains an excess of insecurity as the *fear of crime feedback loop* feeds off itself.

Moreover, it is the affluent fearful who can afford to buy insurance and security. To this end the fearing poor are excluded from the process. As Zedner (2000: 208) has argued:

> The rich and powerful can readily afford personal and property insurance premiums, burglar and car alarms, homes in gated residential areas and even security guards, leaving the poor and unprotected even more vulnerable to those who are thus driven to prey on their more meagre resources.

And as Hudson (2002) has noted in a related context, the objective of new strategies of control is the identification of the different and the dangerous. They are excluded from the club, the apartment, the estate, the shopping centre and even the country. Hope (2000) has referred to this process, quite accurately, as the 'clubbing' of security, suggesting that the 'collective consequence of crime risk avoidance' is the creation of 'risk pools' and that these risk pools are dictated by social position. The logic of collective action, of collectives of active citizenship as it were, 'may act to reinforce a form of *social exclusion* around crime risk' (Hope and Trickett 2004).

So, we might think of these private sector institutions as *servicing* fear of crime amongst other things; fear of crime has become a discursive hook on which to hang the need for securitisation. One enlists these services for 'peace of mind' – to paraphrase one company's advertising slogan, to govern the future by creating various temporal and spatial exclusions. All this is increasingly seen to be the *responsible* thing to do – one joins the security (or secure) club as it were. But these services come at a cost, both social and financial. For individuals (or companies for that matter) to feel adequately compelled to invest in these services there must exist the collective (or individual) notion that financial outlay will be exceeded by the potential savings the service has to offer. One is constituted as a rational actor, and the rational actor must feel compelled to consume these services. This has resulted in a situation whereby some companies engage in the production of advertising, promotion and other forms of media profile that present social life as risky and dangerous; a world so disorganised and untameable that these new service industries are a safety requirement for the responsible self-governing subject. Indeed, Shearing and Stenning (1985) argue that with the growth of these services has emerged a whole 'new class of delinquent', the individual or group who does not responsibly take up the preventative services on offer. So, this neo-liberal rationality based on small government and a free market dovetails nicely with the governmental tactics discussed in the previous chapter. Thus, these industries play on, and often attempt to sensitise us to, fear of crime, or at least fears about particular forms of crime; a 'responsible' *fearing subject* consumes insurance, private security and security hardware. Moreover, some companies can even increase their competitiveness by linking with other social institutions and with local communities – the involvement of insurance companies in Neighbourhood Watch schemes being a pertinent example of this strategy.

Governments have been active in encouraging this engagement with the private sector. As Sarre (1997: 67) has pointed out, many governments have adopted strategies encouraging specialist forms of social ordering such as the services offered by private policing and security firms. Indeed, he claims they have in recent times been embraced as 'junior partners' in the collaborative production of community safety (also see Minton 2002). This fills the void left by the retreat of the state and is consistent with the neo-liberal ideal of 'governing at a distance' (O'Malley 1992). The social ceases to become a target of government, rather it is communities constituted through actuarial calculus or the economic ability to purchase a service. Here the terms *state* and *social* are being replaced by the terms *individual* and *community*, or so Barbara Hudson (2002) puts it drawing on the work of Rose (1995) and Stenson (1995). Adam Crawford (1998), critical of the encroachment of business into this area, notes that 'issue networks' and 'policy communities' are becoming more important than the state and that they have no accountability to the people they target, only their members and shareholders.[4]

Of course private policing, insurance companies and security firms are not new. Private policing dates back to well before the emergence of the public forces and services we have taken largely for granted. What is new is that with the emergence and quantification of fear of crime they now have an additional and quantifiable object to service or to suggest they can service. Zielinski (1995:1) argues that in the North American context, as a result of political rhetoric and fear about crime, the private security industry is 'profitably positioned at the intersection' of the 'right-wing's most cherished crusades: privatisation and law and order'. However, I wouldn't wish to suggest that this move to have a mix of private and public institutions operating simultaneously is confined to 'right-wing' governments or politicians. Rather, governments of varying political hues have been active in encouraging strategies that are broadly based on neo-liberal rationalities even if neo-conservative governments might have been more unrelenting in this pursuit.

Paradoxically, private sector involvement makes the government of fear of crime all the more difficult – that is if we assume the government of crime fear is really about fear reduction (and as I've argued in this book I'm not sure that it is). With consumer demand in this area given over to the private sector the tenuous balance of governing fear becomes increasingly more fragile. This situation is partially responsible for some of the ambiguities contained in governmental policy on fear of crime. Neo-liberal rationalities, leaner government and governing-at-a-distance, brings with it the desire for private sector involvement in many areas of social life; including crime prevention. This in turn opens up 'crime fear' to the market economy. Paradoxically, this shift necessitates increased governmental activity – in this case regulation by public authorities – in trying to explain crime fear, 'define it down', and/or declare it 'irrational'; ultimately some attempt to counter the sustained campaigns of both government itself and the private sector.

She sells Sanctuary (Cove)

While the growth in what has been termed in the US 'defensive architecture' has influenced the construction and renovation of public buildings since the early 1970s – much of which seems to misinterpret or misrepresent Oscar Newman's (1972) argument of the need for 'defensible space' – the growth in the defensible family dwelling began 10 years later. Yet even earlier Jane Jacobs had sounded the death knell for truly public space in American cities, lamenting the loss of 'diversity, intricately mingled in mutual support' (1989/1961: 241). This growth has ominously mirrored the growth in fear of crime discourse and the surveying of crime fear. 'Post-modern urbanism' (Dear 2000; Ellin 1996) has led to a proliferation of architectural styles, as it has led to the 'wallification' of many Western cities and suburbs. Davis (1998) notes that within a new 'ecology of fear' various zones of exclusion and containment separate those who can afford to secure themselves from those who should be quarantined. Flusty (1997) identified the proliferation of a variety of types of 'interdictory spaces'[5] designed to repel would-be users. The gated community is perhaps the perfect embodiment of his notion of 'crusty space' – 'a space that cannot be accessed due to obstructions such as walls, gates and checkpoints' (Flusty 1997: 49).

The growing popularity of the so-called gated community is perhaps the most grand-scale embodiment of a lifestyle change driven by the marketisation of the imperative for private citizens to take responsibility for reducing their risk of victimisation. Here sanctuary and security are purchased side by side in a complete lifestyle package. A gated community is best defined as a residential housing development in which houses, streets, footpaths, parks and other amenities (often sporting facilities for example) are physically enclosed by barriers, 'crusty spaces'. These barriers are most often walls and fences but sometimes also consist of natural barriers such as nature reserves, embankments or creeks. Most gated communities have, as one might expect, gates, or other forms of barrier that impede general public access. In many cases the gates are kept locked 24 hours a day and access is only granted to residents or visitors with 'appointments'. Access is usually granted only by a security guard at the gate or by electronic identification card. Most gated communities have a community organisation or planning group that represents residents' aspirations and views for the community; they are both a body corporate and an artificially constructed community group. These groups are usually catalysed by an estate's developers. That is, a 'sense of community' is artificially constructed as it were. Social capital, where it is evident, is by nature more bonding than bridging – to employ Robert Putnam's (2000) characterisation. Services normally provided to ratepayers via local and other levels of government are usually replaced by privately funded services. These can include community transport, rubbish collection, street maintenance and the like.

In many respects these types of development are not new, and date back to ancient walled towns and fortified Roman camps – the latter in turn gave rise to many British towns (Ellin 1997). Then as today the reasons for such walls were multiple. They were not simply a response to fear but also economic and political (Bannister and Fyfe 2001). Year-round gated living in the modern Western world began in 1850s North America in wealthy communities such as Llewellyn Park in New Jersey (Low 2004). However, in the 1980s gated communities crossed over to the mainstream as it were. They were no longer the exclusive provenance of the super rich, but of the growing aspirational classes as well. Throughout the 1990s and beyond this aspirational consumer base has grown. The phenomenon of the gated community has fascinated criminological, sociological and anthropological researchers since it first began its late-modern renaissance. In the USA it was recently estimated on the strength of census data that 5.9 per cent of households live in gated communities (See Sanchez and Lang cited in Low 2004). This growth is also reflected – if not yet numerically mirrored – in

Australia,[6] the UK and New Zealand, and in each of these countries the growth shares a similar history. The growth of these communities in South Africa, south-east Asia and the Middle East also reflects similar attitudes to security and exclusion, although each locality has its culturally specific history in relation to this.

In the suburban sprawl of greater western Sydney, NSW, Australia, as in much of the Western world, gated communities proliferated over the decade from 1995 to 2005. 'Master-planned estates', many aimed at the constitution of lifestyle packages, and many trumpeting their security credentials, have become a magnet for what have come to be termed in Australian political parlance the 'aspirational' classes. While once Sydney's urban fringe was populated by young low-income first-time buyers, the new master-planned estates are peopled by second- and third-time buyers. These are generally upwardly mobile middle and higher income earners (Gwither 2005). They not only seek sanctuary and security from physical victimisation, but also protection for their assets – most specifically their property and their lifestyle. Legally, residents can prevent outsiders from entering the estate as it is on community title. This makes what would normally be public streets private property. And herein lies the difference between gated communities and secure apartment blocks. In a gated community the street and its amenities, generally seen as a public space, is privatised.

It is probably no coincidence that the growth in gated communities has somewhat mirrored growth in crime fear discourse. The post-modern city has been characterised as an environment in which fear has impacted on form and form has impacted on fear (Ellin 1996). Again, with the discourse of crime fear, developers of gated communities find a healthy consumer stream to tap into and it is reflected in the way residents talk about life in these communities (Gwither 2005; Low 2004). What their proliferation no doubt reflects, questions of the level of crime fear aside, is that fear has become a marketing tool as well as a market driver. Sanctuary can be purchased, at a price, and a price now vaguely affordable to the middle and aspirational classes. And, for the responsibilised consumer, the *fearing subject*, such a purchase is often both desirable and reasonable. Paradoxically though, it is often an aspiration that is at odds with one's own best judgment. As Setha Low (2004: 11) argues in the US context:

> Living in a gated community represents a new version of the middle-class American dream precisely because it temporarily suppresses and masks, even denies and fuses, the inherent anxieties and conflicting social values of modern urban and suburban life.

It transforms Americans' dilemma of how to protect themselves and their children from danger, crime, and unknown others while still perpetuating open, friendly neighbourhoods and comfortable, safe, homes. It reinforces the norms of a middle-class lifestyle in a historical period in which everyday events and news media exacerbate fears of violence and terrorism. Thus, residents cite their "need" for gated communities to provide a safe and secure home in the face of a lack of other societal alternatives.

It is precisely this *need* that Low refers to that is of interest. The choice is that in a securitising world there is no choice. The imagined *fearing subjects* of governmental literature and discourse, discussed in the previous chapter, are implored to reduce their risks of victimisation through choices they make about lifestyle, about how they order and secure their lives socio-spatially. Of course this literature and information does not *prescribe* life in a gated community. However, once the governmentally inspired responsibilising discourses are further mobilised by private sector, and options for reducing risks and fears are offered in lifestyle packages one can purchase, it is not surprising that gated housing estates are growing in popularity when one might feel a duty to one's family to purchase on such an estate. The advertising campaigns of developers tap into an already available discourse on crime fear and security. Once again, it's of little intellectual worth simply to point the finger at the private sector for playing on our anxieties – of course they do and will. The more pressing issue is around how these issues of fear for our safety have become so pervasive. And, as I've been arguing throughout this book, there is no conspiracy, no single institution one can point the finger at as it were. Rather, the *fear of crime feedback loop* is a multi-faceted beast. The aspiration for a gated lifestyle both feeds off, and feeds into this loop, as does the advertising of this fear of crime service industry.

One recent advertising campaign for apartments on the Macquarie Links estate in Sydney's south-west tells prospective clients they are purchasing *inter alia*:

> ... full security including smart card access to the garage, restricted card access to only your floor via private elevator (only 2 apartments per lift per floor). Visitors identified by audio visual link, will only be able to access that specific floor. (11 October 2004 Monarch Investments)

The quotation that headed this chapter was similarly advertising homes on this estate, homes that are both 'exclusive and security safe'. The same is true of the way in which gated communities are advertised in the US and the UK. The advertising for one community in North Carolina is a pertinent example. The first attribute mentioned is the area's low crime rate:

> Only 112 homesites are available at this charming community located in Southport, NC, which boasts the lowest crime rate in the Carolinas.[7]

Although the reasons why residents purchase homes in gated communities are many and complex, the vast majority of research into their growth concludes that concern about crime or fear of crime is towards the top of any list. Although, as Low (2004: 231) rightly concludes, this fear of crime is very multi-faceted:

> At a societal level, people say that they move [to gated communities] because of their fear of crime and others ... At a personal level though, residents are searching for the sense of security and safety that they associate with their childhood. When they talk about their concern with 'others', they are splitting – socially and psychologically – the good and bad aspects of (and good and bad people in) American society. The gates are used symbolically to ward off life's unknowns, including unemployment, loss of loved ones, and downward mobility.

A recent journalistic piece in *The Sydney Morning Herald* (O'Sullivan, 4 March 2005: 12) also adds substance to why exactly people settle in gated communities. Unsurprisingly, the questions of security and crime fear are at the fore, even as they are being downplayed. As one 36-year-old resident says:

> It's safe because it's a community ... we know all the people, they all look out for each other. It is very secure for kids. It is not so much a worry-about-crime thing, just a good feeling of community ... The gates are only closed at certain times, so friends can drop in. There is always a very friendly, neighbourly sort of atmosphere. (cited in O'Sullivan, 4 March 2005: 12)

And this resident is not alone. Another noted on the topic of security that 'You look at Sydney today and it is a dog fight ... we are very happy here ... [Security estates are] the way of the future' (cited in O'Sullivan 2005). Yet, the developer Monarch, through their project manager, noted that 'the gates were closed because of residents' perception of crime [not at the wishes of the developer]. I wanted people to drive through and have a look. It's a hassle if you want to visit someone.'

The debate over the pros and cons of gated communities in western Sydney became intense early in the decade with politicians, academics, journalists and planners all participating. The debate is, however, a particularly sticky one for politicians, particularly politicians traditionally of the left. To be seen as supporting the proliferation of gated communities can be interpreted as a slap in the face for those who cannot afford or choose not to live in such a locality, while to be seen opposing them can be politically dangerous as it might not only alienate those living in such an estate, but also those who aspire to such a lifestyle. All these people add up to a not insignificant minority of western Sydney's voting public. Moreover, the private provision of services fostered in gated communities has its own attractions for government. Again this fits neatly with the neo-liberal ideal of a smaller, more 'hands-off' approach to governance, saving local council tens of thousands of dollars in service provision.

Minton (2002: 4) makes the point that gated communities have a negative effect on broader community spirit:

> Although statistics show crime levels are declining this increasing polarization [of communities] is feeding our growing culture of fear, with the vast majority of the population believing crime is rising. One of the consequences of this false perception is the growth in private security forces ...

Minton (2002) goes further arguing that the current British Government's desire to embrace a 'wider police family' including neighbourhood officers, private security firms and the like feeds into the take-up of private services; what I would call the fear of crime service industries. This governmental imperative has been backed up by legislative change to the Private Security Industry Act 2001 and the Police Reform Act 2002, providing extra powers for security workers.

Graham and Marvin point to processes whereby fortified residential and work spaces are increasingly connected by private roads, private shopping streets and enclosed malls with private security, CCTV and private transportation. They suggest that new secessionary spaces are being created which allow for the unfettered, if spatially delineated, movement of the affluent. Here, 'infrastructure networks are being "unbundled" in ways that help sustain the fragmentation of the social and material fabric of cities' (Graham and Marvin 2001 cited in Atkinson and Flint 2004).

Thus, the privatisation of these spaces has broader ramifications than simply the segregation of the feared and the fearful. Atkinson and Flint (2004: 4) suggest that the notion of 'splintering urbanism' is a useful way to view changes associated with the proliferation of gated communities. That is that residential segregation does more than lead to the withdrawal of certain groups into spatially fixed enclaves – the 'white flight' phenomenon as it has been termed. Rather, this segregation also impacts public service providers, policy-makers and the broader socio-spatial realm (see also Garreau 1991). The wealthy (or aspirational) no longer need be confronted by, and as a result ontologically negotiate, strangeness or difference. This lack of contact leads to more, not less, anxiety about possible victimisation with such setting contributing to paranoia and distrust (Ellin 1996). Moreover, as Hope (2000) suggests, this has the effect of placing those unable to afford the fortification at increased actual risk as state provision recedes and what were more attractive targets become increasingly defended.

Thus gated communities constitute part of a growing socio-spatial archipelago. Socio-spatial networks of leisure, schooling and the workplace are linked via paths which provide various forms of privatised sanctuary from unwanted social contact. Atkinson and Flint (2004: 4) suggest that:

> each of these spaces more or less segregates its occupants from social contact with different social groups … [T]he impact of such residential division resembles a seam or partition running spatially and temporally through cities, … time-space trajectories of segregation.

As these proliferate the 'choice' to move into such a community will become increasingly difficult to reject; a 'choice' not unlike the one you might make in sending your child to a private school when you bear witness to the steep decline in public/state provision under the neo-liberal rhetoric of 'choice'.

Private security

Public policing organisations in much of the world continue to grow in size and numbers of recruits, yet simultaneously there are moves to 'outsource' many policing functions (Button 2002) in the name of expanding security. In 2004 for example the London Metropolitan Police passed a milestone by reaching a total of 30,000 officers. Likewise, police numbers in Australia are at record highs with NSW alone having 13,300 officers in the ranks. Public police throughout Australia numbered approximately 45,200 sworn officers in total (AIC 2006). Yet, security providers employed approximately 80–100,000 in 1999 (Prenzler and Sarre 1999).[8] The private sector accounts for at least two-thirds of that number. The picture is the same in much of the Western world with private police outnumbering by up to two to one the number of public police (Button 2002). In the USA and Canada the ratio is roughly two to one with average revenues in the US exceeding $52 billion (Johnston 2000). Whichever way we look at it this is a massive industry, enjoying massive growth, employing massive numbers globally.

Loader (cited in Button 2002) classifies these cohorts of police as both 'policing through government', denoting that services might be coordinated by government but provided by private bodies, and 'policing beyond government', referring to private services that individual citizens might purchase. Certainly the relationship between government and private policing is an increasingly close one with governments more than happy to explore public–private partnerships and to hive off or contract out elements of policing traditionally conducted by the public police.

How does this growth in private policing relate to fear of crime? While I'm not suggesting that the invention of fear of crime is somehow directly responsible for this growth in private policing/security, I would suggest that the privatisation of policing and security fits neatly in broader neo-liberal governmental rationalities which emphasise personal responsibility and attempt to govern at a distance. Moreover, as I have suggested, once fear of crime becomes a technology of government, a responsibilising mechanism, the private sector is poised to service this. We need only explore the advertising rhetoric of this private sector to identify its position in the *fear of crime feedback loop*.

The home page of Guardian Eagle Security[9] in the USA exemplifies the private security industry's use of fear of crime as a commercial tool. A visitor is bombarded with crime 'facts' which are no doubt meant to encourage the consumption of their products. Flashing banners tell us the following: 'RAPE occurs every 6 minutes; VIOLENT CRIME occurs every 19 seconds; THEFT occurs every 4 seconds; MURDER occurs every 27 minutes', and on it goes.

One Australian security firm uses the advertising slogan 'What is your safety worth?'[10] This particular company provides a number of security 'solutions' such as camera surveillance, 'access control', home alarms and the like. Its website shows visual imagery of a residence being broken into by a man dressed in black, wearing a beanie, and wielding a crowbar. The classic shadowy unknown stranger of fear of crime discourse perhaps?

Another company provides a free downloadable 'information' booklet on 'security'. Again, this plays on our fears, not just of being burgled but of outcomes much more serious:

> The main reason a fair percentage of people buy security systems is because they were burgled recently. They suffered from the "it'll never happen to me" syndrome. Also it's surprising how many people contact us and mention that not only were they robbed, but it happened while they were in bed asleep. Many believe home and content insurance is sufficient. Insurance companies can't replace the life of a loved one … Burglaries at night are becoming more common because, with a well planned exit they can just take off when they hear you or see a light come on. (Would you really investigate in the dark?) Some burglars aren't normal human beings and will confront you. How do we know all this? The burgled have told us![11]

By now it is obvious how many of these companies play on our fears. And why wouldn't they? After all this is precisely what they are servicing, what they are securing. This final example could not make it any clearer:

> Two of the largest investments you're ever likely to make are in your family and personal residence. Physically protecting both is no longer an option. Like it or not, the times demand you thoroughly plan and install a professionally featured home security system. Your family deserves nothing less. That's where [company name] can help.[12]

And:

> In the time it takes you to read this sentence, one burglary will be committed in the U.S. In this same time, a fire department will be responding to a fire somewhere in this country, both according to reports compiled by the FBI.
> **DON'T BECOME A STATISTIC**
> 1. One out of every five homes will experience a burglary, fire, or carbon monoxide poisoning within the next six years.
> 2. 38% of assaults and 60% of rapes occur during a home invasion … (emphasis original).

One would be positively engaging in a dereliction of duty, of responsibility, not to sign up. So while governmental discourse responsiblises us to manage our own risk through potentially fearful images and narratives, the private sector provide the services such responsibilisation impels us to purchase.

CCTV, security hardware and software

The proliferation of closed-circuit television (CCTV) has also proved to be a bonanza for the private sector. Not only can this service be sold to private citizens and businesses, but also to government as CCTV becomes a fixture in public spaces. While CCTV started life as technology used largely by the private retail sector, it has now become omnipresent in public spaces, spurred on by governmental interest into reducing the fear of crime it helped to invent. CCTV's gradual dissemination from private into public space is well explained by Norris and Armstrong (2000: 81):

> CCTV has moved from the private domain of the shop, to the semi-public domain of the underground system and football stadium, to the fully public domain of city streets ... where there is routine photographic surveillance of the mass of the population (regardless of status or criminal history).

Norris and Armstrong (2000) note that in the UK the attraction of CCTV for government was not only that it dovetailed neatly with ideological demands to privatise but that it was also economically attractive. While initial capital costs of installation – coordinated through local government – was met by the Home Office this funding was competitive and would be granted only on the condition of private partnerships with business. Indeed, for an initial outlay of around £37 million, around £100 million was generated. Moreover, the Home Office bore no responsibility for meeting ongoing running costs. These were to be met by local councils. This initial 'investment' has led to the UK population being one of the most surveilled populations in the world, despite questions about rights and privacy, and whether such surveillance actually prevents crime (Short and Ditton 1996). Indeed, one of the arguments against the proliferation of CCTV, that it simply displaces offending to other areas, has been co-opted by advocates of the technology. As Norris and Armstrong (2000) suggest, evidence of displacement to areas without CCTV coverage simply places pressure on such areas to instal it. Local councils are responsibilised to take action by providing further CCTV coverage – lucrative for the private sector.

In Australia the most active client of this technology, apart from business, is local government. Indeed, CCTV now usually constitutes a fundamental element of most local government crime prevention plans. In 1998 the City of Sydney Council began the implementation of what was known as *The Safe City Strategy*. As part of this strategy – which also included CPTED, partnership and lighting initiatives – '48 Street Safety Cameras' were installed in crime 'hotspots'. What is perhaps most striking is that the evaluation of the programme, commissioned by Sydney City Council and conducted by the NSW Bureau of Crime Statistics and Research, was focused almost entirely on public perceptions and fear of crime (Coumarelos 2000). Indeed, it largely sought to examine whether a public education campaign accompanying the *Strategy* had any effect on public perceptions of crime. In conclusion the authors note that the study was only able rudimentarily to explore 'short term' rates of offending, noting that the 'crime analyses were not clear cut' (Coumarelos 2000: 53). In contrast, the report was able to note that some 85 per cent of respondents thought the CCTV made the city safer. Indeed, 274 of the 1,808 respondents (15.1 per cent) suggested installing more CCTV cameras when they were asked to provide suggestions for further safety initiatives (Coumarelos 2000). This was second only to the suggestion of more, and more visible, police.

As Coleman and Sim have put it, 'camera networks, and the official discourse that surrounds them, provide an indication of the increasing importance of 'fear' in the governing process' (2005: 111). The clearly articulated rationale for CCTV is not so much that it reduces crime, although this is certainly a claim made by its advocates; rather, it is that it reduces fear of crime. Indeed, there is evidence to suggest that crime fear (at least as measured) has fallen in areas where CCTV has been installed – so long as this installation has been accompanied by an information campaign aimed at highlighting the installation of the new technology (Wilson and Sutton 2003). The CCTV industry has been a great beneficiary of the invention of fear of crime and the very images it captures – in terms of the commission of crime – serve to reinforce its legitimacy and the need for its expansion. For, despite the fact that the offences captured on film are obviously not being prevented, the evidential application can be championed. Moreover, such images scandalise us and play on our fears, so increasing our – and governments' – appetite for the technology. While the murder of toddler Jamie Bulger in February 1993 provided one such catalytic moment in the UK, provoking calls for the expansion of CCTV systems and silencing opposition, CCTV footage of 'race riots' in Sydney's south in late 2005 made their utility seem self-evident and a political storm was provoked when it was found that police had withheld its public release. Not only do we think it provides us with security, we also wonder at its ability to scandalise and confront us. And while we might no longer be able to differentiate between 'reality television' and televised reality, the private sector is more than happy to provide us with both. As Coleman and Sim (2005: 111) point out:

> In the regenerating city the rise of street camera surveillance, and the fear this feeds off and reinforces in relation to certain forms of crime, has instigated a process of governance through street crime ... [T]hese discourses have targeted the least powerful inhabitants of the city and can be understood as components of a broader landscape of risk propagated and given prominence in times of social, political, and economic upheaval.

Further, while we await the perfection of bio-metric identification systems and other new technological innovations to further service our crime fear we consume security of ever increasing varieties: alarms, sensor lights, deadlocks, intercoms, mobile phones, roller-shutters, bars, grates, guard dogs and other rudimentary forms of security device. Indeed, in many cases the consumption of some such devices is mandatory for many of us who wish to insure our houses, contents and sometimes motor vehicles. And we all know that to forgo such insurance would be highly irresponsible.

Insurance

> One of the first and most salutary effects of insurance is to eliminate from human affairs the fear that paralyses all activity and numbs the soul ... Delivered from fear man is king of creation ... (Chauffon (1884) cited in Ewald 1991: 208)

Insurance companies tend to be less outwardly focused on crime victimisation and accordingly fear of crime, but it is no less part of what François Ewald (1991: 198) calls their *insurantial imaginary*, particularly the *insurantial imaginary* of late modernity. This imaginary delineates the ways in which, in a given social, moral, juridical, political and/or economic context, necessary uses for the technology of insurance can be found in the 'market for security'. For insurance and insurers – which it must be noted come in many different forms, many of which have little to do with crime – crime constitutes only one risk amongst a growing number of others they service. Nonetheless, insurance as a technology is built around a calibration of risk – or at least the assumption that actuarial risk can be calculated: the knowability of risk. As Ewald (1991: 199–200) notes, insurance

> is the practice of a certain type of rationality: one formalised by the calculus of probabilities. That is why one never insures oneself except against risks … Today it is hard to imagine all the things which insurers have managed to invent as classes of risk – always, it should be said, with profitable results. The insurers' activity is not just a matter of passively registering the existence of risks, and then offering guarantees against them. He 'produces risks', he makes risks appear where each person had hitherto felt obliged to submit resignedly to the blows of fortune.

Indeed, fear and insurance are intimately linked. They are both made intelligible *vis-à-vis* the calculation of risk. Ewald goes on to note that the term risk is a neologism of insurance derived from the Italian word *risco*, 'that which cuts' (reef), and consequently 'risk to cargo'. No doubt we now apply the term much more liberally, nonetheless an identified risk still begs for a technology to insure against it. And if, as Beck (1992) suggests, late modernity is organised around the distribution of 'bads', or risks to insure against, certainly crime is one of the most potently symbolic of these. So while the actuarial calculation of risk fixes insurance premiums, notwithstanding other market forces, the same type of calculation also makes intelligible a normative calculation of fear of crime. But where risk makes insurances against 'bads' a function of 'rational' calculation, fear of crime, being by nature in excess of and in binary opposition to risk, intensifies our appetite for private insurance technologies.

This growing range of insurance technologies is increasingly tailored to the individual. Thus, we turn to insurance more readily for the certainty lost to us under neo-liberal rationalities which both encourage and responsibilise the individual, and show less interest in the collective welfare or 'social insurance' of the population. Indeed, these rationalities positively repudiate the notion that the social pooling of risk, perhaps best exemplified in the growth of a welfarist mentality into the mid twentieth century, can act as an adequate responsibilising or socialising principal. This is seen as draining resources, individual incomes, inhibiting commercial risk taking, stifling responsibility, and not providing enough security (Rose 1999). This shift, beginning in the late twentieth century, is what O'Malley (1992) has identified as the move to *private prudentialism*. So as private, individualised insurance increases its range of domains, the social risks we have insured against collectively since the late nineteenth century have seemingly diminished in importance. As Hudson (2003) puts it, modernity's success is that we live with the belief that we have mastered many traditionally collective risks around health and the like. Thus, it is not that insurance is somehow only a function of neo-liberal mentalities and rationalities, rather its traditional ethos of collectivism is equally suited to welfarist rationalities of governance. However, in a period where fear and securitisation go hand in hand with neo-liberal governmentalities, private insurance becomes both attractive and part of individual and civic – depending on its specific form – responsibility. While collective or public insurance reduces, the private expands. Hudson (2003) suggests this increasing distance from many traditional 'social' kinds of risk encourages a hyper-attention to those risks which are readily perceptible, from which state protection is unlikely; risks largely of fellow citizens on the street.

How are our fears and insecurities mobilised by insurers? A prominent US company[13] for example lists crime, or burglary to be precise, as only one safety problem to be insured against amongst 18 others on a list of safety tips. The story is similar with many other companies. However, these companies often have long tentacles and numerous ways to capitalise on the fear factor. NRMA Insurance in Australia, for example, have sponsored Neighbourhood Watch programmes, and sell security systems, as well as selling insurance:

> NRMA Insurance is no stranger to burglary, break-ins and fires. We've been dealing with them every day through our insurance claims. It's that same experience we are using to assist you improve the level of security for your family, home and belongings, through our NRMA Home Security service which provides alarms and monitoring services. While insurance can cover the loss of most of your possessions, no insurance can cover the sense that someone has invaded your space, which inevitably follows a break-in. Nor can it help save your life in the event of a fire or personal emergency. An NRMA Home Security alarm provides you with real protection against intrusion.[14]

So, while the spin of the insurers is generally somewhat more moderate than security firms and the like, its reach and responsibilising techniques are potentially much broader. We often have very little autonomy in avoiding insurance purchases for a number of reasons. Home insurance is a condition of a mortgage; third party car insurance a condition of registration; life insurance part and parcel of superannuation – itself an insurance for a future free of public provided pensions. This network of risk reduction uses fear as a commodity, a motivation for reasonable risk reduction.

Moreover, as noted above, you can sometimes secure a discount on insurance premiums where your home for example has a particular type of alarm installed, or where you are a member of Neighbourhood Watch. Your vigilance is to be rewarded, and if fear drives you to such measures, should it not be celebrated? But your responsibilities do not stop there. On top of paying your premium you must, when it comes to many forms of insurances against crime, show 'reasonable care' that you are not complicit in placing youself or your belongings at risk, thus providing the insurer with a possible binding 'out' clause. Moreover, other 'minimum security conditions' may apply, making various forms of security – specific types of window and door locks and perhaps other forms of security service – a binding condition of the insurance.

Phone home! Fear and the ambivalence of technology

As I write this section, images of the 2005 London Underground bombings are being beamed by satellite into my Sydney home only minutes after the event. Within a couple of hours digital video image files captured on the mobile phones held by those trapped on the Underground trains bring the full horror of the bombing home – literally. The grainy images show ghostly and blackened figures, moving and/or being ushered towards the slightly pixelated glowing lights of a nearby tube station. It is a scene loaded with religious imagery as commuters escape into the light from the (presumed at that time and subsequently confirmed) Islamic fundamentalist inspired horror – albeit of the 'home-grown' variety. I rode the same Underground train only three weeks earlier as I researched this book at the British Library, a block away from King's Cross station, the site of the worst of the carnage wrought when four suicide bombers almost simultaneously detonated four explosive devices in central London. I had also stayed in a hotel only a block away from Tavistock Square where a London 'double-decker' bus was targeted. As the rescue scene becomes a crime scene, it is noted in the up-to-the-minute press coverage that hours of CCTV footage of the Underground will be forensically studied for clues to the identity of the bombers. This process was subsequently successful with video evidence being used to identify those responsible. Within two hours of the bombing an Islamic extremist group with 'links to al Q'aeda' were claiming responsibility for the bombing on an 'Islamic website' which will itself become a site of forensic investigation, speculation and media analysis. Within three hours I've e-mailed friends who live and work in that area of London to confirm their well-being. One had luckily walked instead of catching the tube that morning. On their way to work he and another friend heard the bus explosion in Tavistock Square. A graduate student I supervise was on the King's Cross train that was bombed. She luckily escaped with mild smoke inhalation but described the terror of her ordeal by e-mail:

> ... Phone lines were down for ages. But ... guess what? I'm OK. Yay ... I was on the Piccadilly train that was bombed leaving King's Cross but I was fortunate to get [away] with just smoke inhalation and a prolonged case of trainophobia, which is more than can be said for the people in the carriage next to me. To whoever it was that gave me the advice to always travel in the last carriage of the tube because it is the easiest to escape if something happens ... thank you thank you thank you thank you ...[15]

Saved by responsibilisation perhaps?

One of the first emergency measures actioned by the British policing agencies was to disable the mobile phone network for fear that phones could be used to detonate more bombs – mobile phones had been used in the Madrid bombings of 2004 to detonate the blasts and there was an early assumption that they were used in London as well. The mobile phone can now be a technology for security, for terror, for information and for the detection of criminals. In the London bombings it either played, or was thought to play, the role of all of these at different points. Phones have also increasingly become accessories in the commission of crime; not just to detonate explosive devices but, as recent moral panics about 'happy slapping' in the UK and mobile phone photographing in changing rooms show, in order to carry out a whole range of new offences. For example, mobile phones were used to coordinate the 'gang rape' of a number of teenage girls in Sydney's west in 2000. In 2005 SMS phone messages were used to coordinate the racialised riots in Sydney's south-east.

Mobile phones are now everywhere, an omnipresent web of communications. They have all but become an extension of ourselves. However, not a decade ago, with mobile phones more expensive and much less numerous than they are today, mobile phone companies were explicit in the advertising campaigns that the mobile phone was *inter alia* a personal security device. Today many parents justify the expense of a mobile phone for their children under the guise of a personal security device: 'They travel on public transport'; 'I can always contact them.' Indeed, phones can now be linked up to a Global Positioning System

(GPS) so that the phone user's position can be monitored (Williams 2006: 1). Devices that go by names such as the 'iKids phone' are aimed at increasing parents' peace of mind by enabling them to know the location of their children at all times. In the USA all mobile phones are now required to double as locators for emergency services so that any individual can be pinpointed within a distance of 150 metres. This technology continues a tradition of mobile phone advertising and marketing that emphasises security credentials.

In one of the most memorable examples one company's TV advertisement depicted a young woman's car broken down in what can only be described as an urban dystopia. The young girl's horror at her predicament amongst the symbols of a dilapidated, disorganised and dysfunctional city, darkness, dampness, graffiti, strewn garbage, unfinished roadworks and the like, evoke fears of the unknown *other*. This commercial attempted to tap into the very nameless and faceless fears we construct out of these contingent situations. It also tapped into the governmental discourses of responsibilisation discussed in the previous chapter. To be safe one should purchase mobile phone technology; not just for oneself, but for other vulnerable members of one's family. Of course, with mobile phone in hand, daughter can phone both father and the privately run automobile road service – the responsible motorist would obviously be a member of this and would no doubt have received a minor discount on this membership when he or she purchased it along with their car insurance.

The point here is that even as this technology is sold on its fear reducing credentials, it is actually ambivalent. It can create new risks and fears even as it might promise to reduce others. The same can be said for the internet and other forms of new technology. Indeed, Norris and Armstrong (2000) remind us that CCTV was used to identify members of, and repress, the pro-democracy movement in China after the Tiananmen Square protests – CCTV that was sold to the Chinese Government by Siemens Plessey as an advanced traffic control system. Technology may be politically neutral, but the uses to which it is put rarely are.

The media, representation and fear of crime

When it comes to news coverage there is little doubt that the old adage of 'if it bleeds it leads' remains largely accurate. However, this statement needs to be tempered through the knowledge that not all mass media outlets are born equal, and that the fearful themes taken up and projected by some media outlets are not born in discursive voids.

When it comes to crime reportage, Stan Cohen's 1972 argument about crime stories still rings true. Although his analysis saw the media as very central to the production of moral panics, I would now suggest that it is on site amongst many in the *fear of crime feedback loop*:

> The mass media operate with certain definitions of what is news worthy. It is not that instruction manuals exist telling newsmen that certain subjects (drugs, sex, violence) will appeal to the public or that certain groups (youth, immigrants) should be continually exposed to scrutiny. Rather, there are built in factors, ranging from the individual newsman's intuitive hunch about what constitutes a 'good story', through precepts such as 'give the public what it wants' to structured ideological biases, which predispose the media to make certain events into news. (Cohen 1972: 45)

As an incident makes its way into the media, as it becomes news, it also becomes extraordinary, different, non-routine. When television news highlights an event it simultaneously obscures the 'quotidian setting' of the event's actuality (Gooding-Williams 1993). The media rarely acknowledge complicated and contingent processes by which events develop out of the often-mundane situations that produce them. Thus, it is the elevated event, pure event, de-contextualised and de-historicised, which is flashed and reflected, often fleetingly, on to the psyche of the 'news'-consuming public or community.

There is no doubt then that crimes involving violence make good 'bad' news stories. A gruesome murder is likely to gain weeks of media exposure, be one of the top stories in any news bulletin, and create much public comment around such issues as capital punishment, the erosion of society's moral fabric, the need for more police, and the un-safety of the streets. This is particularly the case when a stranger commits a murder or when the victim is deemed an 'innocent victim' (Carrington 1998: 187), usually someone who could be 'one of us', one who has been responsible. These cases are of course relatively rare. Statistically in Australia, as in the Western world more generally, most murders are committed by members of the victim's own family or by close acquaintances.[16] As Madriz (1997: 187) argues, with few exceptions, the media do not portray husbands, boyfriends, lovers, or other acquaintances as predators even if such an event makes the news.

In the world of the mass media reportage feeds on reportage as certain stories take precedence over others. Smith (1984) concluded, in his study of provincial press in Birmingham, that 70 per cent of the total column space devoted to crime was devoted to violent personal crimes – including mugging – when these crimes constituted only 5 per cent of the total number of offences reported to police. Therefore, according to Smith, what the media presents as being representative of all crime is actually representative of only a very small minority of offences. The proliferation of media sources (not necessarily through media companies) now ensures a big story's exposure to a massive population. Most importantly specific stories can become discursively connected to the broader arguments and debates around 'crime' and law and order. The panic in Britain in 2005 around incidents of 'happy slapping', the identification of 'hoodies', 'anti-social behaviour' and 'respect' are examples of just this. These panics connect with discourse on crime more generally, and suddenly both the moral fabric and our personal safety are in peril. Such conflation makes it possible for newspapers like *The Daily Telegraph* in Sydney to run front-page headlines like 'Crime; we're losing the fight' (*The Daily Telegraph*, 2 May 1997). This way almost any crime story has the potential to draw on people's already available fears and concerns about crime, and to feed the *feedback loop* with 'law and order common sense'.

Hogg and Brown (1998) explored the discursive mechanisms whereby the reportage of crime rates and crime statistics, almost without fail, point to increases in crime. This is despite the fact that in many of these same cases any informed readings of the statistics in question would be at odds with such reportage. If the statistical data being reported tends to point to a drop in specific crime rates Sydney's *Daily Telegraph* routinely points out that the information is collated by '"ivory tower academics and bureaucrats" who know nothing of real life …' (Hogg and Brown 1998: 20). Here, factors affecting the correlation of crime statistics are highlighted as examples as to why these statistics are flawed. For example, it reports that drops in 'official' crime rates are due to the fact that people are unwilling to report crime for a variety of reasons, mostly that they think nothing will be done about it or they are scared to report. Thus, drops in crime rates are explained away as being due to the 'common sense' notion that 'crime has become so common that victims no longer bother to report it' (Hogg and Brown 1998: 25). However, if 'official' crime statistics point to increasing crime the opposite tactic is applied. The increase in crime is real, this is 'common sense' that should not be explained away by factors such as increased reportage. Thus, the public 'common sense' understandings about increases in crime are confirmed and the newspaper feeds its target demographic the 'bad' news it already knows to be a 'true' reflection of the ever-deteriorating social climate.

Moreover, crime is routinely (re)presented in the media as being 'worse than ever'(Hogg and Brown 1998; Pearson 1983). Such reportage suggests that the peaceable days of the past have been replaced by violence and disorder. Hogg and Brown refer to this discourse as 'law and order nostalgia':

> The depiction of crime as a problem of novel proportions is heightened in the press by juxtaposing the menacing present with nostalgic references to an apparently harmonious and peaceful past ... Such nostalgia is largely misplaced and misleading ... [S]imilar things have been said in ... 1844 as in the 1970s, '80s and '90s. (Hogg and Brown 1998: 27)

Thus, each successive generation seems able to have its own 'crime wave' or 'moral panic', and for each successive era the reportage has remained surprisingly similar. Each era understands itself as being quite different from the past, as being a period that is much more violent and much more dangerous than the preceding one. Further, Hogg and Brown (1998) point to the discursive mechanisms whereby local crime stories are explicitly associated with crime in other 'more violent' or unruly cities or 'crime hot spots', New York and Los Angeles being the often-quoted examples in the Australian press in the 1990s, although at the time of writing it is more likely to be Baghdad.

It has also been suggested (Madriz 1997: 113) that the media reconstruct reality in ways that present us with understandings about crime that privilege the predatory stranger; they construct what Madriz refers to as 'media icons'. The sources of these icons are not just exclusively the evening news and the print news media. Rather the images presented by these news sources connect discursively with TV drama and film images to become a constant presence in the average home. Madriz (1997: 98) further suggests that discourses on dangerous strangers (or outlaws) are often racialised and that fear of crime becomes merged with a fear of racial difference discourse.[17]

All this suggests that one business sector set to profit out of crime fear is the media. Of course, media institutions have long been a champion of crime fear. However, it is no oversight on my part that I place the media last in my analysis in this book. It is not that I think this element of the analysis any less important that any other. It is, rather, that I see the other elements of the analysis as *equally* important as any analysis of the media. Yes, of course the media has had a role in intensifying the discourse around fear of crime. However, like the other elements of the *fear of crime feedback loop*, the media both feed off and feed a broader fear of crime discourse the likes of which I've identified. They are, however, not the *origin*. That is, they are one site of, or one element of, the *feedback loop*; they are not the catalyst, the cause, or indeed the central problem, as much criminological and sociological analysis seems to assume. I would suggest that blaming the media for fear of crime has only led to a lack of reflexivity to the role of social scientific, governmental, and political discourses in the development of crime fear – the very institutional discourses, the very sites of knowledge/power that provide the media with a regime of truth through which to discuss crime fear.

Barry Glassner's (1999) analysis is spot on in regard to the need to de-centre the media in any analysis of crime fear. As he suggests, in some cases news organisations run stories which allay the very fears they aroused in order to lure audiences. He gives specific examples where the *Washington Post* and *New York Times* published pieces specifically allaying fears of schoolyard shootings, and supporting tighter gun restrictions respectively. But he goes even further to suggest, 'As a social scientist I am impressed and somewhat embarrassed to find that journalists, more often than media scholars, identify the jugglery in making small hazards appear huge and huge hazards disappear from sight' (Glassner 1999: xxiv).

All this is not to suggest that the media should be ignored as a site of knowledge/power in relation to crime fear. For as our sources of information multiply so the 'legitimate' or 'official sources' of information such as crime statistics decrease in their truth value. A number of theorists have identified suspicion of expert knowledge as being a component of late modernity (Beck 1992; Giddens 1993; Hudson 2003). As Pratt (1997: 15) notes, our assessments of risk under neo-liberal rationalities are likely to be 'based on remote sources of information, found predominantly in an increasingly prolific mass media and the centrality of crime reporting to its presentation, a presentation whereby the "reality of crime"' confirms and increases anxieties and fears now associated with venturing into public space (1997: 151).

This discussion is not an attempt to cover every aspect of the media or media coverage and how these intersect with the fear of crime. To attempt to do so would be to over-generalise the role of the media given that media institutions and their reportage of crime vary from town to town, from city to city, and country to country. Meta-narratives explaining media coverage and its effects are destined to fail; in the media world there is always an exception to any general rule. Further, some theorists question whether a separate discussion on the media is of any analytical use at all. Young (1996) argues that crime is imagined through a multiplicity of discourses, practices and institutions she calls the 'crimino-legal complex'.[18] Within this 'crimino-legal complex' Young includes:

> The knowledges, discourses and practices that are deemed to fall
> under the rubric of criminology, criminal justice and criminal law
> … I wish to include all these, together with popular discourses
> that are manifested in the media, cinema, and advertising, in
> order to convey the sense that 'crime' has become (been made?)
> a potent sign which can be exchanged among criminal justice
> personnel, criminologists, politicians, journalists, film-makers and,
> importantly, (mythically) ordinary individuals. (Young 1996: 2)

Given Young's analysis we might rightly question the merits of reifying
the media and media discourse in any way at all. For its functioning
must surely be intimately interlinked in exchanges – in 'signs of crime' –
with other discourses of the 'crimino-legal complex'. However, I do not
think we have to imagine the media as discursively discrete from this
complex to make some of its operations subject to analysis. Rather, we
must constantly reflect on the fact that the media discourses, narratives
and practices that are analysed below do not function autonomously. I
have attempted to situate this interactivity in terms of the *fear of crime
feedback loop*. This feedback loop, like Young's crimino-legal complex,
is an attempt to draw in the multiplicity of entities that enable fear of
crime to function. The case study below is an excellent illustration of
this interactivity. For here, as we shall see, the media actually pick up
on discourses of criminology and the social sciences, the fear of crime
component of the victim survey.

Thus, to suggest that there is an intersection between the media and
fear of crime is not to suggest that there is a direct causal link between
the two. Rather, I want to suggest that, on the one hand, what and how
the media reports in regard to crime is mediated through imagined
– often borrowed – narratives about crime (Sparks 1992; Young 1996)
and that understanding the discursive operation of these narratives
is important to understanding how media institutions situate their
readership. To relate back to the last chapter, media institutions too
imagine a particular form of consuming (fearing?) subject. I want to
suggest that the public consume (read) crime stories in a multiplicity
of ways and that whether this consumption leads to increased fear of
crime is dependent on the lived experiences of the consumer and their
cultural context amongst other factors (Walklate 1998).

While much of this is well-traversed terrain the case studies I want
to explore are somewhat different. I want to explore the way in which
the media is increasingly becoming a monitor of crime fears. By this I
mean that the media is increasingly taking a quasi social-scientific role
in measuring fear of crime by way of fear surveys, phone-ins and the
like. This is not surprising when we consider that these same crime

fears are what helps sell papers or attract viewers to nightly news bulletins.

Fear surveys

Apart from sensationalising crime stories, and thus possibly increasing public concern and fear about crime, some elements of the media have in recent years, like pollsters and social researchers, taken a much greater interest in the fear of crime as a concept – something to measure and report on in and of itself. Pratt (1997: 150) argues that this new interest coincides with a shift in the way individuals conceptualise their own bodies and indeed their liberty. Thus, our fears and risks are reported back to us, the print media and television news and current affairs show us ourselves in numbers, and there is nothing more compelling to the viewer/reader than that which presents us to ourselves. Baudrillard (1988) has argued that people have become public; that we now enjoy the luxury of witnessing the fluctuations of our own opinions in the daily reading of various opinion polls. We witness these not as truth, according to Baudrillard (1988: 212), but as 'a game of truth effects in the circularity of questions and answers'. This is not unlike the *feedback loop* I've outlined in this book, I'd suggest. Thus, segments of the media now embark on their own elementary forms of fear of crime survey. These days governmental statistics on fear, which less than three decades ago were the only information available apart from the odd poll, have been joined by many new types of statistical surveys and studies that borrow the general format. Indeed, as these new 'regimes of truth' about fear of crime have proliferated so has the contestation of governmental statistics, the suspicion of expert knowledge. Pratt (1997: 152) argues – in a broader context – that official crime statistics have become:

> One amongst a number of statistical sources of information on crime that have been made available to us. These include university-organised crime surveys, independent victim surveys, self-report studies, surveys conducted by the phone, those organised by sections of the media and so on. All of these indicators claim to represent the reality of crime – albeit a different version of this reality: a reality which by and large portrays the risk of crime – particularly sexual and violent crime – as being significantly greater than when computed from official crime statistics.

In this final section I will focus on two examples of the final type of survey Pratt refers to; that of the survey organised by, or at least through, the media, giving two examples from the Australian press. Their prominence, one in a high-circulation Sydney daily, the other as a front page story in a local Sydney suburban weekly publication, illustrates well how such surveys and their reportage form part of the *fear of crime feedback loop*. They also illustrate how the discourse of the fear of crime survey has been democratised, for better or worse.

'The Daily Telegraph Law and Order Survey'

The Daily Telegraph is a high-circulation Rupert Murdoch owned (News International) tabloid newspaper based in Sydney. Its populist editorial tone is well established and its penchant for law and order and crime stories equally well understood, as has been noted in the discussion above. In July 2004 *The Daily Telegraph* published a two-page central spread, 'The Law and Order Survey 2004' (3 June 2004: 14–15). The paper has run similar surveys prior to this and will no doubt run more. Readers were asked either to fill in the survey manually and send it reply paid to *The Telegraph*; or to complete the survey online. Readers were told the survey was 'asking readers to tell us – and the police and judiciary – what concerns them about law and order in NSW'. It went on to tell us that the questionnaire had 'been compiled with the help of senior police and a legal expert' but did not publish their names. What becomes clear from a perusal of the survey's 66 questions is that it is largely a fear of crime survey with the aim of identifying specific public concerns for its readership. What's more, its leading questions tap into the very forms of authoritarian populism the paper regularly trumpets and many of the current issues it champions. Importantly, the survey also followed a number of highly publicised offences and events in Sydney: the gang rape of a number of young women by 'ethnic gangs', a concern over the attempted abduction of young children (later proven to be a largely baseless moral panic), discussion about the length and severity of sentences for serious offenders, and finally terrorism.

The very first question asks respondents, 'Which of the following do you have in your home? House alarm, House alarm with back-to-base facility, sensor lights, dogs (for security), deadlocks, bars/grills on windows, video surveillance cameras, roller shutters on windows, any weapon (please state).' This early establishing of respondents' risk reduction measures is followed by a question on what types of crime you have fallen victim to in the past five years, followed by a third question asking, 'How safe do you feel in your own home?' Following lists of questions on; the police, one of which asks, 'Do you believe that it is the sole responsibility of NSW Police to reduce crime?'; gangs, one of which asks, 'Are you aware of any criminal gangs operating in your area?'; the judiciary, one of which asks, 'Do you believe judges/ magistrates are in touch with the community in regard to issues of [lists a number of serious offences]', the survey goes on to ask what might be considered a number of stock fear of crime questions: 'Do you feel safe on public transport at night?'; 'Do you feel safe walking on the streets at night?' and the like, and then moves on to a number of questions about terrorism: 'Do you think there will be a terrorist attack within Australia within the next 12 months?' Finally, 'Which of the following concerns you the most, assault, home invasion, terrorism, murder, war, theft, sexual assault, rape, safety of your children, none?' We might answer the final question with 'the frightening tone of our daily newspaper' if it were an option, but this is not the point I want to make. Rather, it is that this survey format, specifically tapping into the fear of crime discourse I have identified above, has been popularised and normalised to such an extent that readers of *The Telegraph* are completely cognisant with the style and format. Moreover, the paper is more than willing to give up two full pages to the process, presumably evidence of the commercial rewards such an investment might reap.

Nine days later in a 'special report' the 'survey results' were published (12 July 2004: 12). Or were they? In fact the results of only 13 of the 66 questions were ever published. Rather, the results that were selectively published were those that were ideologically or discursively aligned with the 'exclusive' headline aimed, in no uncertain terms, at the judiciary: 'YOU'RE OUT OF TOUCH, Judges and magistrates are out of touch with the community on every type of crime and penalties should be toughened, an exclusive law and order survey for *The Daily Telegraph* has found' (Miranda and Wockner 2004: 1). Indeed, the results that were published painted a picture of an anxious public commonsensically blaming for their anxieties a soft criminal justice system that 'favours criminals' – the authoritarian populist stance. The other topic area that was published was that of the question of terrorism. Here terrorism is not only on the radar, as it were, it has rocketed towards the top of our fear list. And even as we reflect on our responses published before us we can feel political responses being formulated, responses not just aimed at governing the crime we perceive, but the fear of this crime itself.

'The Hills News'

'CRIME FEAR IMMENSE' announces the headline on the front page of the *Hills News*, a small weekly paper distributed in the Castle Hill area of Sydney (Gainsford 1998: 1). The front pages of these smaller and local publications in Australia regularly carry local crime stories.

However, this story is not about any particular crime, it is about fear of crime. This story begins:

> A survey of 300 local people aged between 13 and 23 has revealed widespread fear of violent crime in Baulkham Hills Shire. The survey conducted by the newly formed Hills Community Safety Council to help strategies to combat crime in the district … (Gainsford 1998: 1)

So while this survey is not conducted 'exclusively' by the *Hills News*, it is unproblematically reproduced for and by the paper. The Hills Community Safety Council's credentials are established early in the piece by way of its 'youth representative', being also the 'shire's Australia Day young citizen of the year'. The article goes on to outline the findings of this 'survey' but precedes these by emphasising that 'of the 300 interviewed, 27 had friends who had been stabbed in the Hills district in the past three months'. Putting to one side the glaring methodological flaws in the survey design[19] I will take a closer look at the results of the survey. They were represented in the *Hills News* as follows:

- 81 per cent of adolescents under 18 years of age said they were scared of getting stabbed by the increasing number of gangs in the Hills district.

- 78 per cent said their major fear was that gangs from Parramatta, Blacktown and Penrith districts were coming into Castle Hill because it was a richer area.

- 72 per cent said transport in the Hill district had failed them and they were scared to go out at night because they could not get transport home and were stranded at bus stops late at night.

The paper went on to report:

> […] These results showed that there is immense fear over the increasing amount of violent crime and that adolescents live from day to day with the constant threat of being attacked. (Gainsford 1998: 1)

It is not clear of course just how these summations were translated from the survey results to the 'news' article. What is clear is that it is unlikely that any credible survey design could have produced the results as they are shown. The first 'finding' suggests unproblematically that there are an 'increasing number of gangs' in the Hills district. If the suggestion that the 'number of gangs in the Hills district had increased' was included in the survey design there is no doubt that the findings would be flawed. Further, respondents replied that they were 'scared of getting stabbed' as a result of these gangs. Who would not be 'scared of getting stabbed'? If, as seems to be suggested in the article, the survey was conducted verbally, how could these questions be verbally posed without leading the respondents?

In the second finding above we see the adoption of the powerful motif of crime being committed by strangers from elsewhere. This topic also touches a nerve in terms of class, and borders, purity and locality – the unruly others moving in to threaten the propertied and law-abiding citizens of the Hills metropolis. Dumm (1993) suggests that the freedom and mobility of dangerous others has historically been of concern to the propertied and political authorities (Bauman 1993; Sibley 1995). It is worth noting that the Hills district represents or imagines itself as the up-market locality in Sydney's north-western suburbs. It is also the centre of evangelistic Christian resurgence, thus, concerns about property might be high on the priorities of the *Hills News* readership.

The third point in the list of 'findings' regarding public transport also raises methodological issues – although it must be added that the public transport system in western Sydney is indeed abysmal. For example, it is easy to see how respondents might reply that public transport had failed them and may leave them stranded; however, it is difficult to know how a question might be structured that then connects this to being 'scared to go out'.

Not surprisingly the article ends with calls for a crackdown on crime, tougher laws, and more police powers, all justified through the survey format. We are left with the unproblematic inferences that violent crime is rising in the area, more gangs are forming, young people are afraid to go out of their houses, dangerous others are invading the area, fear is rising, criminals are not punished, and the list goes on.

However, of more interest is the discursive narrative through which this 'survey' operates. Its truth-value is not constituted in and of itself. The survey format, as I have suggested, gains legitimation through being a tool of social science; it emerges into a particular regime of truth. Moreover, it speaks to 'real people'. The surveyed are the 'readership' and other 'locals'. The readership can reflexively view themselves in enumerated categories and be informed as to how they might conduct themselves and what precautions they might take. Readers of newspapers, it has been suggested by news editors, are interested in what editors call 'local, local news'.[20] They want to know about the local business community, their child's school, their neighbourhoods.

So the local fear survey has particular salience. It is personal. That is not to say it necessarily increases fear in every individual although it does sensitise the reader to the notion of fear of crime as a concept – an emotion one *might* feel. Maybe, as Baudrillard (1988) suggests, the readership treat such surveys ironically? And, as Sparks (1992) has suggested, some readers may even revel in the increasingly risky nature of their local environment. However, we can conclude that, at the very least, such surveys must result in an intensification of discourse around fear of crime, and consequently an intensification of the *fear of crime feedback loop*. Perhaps most importantly, they sell papers to a public hungry to reflect on their fear of crime.

Conclusion

This chapter has attempted to discuss the dimensions of private interests in fear of crime discourse and how these feed into and feed off the *fear of crime feedback loop*. Since fear of crime was discovered in the 1960s, a host of industries has assembled around it which service it in a variety of ways. Crime fear discourse makes it possible to advertise the securing credentials of an array of security hardware and software, private policing, private security, real estate and lifestyle goods. These become part of what Garland terms the criminologies of the self (1996).

Insurance, private policing and security, security hardware and software, CCTV and the like all have a stake in fear of crime discourse. In the securitisation required of the individual under neo-liberal governmental rationalities one is responsible for the consumption of such services. Simultaneously the state provision of services and public insurance is pared back and replaced only with a more pro-active set of functions around the security of sovereignty. The war on terror carried out at the level of the policing of asylum seekers has been a prime example.

Meanwhile it is win-win for elements of the media only too willing to tap into these desires and even borrow the very social scientific regimes of truth legitimated via the history of fear of crime research. In drawing attention to these practices, discourses and narratives that circulate within media institutions and their reporting I have also tried to reiterate that these do not operate in a vacuum; that the media is one institution amongst many that inform, function and are informed by such narratives.

Notes

1 http://www.domain.com.au/real_estate/sale/nsw/liverpool_ – _fairfield/ macquarie_links/real_estate.aspx
2 One such estate in western Sydney employed media personality Ita Butrose as their public advertising face so that the estate could be marketed to an aging and apparently fearful population.
3 ABC Television Australia, 7.30 Report, September 2005.
4 See discussion in Hudson (2002).
5 Flusty's (1997) five main types being stealthy space – a space that is camouflaged or obscured; slippery space – space that cannot be reached due to missing or contorted paths or entry points; crusty space – cannot be accessed due to walls, gates or checkpoints; prickly space – cannot be comfortably occupied; jittery space – monitored or patrolled space.
6 There are estimated to be around 100,000 people in Australia living in gated communities although the level of security varies greatly from community to community and even within communities.
7 http://www.private-communities.org/communitydetail.asp?communityid =12 accessed 2 July 2005.
8 Prenzler and Sarre (2005: 15) note that obtaining such figures is notoriously difficult. However, while suggesting that the number of police and security officers in Australia have not expanded at rates some critics suggest, they estimate an expansion of 31.1 per cent from 1996–2001 compared with an expansion of 6.5 per cent for public police and 6.0 per cent in population.
9 http://www.guardianeagle.net/ accessed 5 January 2006.
10 http://www.signalsecurity.com.au/ accessed 4 July 2005.
11 http://www.securepro.com.au/index.php?fuseaction=home.main accessed 8 July 2005.
12 http://www.kingssecurity.com.au/home_security/home_security.php accessed 7 July 2005.
13 http://www.amica.com/aboutUs/safety_tips/homeSafety.html accessed 7 June 2005.
14 http://www.nrma.com.au/pub/nrma/home/home-security.shtml accessed 7 May 2005.
15 Personal communication printed with consent of the author whose identity has been withheld.
16 Between 1989–1996, 68 per cent of homicides in Australia were committed by family members or acquaintances. Only 16 per cent of homicides in Australia were committed by strangers to the victim. Note: these figures are for homicide which includes both murder and manslaughter (AIC 1998). It could be surmised that the figure for murder would be lower than 16 per cent.
17 Also see Sibley (1995).
18 I should point out that Young specifically credits Peter Rush with coining this term.

19   There is no indication of exactly what was asked in the survey nor how the survey was structured. Additionally, there is no indication as to how the survey was operationalised, how the sample group was chosen, what methodologies were used, how the survey was delivered, whether it was written or oral, how the results were correlated. Of course it is possible that this survey methodology was rigorous. However, it seems unlikely that 'Ms Stevens [who] visited local youth groups, community organisations and local shopping centres to compile the survey over a weekend' (*Hills News*, 26 May 1998) would be capable of such rigour without help from a number of researchers.

20   cf. interview with Judy Pace-Christie (editor of *Florida Today* newspaper), ABC Media Report, 24 June 1999.

Chapter 8

Conclusion: don't mention the F word

Fear of crime was 'discovered' in either 1965 or 1967. Or so goes the conventional wisdom of what seem at first glance some very reasonable and logical accounts of the history of fear of crime. This discovery was made possible by the development of the large-scale victim survey, and in particular the trilogy of surveys conducted at the behest of the US President's Commission in 1965 whose report, as we have seen, was published in 1967. And there is indeed logic in these accounts of the unfolding of events. Fear of crime as we understand it today did indeed become a criminological concept and an object of social scientific enquiry at this point in time, of that there is little doubt. Moreover, the President's Commission Report and its attendant research was indeed a pivotal event in this becoming, this conceptualisation. However, following this historical account through to its logical conclusion leads us to two propositions about the nature of this discovery, both of which I have intimated here are flawed and unsupported by the available historical evidence; and both of which are at odds with the genealogical account I have outlined.

The first is that crime fear increased (and was thus discovered) as a result of escalating recorded crime rates and general political disorder, or at least the perception of increasing crime. This, it is argued, had its genesis in the USA in the early to mid 1960s. Of these accounts liberal interpretations argue that this was the result of political manoeuvring and/or inflated or misrepresented statistical data on recorded crime. In short it was the result of moral panic whipped up by conservatives and devoured by the almost equally conservative media. On the other hand conservatives would suggest that this discovery was due to the reality of rising crime and the breakdown of general moral order in the counter-cultural 1960s; that is, a breakdown in both formal and informal social control (Wilson and Kelling 1982: 29–38). I will return to these propositions.

The second logical proposition we could reach would suggest that crime fear had always existed but that it was only through the development of new methods of detecting and calculating it, of the evolution of technological and social scientific innovation, that we were able to identify this problem. Such an account would emphasise the development of the victim surveys, the democratisation of social scientific knowledge, and the work of pollsters and the like in identifying and enumerating a problem in need of prompt policy treatment.

The first set of propositions suggests an historical rupture of monumental proportions, and if we accept this, a rupture that has taken place across much of the Western world in the years between 1965 and 1982 – a veritable explosion in crime fear related to crime's politicisation or simply its vast increase. Such a claim seems somewhat tenuous, particularly as there have been numerous historical periods of high crime rates that did not result in the discovery of fear of crime. As suggested, some of these accounts also emphasise the political origins of fear of crime, yet despite the undeniable salience of fear of crime it is not simply an invention of politics, certainly not party politics at least.

The second conclusion suggests the existence of a phenomenon that continues in a-historical sameness and privileges a teleological history of social scientific enquiry. This envisages social scientific knowledge as progressively uncovering the truth about the social world; a modernisation myth of the march of scientific progress, if you will. Here fear of crime is simply a new observable 'object' discovered via the development of enlightened means of observation and calculation.

I've suggested that both of these interpretations are flawed. Indeed, they rely on deferring the primary unanswered question of the fear of crime debates; that is, the question of 'what is fear of crime?' I would suggest the answer to this question is actually quite simple. That is, fear of crime is *nothing* in and of itself. No such objective thing actually exists. Although I must admit this conclusion is not completely original; Jason Ditton noted back in the 1990s that 'fear of crime does not exist'.

Of course, the point of all this is that once we establish that fear of crime does not exist in an objective form, and we no longer defer the original question of 'what is fear of crime?', conventional histories of fear of crime become somewhat obsolete. Thus, I have attempted here to apply a new approach and subsequently a new set of questions to the issue of crime fear. The questions I have asked in this book are largely Foucaultian ones and were formulated with an eye to the historical impasses I have just outlined:

1 Through which forms of knowledge/power, and via which discursive surfaces of emergence, has fear of crime become an object of social scientific enquiry and criminological concept?

2 How has this discourse of fear of crime subsequently come itself to have power effects?

3 Through which rationalities and mentalities are the power effects of fear of crime able to be exercised, and what are the consequences of this?

I have called this assemblage of discursive affects, and effects, this node of power/knowledge, the *fear of crime feedback loop*. The notion of a *feedback loop* dispenses with the idea of a central reality, and objectivity, to fear of crime, but highlights both the production of and the productive effects of fear of crime the concept.

These questions have also assumed a particular set of productive relationships between the power effects of social scientific knowledge and the human subjectivities it reports on. That is, bodies are not inert. The second flawed explanation of fear of crime I outlined above makes the assumption that, not only has fear of crime always existed, but that human subjects have always responded to it – it was only with its 'discovery' though that we enumerated it and gave it a name. However, my method here assumes that, not only have an infinite variety of appalled responses and reactions to crime historically existed, but that these are produced, inscribed, and mutated by *inter alia* the very social scientific methods, explanations and analysis we use to understand them in our research.

Once the researchers and pollsters began enumerating crime fear and called it fear of crime, an object was not discovered – rather, a discourse and problematisation was born; a concept was invented. This new node of knowledge had power effects. It could be a political tool; it could be a tactic of government in the management of risk; it could sell security; it could sell newspapers; and, perhaps most importantly, once it had a name, it could be experienced as an emotional state. And experience it we have. Its enumeration allows us to view our own fearfulness about crime in any number of statistical studies, local newspaper polls, websites, women's magazines and the like – view them as 'new regimes of truth'. We are now so obsessed with crime fear our police forces see its reduction as almost as important as the reduction of crime itself. The history of fear of crime is a cogent lesson in the unintended consequences and power effects of both social enquiry and political rationalities. As researchers we should, I suspect, always seek to problematise the notion of fear of crime; render it contingent. Likewise, we must abandon positivistic notions that fear of crime is a stable object of knowledge that can be attributed specific causality. As Derrida (1977: 342) suggests, 'it is a question of explicitly and systematically posing the problem of the status of a discourse ... A problem of *economy* and *strategy*'.

The difficulty of reducing fear of crime and concerted critical attacks on its legitimacy have seen it, in the past few years at least, become a slightly more marginal concern for criminology – if not government. Nonetheless, the enumeration of fear of crime continues as if the plethora of problems critical scholars have identified in regard to it mean nothing in light of good accessible time series data, no matter how flawed. I could pronounce fear of crime dead, a thing of the past. And perhaps in part that was what this book was meant to do, I cannot speak from outside the discourse I seek to problematise. However, I fear the baton has already been passed to that great fear of the early twenty-first century, terror. And long, I expect, will it reign over us.

References

AIC (2006) 'Sworn Police Officers in Australia', *Crime Facts Info*. Canberra: Australian Institute of Criminology.

Akers, R. L., LaGreca, A., Sellers, C. and Cochrane, J. (1987) 'Fear of Crime and Victimisation among the Elderly in Different Types of Communities', *Criminology*, 25 (3): 487–506.

Allen, J. (1988) 'The Masculinity of Criminality and Criminology: Interrogating Some Impasses', in M. Findlay and R. Hogg (eds), *Understanding Crime and Criminal Justice*. North Ryde: The Law Book Co.

Allen, J. (1990) *Sex and Secrets: Crimes Involving Australian Women Since 1880*. Melbourne: Oxford University Press.

Anderson, S., Kinsey, R., Loader, I. and Smith, C. (1990) *The Edinburgh Crime Survey*. Edinburgh: Scottish Office.

Anderson, S., Kinsey, R., Loader, I. and Smith, C. (1991) *'Cautionary Tales': A Study of Young People in Edinburgh*. Edinburgh: Centre for Criminology, University of Edinburgh.

Antilla, I. (1964) 'The Criminological Significance of Unregistered Criminality', *Excerpta Criminologica*, no. 4: 441.

Argana, M.G. (1975) 'Development of a national Victimisation Survey', in I. Drapkin and E. Viano (eds), *Victimology: A New Focus, Volume III: Crimes, Victims and Justice*, Vol. III. Lexington: Lexington Books.

Arrigo, B. (2001) 'Deconstruction', in E. McLoughlin and J. Muncie (eds), *The Sage Dictionary of Criminology*. London: Sage.

Atkinson, R. and Flint, J. (2004) 'The Fortress UK? Gated Communities, The Spatial Revolt of the Elites and Time Space Trajectories of Segregation', *CNR*: unpublished conference paper.

Bannister, J. and Fyfe, N. (2001) 'Introduction: Fear and the City', *Urban Studies*, 38 (5–6): 807–813.

Barclay, D. (1950) 'Parents Advised on Sex Crime Fear', *The New York Times*, 6 June 1950: 33.

Baudelaire, C. (1972) 'The Painter and Modern Life', *Selected Writings on Art and Artists*. Harmondsworth: Penguin.

Baudrillard, J. (1988) *Selected Writings*. Stanford California: Stanford University Press.

Bauman, Z. (1993) *Postmodern Ethics*. Oxford: Blackwell.

Baumer, T. (1978) 'Research on Fear of Crime in the United States', *Victimology: An International Journal*, 3 (3/4): 354–364.

Baumer, T. (1985) 'Testing a General Model of Fear of Crime: Data From a National Sample', *Journal of Research in Crime and Delinquency*, 22(3): 239–255.

Beck, U. (1992) *Risk Society: Towards a New Modernity*. London: Sage.

Beirne, P. (1993) *Inventing Criminology: Essays on the Rise of 'Homo Criminalis'*. Albany: University of New York Press.

Beirne, P. and Messerschmidt, J.W. (2006) *Criminology*, Vol. 4. Los Angeles: Roxbury.

Bennett, T. (1994) 'Confidence in the Police as a Mediating Factor in the Fear of Crime', *International Review of Victimology*, 3: 179–194.

Biderman, A., Johnson, L., McIntyre, J. and Weir, A. (1967) 'Report on a Pilot Study in the District of Columbia on Victimisation and Attitudes Toward Law Enforcement', *President's Commission on Law Enforcement and Administration of Justice, Field Surveys 1*. Washington DC: US Government Printing Office.

Black, D. (2004) 'Terrorism as Social Control', in M. Deflem (ed), *Terrorism and counter terrorism: criminological perspectives*. Amsterdam: Elsevier.

Blair, W. (1949) 'Opinion Polls Held Aids of Democracy', *The New York Times*, New York, 12 February 1949: 15.

Box, S., Hale, C. and Andrews, G. (1988) 'Explaining Fear of Crime', *The British Journal of Criminology*, 28 (3): 340–356.

Braithwaite, J. (1989) 'The State of Criminology. Theoretical Decay or Renaissance?' *Australian and New Zealand Journal of Criminology*, 25 (3): 333–355.

Braithwaite, J., Biles, D. and Whitrod, R. (1982) 'Fear of Crime in Australia', in H.J. Schneider (ed), *The Victim in International Perspective*. New York: Walter deGruyer.

Brake, M. and Hale, C. (1992) *Public order and private lives: the politics of law and order*. London: Routledge.

British Conservative Party (1970) 'Election 1970 Tory Manifesto', *The Times*, London, 27 May: 8.

Burchell, G. (1993) 'Liberal government and techniques of the self', *Economy and Society*, 23 (3): 267–282.

Burke, R.H. (2005) *An Introduction to Criminological Theory*. Cullompton: Willan.

Bush, G. (2005) Press Release: 08/03/2005.

Button, M. (2002) *Private Policing*. Cullompton: Willan.

Caldeira, T. (2000) *City of Walls: Crime, Segregation and Citizenship in São Paulo*. Berkeley: University of California Press.

Carach, C. and Mukherjee, S. (1999) 'Women's Fear of Violence in the Community', in A. Graycar (ed), *Trends and Issues in Crime and Criminal Justice*. Canberra: Australian Institute of Criminology.

Carrington, K. (1994) 'Postmodernism and Feminist Criminologies: Disconnecting Discourses?', *International Journal of the Sociology of Law*, 22: 261–277.

Carrington, K. (1998) *Who Killed Leigh Leigh: A Story of Shame and Mateship in an Australian Town*. Milsons Point: Random House Australia.

Carrington, K., Gow, J., Hogg, R. and Johnson, A. (1996) *Crime, Locality and Citizenship: Interim Research Report*. Sydney: Institute of Criminology.

Chevalier, L. (1973) *Labouring Classes and Dangerous Classes in Paris in the First Half of the Ninteenth Century*. New York: Howard Festig.

Chiricos, T., Hogan, M. and Gertz, M. (1997) 'Racial Composition of Neighbourhood and Fear of Crime', *Criminology*, 35 (1): 107–131.

Clarke, R. (1980) 'Situational crime prevention: theory and practice', *British Journal of Criminology*, 20: 136–147.

Cohen, S. (1972) *Folk Devils and Moral Panics: The Creation of the Mods and Rockers*. London: Paladin.

Cohen, S. (1985) *Visions of Social Control*. Cambridge: Polity Press.

Cohen, S. (1996) 'Crime and Politics: Spot the Difference', *The British Journal of Sociology*, 47 (1): 1–21.

Coleman, R. and Sim, J. (2005) 'Contemporary Statecraft and the "Punitive Obsession": A Critique of the New Penology Thesis', in J. Pratt, D. Brown, M. Brown, S. Hallsworth and W. Morrison (eds), *The New Punitiveness*. Cullompton: Willan.

Colquhoun, P. (1799) *Treatise on the Police of the Metropolis*. London: J. Mawman.

Conklin, J. (1975) *The Impact of Crime*. New York: Macmillan.

Coumarelos, C. (2000) 'An Evaluation of the Safe City Strategy in Central Sydney'. Sydney: NSW Bureau of Crime Statistics and Research.

Crawford, A. (1998) *Crime Prevention and Community Safety: Politics, Policies and Practices*. Essex: Pearson.

Crawford, A., Jones, T., Woodhouse, T. and Young, J. (1990) 'Second Islington Crime Survey'. London: Middlesex Polytechnic.

Cruikshank, B. (1996) 'Revolutions Within: Self Government and Self-Esteem', in A. Barry, T. Osborne and N. Rose (eds), *Foucault and Political Reason: Liberalism, Neo-Liberalism and Rationalities of Government*. London: University of Chicago Press.

Darwin, C. (1902) *On the Origin of Species by Means of Natural Selection, or the Preservation of Favoured Races in the Struggle for Life*. London: John Murray.

Davis, F. (1952) 'Crime News in the Colorado Newspapers', *The American Journal of Sociology*, 57 (4): 325–330.

Davis, M. (1990) *City of Quartz*. London: Pimlico.

Davis, M. (1998) *Ecology of Fear: Los Angeles and the Imagination of Disaster*. London: Picador.

De Lint, W. (2004) 'Neoconservatism and American counter-terrorism', in M. Deflem (ed), *Terrorism and counter-terrorism: criminological perspectives*. Amsterdam: Elsevier.

Dean, M. (1991) *The Constitution of Poverty: Towards a Genealogy of Liberal Governance*. London: Routledge.

Dean, M. (1999) *Governmentality: Power and Rule in Modern Society*. London: Sage.

Dear, M. (2000) *The Postmodern Urban Condition*. Massachusetts: Blackwell.

Department of Urban Affairs and Planning (2001) *Crime prevention and the assessment of development applications: Guidelines under section 79C of the Environmental Planning and Assessment Act 1979*. Sydney: Department of Urban Affairs and Planning.

Derrida, J. (1977) *Writing and Difference*. London: Routledge.

Derrida, J. (1991) *A Derrida Reader: Between the Blinds*. New York: Columbia University Press.

Ditton, J., Bannister, J., Gilchrist, E. and Farrall, S. (1999a) 'Afraid or Angry? Recalibrating the "Fear" of Crime', *International Review of Victimology*, 6: 83–99.

Ditton, J. and Farrall, S. (2000) *The Fear Of Crime*. Ashgate: Aldershot.

Ditton, J., Farrall, S., Bannister, J., Gilchrist, E. and Pease, K. (1999b) 'Reactions to Victimisation: Why Has Anger Been Ignored', *Crime Prevention and Community Safety: An International Journal*, 1 (3): 37–54.

Dobash, R.E. and Dobash, R. (1992) *Women, Violence and Social Change*. London: Routledge.

Donzelot, J. (1979) *The Policing of Families: Welfare Versus the State*. London: Hutchinson.

Drapkin, I. and Viano, E. (eds) (1975) *Victimology: A New Focus, Volume III: Crimes, Victims, and Justice*, Vol. III. Lexington: Lexington Books.

Dugan, L. (1999) 'The Effect of Criminal Victimisation on a Household's Moving Decision', *Criminology*, 37 (4): 903–930.

Dumm, T. (1993) 'The New Enclosures: Racism in the Normalised Community', in R. Gooding-Williams (ed), *Reading Rodney King*. New York: Routledge.

Edmondson, B. (1994) 'Most Homes Armed', *American Demographics*, 16 (10): 19.

Egger, S. (1997) 'Women and Crime Prevention', in P. O'Malley and A. Sutton (eds), *Crime Prevention in Australia: Issues in Policy and Research*. Leichhardt: Federation Press.

Ellin, N. (1996) *Postmodern Urbanism*. Oxford: Blackwell.

Ellin, N. (1997) 'Shelter From the Storm or Form Follows Fear and Vice Versa', in N. Ellin (ed), *Architecture of Fear*. New York: Princeton Architectural Press.

Emsley, C. (1987) *Crime and Society in England 1750–1900*. New York: Longman.

Engels, F. (1844) *The Condition of the Working Class in Britain*. Oxford: Chaloner.

Ennis, P. (1967) 'Criminal Victimisation in the United States: A Report of a National Survey', *President's Commission on Law Enforcement and the Administration of Justice, Field Surveys II*. Washington DC: Government Printing Office.

Ewald, F. (1991) 'Insurance and Risk', in C. Gordon, G. Burchell and P. Miller (eds), *The Foucault Effect: Studies in Governmentality*. London: Harvester Wheatsheaf.

Ewald, F. (1993) 'Two infinities of risk', in B. Massumi (ed), *The politics of everyday fear*. Minnesota: University of Minnesota Press.

Farrall, S., Bannister, J., Ditton, J. and Gilchrist, E. (1997) 'Questioning the Measurement of the "Fear of Crime"', *The British Journal of Criminology*, 37 (4): 658–679.

Farrall, S., Bannister, J., Ditton, J. and Gilchrist, E. (1999) 'Social Psychology and the Fear of Crime: Re-Examining a Speculative Model', *The British Journal of Criminology*, 40 (4): 692–709.

Farrall, S. and Gadd, D. (2004) 'Research Note: The Frequency of Fear of Crime', *The British Journal of Criminology*, 44 (1): 127–132.

Farrall, S., Jackson, J. and Grey, E. (2006) Experience and Expression in the Fear of Crime. Unpublished Working Paper No. 2.

Fattah, E.A. and Sacco, V.F. (1989) *Crime and Victimization of the Elderly*. New York: Springer-Verlag.

Fenton, F. (1911) *The Influence of Newspaper Presentations upon the Growth of Crime and Other Anti-Social Activity*. Chicago: The University of Chicago Press.

Ferraro, K.F. (1995) *Fear of Crime: Interpreting Victimisation Risk*. Albany: State University of New York Press.

Ferraro, K.F. and La Grange, R. (1987) 'The Measurement of Fear of Crime', *Sociological Inquiry*, 57: 70–101.

Fielding, H. (1751) *An Enquiry Into the Causes of the Late Increase of Robbers*. Oxford: Oxford University Press.

Fletcher, J. (1850) 'Moral and educational Statistics of England and Wales', *Journal of the Statistical Society of London*, 11: 344–366.

Flusty, S. (1997) 'Building Paranoia', in N. Ellin (ed), *Architecture of Fear*. New York: Princeton Architectural Press.

Foucault, M. (1977) *Discipline and Punish: The Birth of the Prison*, 1st Edition. New York: Pantheon Books.

Foucault, M. (1982) 'The subject and power', *Critical Enquiry*, 8 (4): 777–795.

Foucault, M. (1984) *The Foucault Reader*. New York: Pantheon Books.

Foucault, M. (1991) 'Governmentality', in P. Miller, G. Burchell and C. Gordon (eds), *The Foucault Effect: Studies in Governmentality*. London: Harvester Wheatsheaf.

Freedman, L. (1992) 'The Concept of Security', in M. Hawkesworth and M. Kogan (eds), *Encyclopedia of Government and Politics*, London: Routledge.

Furstenberg, F. (1971) 'Public Reaction to Crime in the Streets', *American Scholar*, 40: 601–610.

Gainsford, J.H.N. (1998) 'Crime Fear Immense', *Hills News*. Castle Hill, Sydney.

Gardner, J. (1990) 'Victims and Criminal Justice', Adelaide: Office of Crime Statistics, Attorney-General's Department.

Garland, D. (1985) 'Politics and Policy in Criminological Discourse; A Study of Tendentious Reasoning and Rhetoric', *International Journal of the Sociology of Law*, 13: 1–13.

Garland, D. (1990) *Punishment and Modern Society: A Study in Social Theory*. Chicago: University of Chicago Press.

Garland, D. (1996) 'The Limits of the Sovereign State: Strategies of Crime Control in Contemporary Society', *British Journal of Criminology*, 36: 445–471.

Garland, D. (1997) 'Governmentality and the Problem of Crime: Foucault, Criminology, Sociology', *Theoretical Criminology*, 1 (2): 173–214.

Garland, D. (2001) *Culture of Control: Crime and Social Order in Contemporary Society*. Chicago: The Chicage University Press.

Garland, D. (2002) 'Of Crimes and Criminals: The Development of British Criminology', in M. Maguire, R. Morgan and R. Reiner (eds) *The Oxford Handbook of Criminology*. Oxford: Clarendon Press.

Garofalo, J. (1979) 'Victimisation and Fear of Crime', *Journal of Research in Crime and Delinquency*, 16: 80–97.

Garofalo, J. (1981) 'The Fear of Crime: Causes and Consequences', *Journal of Criminal Law and Criminology*, 72 (2): 839–857.

Garreau, J. (1991) *Edge City: Life on the New Frontier*. New York: Anchor Books.

Gatens, M. (1991) *Feminism and Philosophy: Perspectives on Difference and Equality*. Cambridge: Polity.

Giddens, A. (1990) *The Consequences of Modernity*. Cambridge: Polity Press.

Giddens, A. (1993) *Politics, Sociology and Social Theory: Encounters with Classical and Contemporary Social Thought*. Cambridge: Polity Press.

Gilchrist, E., Bannister, J., Ditton, J. and Farrall, S. (1998) 'Women and the "Fear of Crime": Challenging the Accepted Stereotype.' *The British Journal of Criminology*, 38 (2): 283–298.

Girling, E., Loader, I. and Sparks, R. (2000) *Crime and Social Change in Middle England: Questions of Order in an English Town*. London: Routledge.

Glassner, B. (1999) *The Culture of Fear*. New York: Basic Books.

Glyde, J. (1856) 'Localities of Crime in Suffolk', *Journal of the Statistical Society of London*, 19: 102–106.

Golant, S. (1984) 'Factors Influencing the Night Time Activity of Old Persons in Their Community', *Journal of Gerontology*, 39: 485–491.

Goldwater, B. (2006) 'Goldwater's speech at the 28th Republican National Convention', *The Washington Post*, www.washingtonpost.com/wp-srv/politics/daily/may98/goldwaterspeech.htm, accessed 29 January 2005.

Gomme (1986) 'Fear of Crime Amongst Canadians: A Multi-Variate Analysis', *Journal of Criminal Justice*, 14: 249–258.

Goodey, J. (1994) 'Fear of Crime: What Can Children Tell Us?', *International Review of Victimology*, 3: 195–210.

Goodey, J. (1997) 'Boys Don't Cry: Masculinities, Fear of Crime, and Fearlessness', *The British Journal of Criminology*, 37 (3): 401–418.

Gooding-Williams, R. (1993) *Reading Rodney King: Reading Urban Uprising*. New York: Routledge.

Gordon, C. (1991) 'Governmental Rationality: An Introduction', in P. Miller, G. Burchell and C. Gordon (eds), *The Foucault Effect: Studies in Governmentality*. London: Harvester Wheatsheaf.

Gordon, M.T. and Riger, S. (1989) *The Female Fear*. New York: Free Press.

Grabosky, P.N. (1995) 'Fear of Crime, and Fear Reduction Strategies', *Current Issues in Criminal Justice*, 7 (1): 7–19.

Greg, W.R. (1835) *Social Statistics of the Netherlands*, 1835.

Grosz, E.A. (1989) *Sexual Subversions: Three French Feminists*. Sydney: Allen and Unwin.

Grosz, E.A. (1994) *Volatile Bodies: Toward a Corporeal Feminism*. Sydney: Allen and Unwin.

Guerry, A.M. (1833) *Essai sur la statistique moral de la France*. Paris: Crochard.

Gunter, B. (1987) *Television and the Fear of Crime*. London: Libbey.

Gwither, G. (2005) 'Seeking Utopia: Master Planned Estates on Sydney's Urban Fringe', in J. Gaffey, A. Possamai-Inesedy and K. Richards (eds) *The Chameleon and the Quilt: A Cross-Disciplinary Exploration in the Social Sciences*, Sydney: University of Western Sydney.

Hacking, I. (1982) 'Biopower and the Avalanche of Printed Numbers', *Humanaties and Society*, 5: 279–295.

Hacking, I. (1983) 'Nineteenth century cracks in the concept of determinism', *Journal of the History of Ideas*, 44 (3): 455–475.

Hacking, I. (1990) *The Taming of Chance*. Cambridge: Cambridge University Press.

Hale, C. (1996) 'Fear of Crime: A Review of the Literature', *International Review of Victimology*, 4: 79–150.

Hall, S., Critcher, C., Jefferson, T., Clarke, J. and Roberts, B. (1978) *Policing the Crisis: Mugging, the State and Law and Order*. London: Macmillan.

Hardt, M. and Negri, A. (2000) *Empire*. Cambridge: Harvard University Press.

Harris, R. (1969) *The Fear of Crime*, 1st Edition. New York: Frederick A. Praeger.

Hawkesbury City Council (2001) *Hawkesbury Crime Prevention Plan*. Hawkesbury: Hawkesbury City Council.

Hayward, K. (2004) *City Limits: Crime, Consumer Culture and the Urban Experience*. London: Glasshouse.

Heartless, J., Ditton, J., Nair, G. and Philips, S. (1995) 'More Sinned Against Than Sinning: A Study of Young Teenagers' Experence of Crime', *British Journal of Criminology*, 35 (1).

Heath, L. and Gilbert, K. (1996) 'Mass Media and the Fear of Crime', *American Behavioral Scientist*, 39: 379–386.

Heren, L. (1969) 'Friendly and Unfriendly', *The Times*, London, 18 November: 8.

Heren, L. (1970) 'News Diary', *The Times*, London.

Hindelang, M.J. (1974) 'Public Opinion regarding Crime, Criminal Justice and Related Topics', *Journal of Research in Crime and Delinquency*, (July): 101–116.

Hindelang, M., Gottfredson, M. and Garofalo, J. (1978) *Victims of Personal Crime*. Boston: Ballenger.

Hocking, B. (2004) *Terror Laws: ASIO, Counter-Terrorism and the Threat to Democracy*. Sydney: UNSW Press.

Hogg, R. (1988) 'Taking Crime Seriously: Left Realism and Australian Criminology', in M. Findlay and R. Hogg (eds), *Understanding Crime and Criminal Justice*. Sydney: The Law Book Company.

Hogg, R. (2002) 'The Khaki Election', in P. Scraton (ed), *Beyond September 11*. London: Pluto.

Hogg, R. and Brown, D. (1998) *Rethinking Law and Order*. Annandale: Pluto Press.

Hollway, W. and Jefferson, T. (1997a) 'Eliciting Narrative Through the In-Depth Interview', *Qualitative Inquiry*, 3 (1): 53–70.

Hollway, W. and Jefferson, T. (1997b) 'The Risk Society in an Age of Anxiety: Situating Fear of Crime', *The British Journal of Sociology*, 48 (2): 255–266.

Hollway, W. and Jefferson, T. (2000) *Doing Qualitative Research Differently: Free Association, Narrative and the Interview Method*. London, Thousand Oaks: Sage Publications.

Holmes, J. (1929) 'Crime and the Press', *Journal of the American Institute of Criminal Law and Criminology*, 20 (1): 6–59.

Home Office (1989) 'The Grade Report', *Report of the Working Group on the Fear of Crime*. London: Home Office.

Home Office (2001) 'Untitled Personal Safety Advice', Vol. 2002.

Hood, R. (2004) 'Hermann Mannheim and Max Grunhut: Criminological Pioneers in London and Oxford', *British Journal of Criminology*, 44 (4): 469–495.

Hood, R. and Sparks, R. (1970) *Key Issues in Criminology*. London: Weidenfeld and Nicolson.

Hope, T. (2000) 'Inequality and the Clubbing of Security', in T. Hope and R. Sparks (eds), *Crime, Risk and Insecurity*. London: Routledge.

Hope, T. (2005) 'The New Local Governance of Community Safety in England and Wales', *Canadian Journal of Criminology and Criminal Justice*, April: 369–387.

Hope, T. and Trickett, A. (2004) 'Angst Essen Steele Auf … But it Keeps Away the Burglars! Private Security, Neighbourhood Watch and the Social Reaction to Crime', *Kölner Zeitschrift für Soziologie und Sozialpsychologie*, 43: 441–468.

Hough, M. and Mayhew, P. (1983) *The British Crime Survey: First Report*, Vol. No. 76. London: Her Majesty's Stationery Office.

Hough, M. and Mayhew, P. (1985) 'Taking Account of Crime: Key Findings from the 1984 British Crime Survey'. London: HMSO.

Hudson, B. (2002) 'Punishment and control', in M. Maguire, R. Morgan and R. Reiner (eds), *The Oxford Handbook of Criminology*. Oxford: Oxford University Press.

Hudson, B. (2003) *Justice in the Risk Society*. London: Sage.

Hunt, A. and Wickham, G. (1994) *Foucault and Law: Towards a Sociology of Law as Governance*. London: Pluto Press.

Innes, M. (2004) 'Signal Crimes and Signal Disorders: Notes on Deviance as Communicative Action', *British Journal of Sociology*, (55/3) pp. 335–55.

Jackson, J. (2004) 'An Analysis of a Construct and Debate: The Fear of Crime', in J. Albrecht, T. Serassis and H. Kania (eds), *Images of Crime II*. Freiburg: Edition Iuscrim/Max Planck Institute.

Jacobs, J. (1989) *The Death and Life of Great American Cities: The Failure of Town Planning*. New York: Random House.

Janson, P. and Ryder, L. (1983) 'Crime and the Elderly: The Relationship Between Risk and Fear', *The Gerontologist*, 23: 207–212.

Johnson, A. (2000) Crime, governance and numbers: a genealogy of counting crime in New South Wales. Unpublished Doctorate, University of Western Sydney.

Johnson, H. (2005) 'Crime Victimisation in Australia: Key Results of the 2004 International Crime Victimisation Survey', *Australian Institute of Criminology Research and Public Policy Series No. 64*.

Johnson, L. (1965) 'State of the Union Address', http://www.infoplease.com/ipa/A0900149.html (accessed 7 May 2005).

Johnston, L. (2000) *Policing Britain*. Harlow: Longman.

Jones, T., MacLean, B. and Young, J. (1986) *The Islington Crime Survey: Crime, Victimisation and Policing in Inner-City London*. Aldershot: Gower Publishing Co. Ltd.

Joyce, P. (2003) *The Rule of Freedom: Liberalism and the Modern City*. London: Verso.

Keane, C. (1995) 'Victimisation and Fear: Assessing the Role of Offender and Offence', *Canadian Journal of Criminology*, 37 (3): 431–455.

Killias, M. (1990) 'Vulnerability: Towards a Better Understanding of a Key Variable in the Genesis of Fear of Crime', *Violence and Victims*, 5: 97–108.

Kinsey, R. (1984) 'The Merseyside Crime Survey'. Liverpool: Merseyside County Council.

Krannich, R., Grieder, T. and Little, R. (1985) 'Rapid Growth and Fear of Crime: A Four Community Comparison', *Rural Sociology*, 50: 193–209.

La Grange, R. and Ferraro, K.F. (1987) 'The Elderly's Fear of Crime: A Critical Examination of the Research', *Research on Aging*, 9: 372–391.

La Grange, R. and Ferraro, K.F. (1989) 'Assessing Age and Gender Differences in Perceived Risk and Fear of Crime', *Criminology*, 27: 697–719.

Lane, R.E. (1966) 'The Decline of Politics and Ideology in a Knowledgeable Society', *American Sociological Review*, 31 (5): 649–662.

Lechte, J. (1995) '(Not) Belonging in Postmodern Space', in S. Watson and K. Gibson (eds) *Postmodern Cities and Spaces*. Cambridge: Blackwell.

Lee, M. (1999) 'The Fear of Crime and Self-Governance: Towards a Genealogy', *The Australian and New Zealand Journal of Criminology*, 32 (3): 227–246.

Lee, M. (2001) 'The Genesis of Fear of Crime', *Theoretical Criminology*, 5 (4).

Lee, M. (2006) 'Fear, Law and Order and Politics', in E. Barklay, J. Scott, J. Donnermeyer and R. Hogg (eds), *Crime in Rural Australia: Integrating Theory, Research and Practice*. Sydney: Federation Press.

Levin, Y. and Lindesmith, A. (1939) 'English ecology and criminology of the past century', *American Institute of Criminal Law and Criminology*, 27: 801–816.

Loader, I. (1997) 'Thinking Normatively about Private Security', *Journal of Law and Society*, 24: 377–394.

Loader, I. (2004) 'Policing, securitisation and democratisation in Europe', in T. Newburn and R. Sparks (eds), *Criminal Justice and Political Cultures: National and international dimensions of crime control*. Cullompton: Willan.

Loader, I., Girling, E. and Sparks, R. (2000) 'After Success? Anxieties of affluence in an English Village', in T. Hope and R. Sparks (eds), *Crime, Risk and Insecurity*. London: Routledge.

Loader, I. and Sparks, R. (2004) 'For an Historical Sociology of Crime Policy in England and Wales since 1968', *Critical Review of International Social and Political Philosophy*, 7 (2): 5–32.

Lombroso, C. (1876) *L'Uomo delinquente*. Milan: Hoepli.

Lombroso, C. (2004/1897) 'Why Homicide has Increased in the United States', in D. Horton and K. Rich (eds), *The Criminal Anthropological Writings of Cesare Lombroso in the English Language*. Lampeter: The Edwin Mellen Press.

Lombroso, C. (1911/1899) *Crime and Its Causes*. London: William Heinemann.

Longaker, R. (1973) 'The Nature of Governmental Secrecy', in P. Melanson (ed), *Knowledge, Politics, and Public Policy*. Cambridge: Winthrop.

Loo, D. and Grimes, R. (2004) 'Polls, Politics, and Crime: The "Law and Order" Issue of the 1960s', *Western Criminological Review*, 5 (1): 50–65.

Low, S. (2004) *Behind the Curtains: Life, Security and the Pursuit of Happiness in Fortress America*. New York: Routledge.

Lupton, D. (1999) 'Dangerous Places and the Unpredictable Stranger', *The Australian and New Zealand Journal of Criminology*, 32 (1): 1–15.

Madriz, E. (1997) *Nothing Bad Happens to Good Girls: Fear of Crime in Women's Lives*. Berkeley: University of California Press.

Maguire, M. (1997) 'Crime Statistics, Patterns, and Trends', in M. Maguire, R. Morgan and R. Reiner (eds), *The Oxford Handbook of Criminology*. Oxford: Clarendon Press.

Maguire, M. (2002) 'Crime Statistics: The "Data Explosion" and its Implications', in M. Maguire, R. Morgan and R. Reiner (eds), *The Oxford Handbook of Criminology*. Oxford: Oxford University Press.

Manly City Council (2001) 'Manly City Council Crime Prevention Plan'. Manly: Manly City Council.

Martinson, R. (1974) 'What Works? Questions and Answers About Prison Reform, *Public Interest*, 35: 22–54.

Maxfield, M.G. (1984) *Fear of Crime in England and Wales*. London: Her Majesty's Stationery Office.

Maxfield, M.G. (1987) 'Explaining fear of crime: evidence from the 1984 British Crime Survey', *Home Office Research and Planning Unit*. London: HMSO.

Mayhew, H. (1862/1968) *The Criminal Prisons of London*. London: Augustus M. Kelley.

McCulloch, J. (2003) '"Counter-terrorism", human security and globalisation – from welfare state to warfare state?', *Current Issues in Criminal Justice*, 14 (3): 283–298.

McCulloch, J. (2004) 'Blue armies, khaki police and the cavalry of the new American frontier', *Critical Criminology*, 12: 309–326.

McDonald, I. (1972) 'When the Only Problem is What to Tell the Census Lady', *The Times*, London, 22 September: 7.

McLaughlin, E. (2001) 'Fear of Crime', in E. McLaughlin and J. Muncie (eds), *Sage Dictionary of Criminology*. London: Sage.

McLaughlin, E. and Muncie, J. (2000) 'Walled Cities: Surveillance, Regulation and Segregation', in S. Pile *et al.* (eds), *Unruly Cities*. London: Routledge.

McMullan, J.L. (1998) 'Policing reform and moral discourse: the genesis of a modern institution', *Policing: An International Journal of Police Strategies and Management*, 21 (1).

Melanson, P. (1973) *Knowledge, Politics, and Public Policy*. Cambridge: Winthrop.

Miller, P. and Rose, N. (1990) 'Governing Economic Life', *Economy and Society*, 19: 1–19.

Minton, A. (2002) 'Mind the Gap: Tackling Social Polarisation Through Balanced Communities'. London: Royal Institute of Chartered Surveyors (RICS).

Miranda, C. and Wockner, C. (2004) 'You're Out of Touch'. *The Daily Telegraph*, 12 July. Sydney.

Mohanram, R. (1999) *Black Body: Women, Colonialism and Space*. St Leonards: Allen and Unwin.

Moore, M. (2001) *Stupid White Men*. Camberwell: Penguin.

Morris, A., Reilly, J. and in collaboration with S. Berry and R. Ransom (2003) *The New Zealand national survey of crime victims 2001*, first published in May 2003. New Zealand Ministry of Justice.

Mugford, S. (1984) 'Fear of Crime – Rational or Not? A Discussion and Some Australian Data', *The Australian and New Zealand Journal of Criminology*, 17: 267–275.

Mythen, G. and Walklate, S. (2006) 'Criminology and terrorism: Which thesis? Risk society or governmentality?', *British Journal of Criminology*, 46(3): 379–398.

Newcastle City Council (2000) 'Newcastle City Council Crime Prevention Plan'. Newcastle: NSW Attorney General's Department.

Newan, O. (1972) *Defensible Space*. New York: Macmillan.

Norris, C. and Armstrong, G. (2000) 'CCTV and the Rise of the Mass Surveillance Society', in P. Carlan and R. Morgan (eds), *Crime Unlimited? Questions for the 21st Century*. Houndmills: MacMillan.

NRMA (1990) 'Neighbourhood Watch'. Sydney: NRMA.

NSW Attorney General's Department (2001) Untitled Web Pages.

NSW Police Service (1995) *Preventing Burglary*. Sydney.

NSW Police (No date) 'Leave it About and it will go Without a Doubt'. Sydney.

Ollenburger, J. (1981) 'Criminal Victimisation and Fear of Crime', *Research on Ageing*, 3: 101–118.

O'Malley, P. (1992) 'Risk, Power, and Crime Prevention', *Economy and Society*, 21: 252–275.

O'Malley, P. (1996) 'Risk and Responsibility', in A. Barry, T. Osborne and N. Rose (eds), *Foucault and Political Reason*. London: University of Chicage Press.

O'Malley, P. (2000) 'Uncertain Subjects: Risks, Liberalism and Contract, *Economy and Society*, 29 (4): 460–484.

O'Malley, P. (2004) 'Globalising Risk? Distinguishing Styles of 'Neo-liberal' Criminal Justice in Australia and the USA', in R. Sparks and T. Newburn (eds), *Criminal Justice and Political Cultures*. Cullompton: Willan.

O'Malley, P., Weir, L. and Shearing, C. (1997) 'Governmentality, Criticism and Politics', *Economy and Society*, 27 (4).

O'Sullivan, M. (2005) 'Behind the urban curtains', *Sydney Morning Herald*, Sydney.

Pasquino, P. (1991a) 'Criminology: The Birth of a Special Knowledge', in P. Miller, G. Burchell and C. Gordon (eds) *The Foucault Effect: Studies in Governmentality*. London: Harvester Wheatsheaf.

Pasquino, P. (1991b) 'Theatrum Politicum: The Genealogy of Capital – Police and the State of Prosperity', in P. Miller, G. Burchell and C. Gordon (eds), *The Foucault Effect: Studies in Governmentality*. London: Harvester Wheatsheaf.

Pearson, G. (1983) *Hooligan: A History of Respectable Fears*. London: Macmillan Press Ltd.

Philips, D. (1977) *Crime and authority in Victorian England: the Black Country 1835–1860*. London: Croom Helm.

Phipps, A. (1986) 'Radical Criminology and Criminal Victimisation', in R. Matthews and J. Young (eds) *Confronting Crime*. London: Sage Publications.

Pike, L.O. (1968) *A History of Crime in England*. New Jersey: Patterson Smith.

Poovey, M. (1995) *Making a Social Body: British Cultural Formation 1830–1864*. Chicago: Chicago University Press.

Poveda, T. (1972) 'The fear of Crime in a Small Town', *Crime and Delinquency*, April: 147–153.

Povey, D., Upson, A. and Jansson, K. (2005) 'Crime in England and Wales: Quarterly Update to June 2005', *Statistical Bulletin 18/05*. London: Home Office.

Pratt, J. (1997) *Governing the Dangerous: Dangerousness, Law and Social Change*. Leichhardt: The Federation Press.

Pratt, J., Brown, D., Brown, M., Hallsworth, S. and Morrison, W. (2005) 'Introduction', in J. Pratt, D. Brown, M. Brown, S. Hallsworth and W. Morrison (eds), *The New Punitiveness*. Cullompton: Willan.

Prenzler, T. and Sarre, R. (1999) 'A Survey of Security Legislation and Regulatory Strategies in Australia', *Security Journal*, 3 (12): 7–17.

Prenzler, T. and Sarre, R. (2005) *The Law of Private Security in Australia*. Sydney: Thompson Law Book Co.

The President's Commission on Law Enforcement and Administration of Justice (1967) *The Challenge of Crime in a Free Society: A Report by the President's Commission on Law Enforcement and Administration of Justice*. United States Government Printing Office, Washington DC.

Putnam, R. (2000) *Bowling Alone: The Collapse and Revival of American Community*. New York: Simon and Schuster.

Quetelet, A. (1984) *Adolphe Quetelet's Research on the propensity for crime at different ages*, translated with an introduction by Sawyer F. Sylvester. Cincinnati: Anderson Pub. Co.

Radzinowicz, L. (1948) *A History of English Criminal Law*, Vol. 1. London: Stevens and Sons.

Radzinowicz, L. (1999) *Adventures in Criminology*. London: Routledge.

Radzinowicz, L. and King, J. (1977) *The Growth of Crime: The International Experience*. New York: Basic Books.

Rafter, N. and Heidensohn, F. (1995) *International Feminist Perspective's in Criminology: Engendering a Discipline*. Buckingham: Open University Press.

Rawson, R.W. (1839) 'An inquiry into the statistics of crime in England and Wales', *Journal of the Statistical Society*, 2: 316–344.

Reedy, L., Hickie, M., Leonard, R. and Simeoni, E. (1994) '"Ask Any Woman" A Report of a Phone-In on Women and Safety in Liverpool Local Government Area', Liverpool: Liverpool City Council.

Reiner, R., Livingston, S. and Allen, J. (2000) 'No More Happy Endings: The media and Popular Concern About Crime Since The Second World War', in T. Hope and R. Sparks (eds), *Crime, Risk and Insecurity*. London: Routledge.

Reiss, A. (1967) 'Studies in Crime and Law Enforcement in Major Metropolitan Areas, Volume 1', *President's Commission on Law Enforcement and the Administration of Justice, Field Surveys III*. Washington DC: US Government Printing Office.

Report of the Special Commission to the National Science Board (1973), in Melanson, P. (ed), *Knowledge, Politics, and Public Policy*. Cambridge: Winthrop.

Robinson, L. (1964) 'Rising Fear Found On Upper West Side', *The New York Times*, New York.

Rock, P. (1994) 'The Social Organisation of British Criminology', in M. Maguire, R. Morgan and R. Reiner (eds), *The Oxford Handbook of Criminology*. Oxford: Clarendon Press.

Rose, N. (1988) 'Calculable Minds and Manageable Individuals', *History of the Human Sciences*, 1 (2): 179–200.

Rose, N. (1991) 'Governing by Numbers: Figuring out Democracy', *Accounting, Organisation and Society*, 16 (7): 673–692.

Rose, N. (1995) 'The death of the social? Refiguring the territory of government', *Economy and Society*, 23 (3): 327–356.

Rose, N. (1996) 'Governing "Advanced" Liberal Democracies', in A. Barry, T. Osborne and N. Rose (eds), *Foucault and Political Reason: Liberalism, Neo-Liberalism and Rationalities of Government*. London: UCL Press.

Rose, N. (1999) *Powers of Freedom: Reframing Political Thought*. Cambridge: Cambridge University Press.

Rose, N. and Miller, P. (1992) 'Political Power Beyond the State: Problematics of Government', *British Journal of Sociology*, 43 (2).

Rothe, D. and Muzzatti, S. (2004) 'Enemies everywhere: terrorism, moral panic, and US civil society', *Critical Criminology*, 12: 327–350.

Sacco, V. F. (1990) 'Gender, Fear and Victimisation', *Sociological Spectrum*, 1: 485–506.

Sarre, R. (1997) 'Crime Prevention and Police', in P. O'Malley and A. Sutton (eds), *Crime Prevention in Australia: Issues in Policy and Research*. Annandale: Federation Press.

Schwendinger, J. and Schwendinger, H. (1975) 'Studying Rape: Integrating Research and Social Change', in C. Smart and B. Smart (eds), *Women, Sexuality and Social Control*. London: Routledge.

Shapland, J. and Vagg, J. (1988) *Policing by the Public*. London: Routledge.

Shearing, C. and Stenning, P. (1985) 'From the Panopticon to Disney World: The Development of Discipline', in A. Doog and E. Greenspan (eds), *Perspectives in Criminal Law*. Ontario: Canada Law Book Inc.

Short, E. and Ditton, J. (1996) 'Does Close Circuit Television Prevent Crime? An Evaluation of the Use of CCTV Surveillance Cameras in Airdrie Town centre'. Edinburgh: Scottish Office Central Research Unit.

Sibley, D. (1995) *Geographies of Exclusion: Society and Difference in the West*. London: Routledge.

Simmons, J. and Dodd, T. (2003) 'Crime in England and Wales 2002/03', *Home Office Statistical Bulletin*. London: Home Office.

Skogan, W.G. (1986) 'The Fear of Crime and Its Behavioral Implications', in A. Fattah (ed), *From Crime Policy to Victim Policy*. London: Macmillan.

Skogan, W.G. (1989) 'Communities, Crime, and Neighbourhood Organisation', *Crime and Delinquency*, 35 (3): 437–457.

Skogan, W.G. (1995) 'Crime and the Racial Fears of White Americans', *The Annals of The American Academy of Political and Social Science*, 539: 59–71.

Skogan, W.G. and Maxfield, M.G. (1981) *Coping With Crime: Individual and Neighborhood Reactions*. Beverly Hills: Sage Publications.

Smart, C. (1995) *Law Crime and Sexuality: Essays in Feminism*. London: Sage Publications.

Smart, C. and Smart, B. (1975) 'Women and Social Control: An Introduction', in C. Smart and B. Smart (eds), *Women, Sexuality and Social Control*. London: Routledge.

Smith, L. and Hill, G. (1991) 'Victimisation and Fear of Crime', *Criminal Justice and Behaviour*, 18: 217–239.

Smith, S.E. (1986) *Fear or Freedom*. Illinois: Mother Courage Press.

Smith, S.J. (1984) 'Crime in the News', *British Journal of Criminology*, 24 (3): 289–295.

Sparks, R. (1992) 'Reason and Unreason in 'Left Realism': Some Problems in the Constitution of the Fear of Crime', in R. Matthews and J. Young (eds), *Issues in Realist Criminology*. London: Sage Publications.

Sparks, R. (1992) *Television and the Drama of Crime: Moral Tales and the Place of Crime in Public Life*. Buckingham: Open University Press.

Sparks, R., Genn, H. and Dodd, D. (1977) *Surveying victims: a study of the measurement of criminal victimisation, perceptions of crime, and attitudes to criminal justice*. New York: Wiley.

Stafford, M. and Galle, O. (1984) 'Victimisation rates, exposure to risk, and fear of crime', *Criminology*, 22 (2): 173–185.

Stanko, E. (1990) *Every Day Violence: How Women and Men Experience Sexual and Physical Danger*. London: Pandora.

Stanko, E. (1997) 'Safety Talk: Conceptualizing Women's Risk Assessment as a "Technology of the Soul"', *Theoretical Criminology*, 1 (4): 479–499.

Stanko, E. (1998) 'Warnings to Women', in P. O'Malley (ed), *Crime and the Risk Society*. Dartmouth: Ashgate.

Stanko, E. (2000) 'Victims "R" Us', in T. Hope and R. Sparks (eds), *Crime, Risk and Insecurity*. London: Routledge.

Steinert, H. (2003) 'The Indispensable Metaphor of War', *Theoretical Criminology*, 7 (3): 265–291.

Stenson, K. (1993a) 'Social Work Discourses and the Social Work Interview', *Economy and Society*, 22 (1).

Stenson, K. (1993b) 'Community Policing and Governmental Technology', *Economy and Society*, 22 (3).

Stenson, K. (1995) 'Communal security as government- the British Experience', in W. Hammerschick, I. Karazman-Moraewetz and W. Stangl (eds), *Jahrbuch fur Rechts und Kriminalsoziologie*. Baden-Baden: Nomos.

Sutton, R.M. and Farrall, S. (2005) 'Gender, Socially Desirable Responding and the Fear of Crime: Are Women Really More Anxious about Crime?', *British Journal of Criminology*, 45 (2): 212–224.

Sykes, J.B. (1976) *The Concise Oxford Dictionary of Current English*. Oxford: Oxford University Press.

Talese, G. (1961) 'Park – Crime Fear Held Unjustified', *The New York Times*, New York, 19 May 1961: 17.

Taylor, I., Walton, P. and Young, J. (1973) *The New Criminology: For a Social Theory of Deviance*. London: Routledge.

Taylor, R. (1988) *Human Territorial Functioning: An Empirical, Evolutionary Perspective on Individual and Small Group Territorial Cognitions, Behaviors, and Consequences*. New York: Cambridge University Press.

Taylor, R. and Hale, M. (1986) 'Testing Alternative Models of Fear of Crime', *Journal of Criminal Law and Criminology*, 77: 151–189.

Thornton, M. (1995) *Public and Private Feminist Legal Debates*. Melbourne: Oxford University Press.

Tierney, J. (1996) *Criminology: Theory and Context*. Pearson: London.

Tobias, J. (1972) 'Forward', in J. Wade (ed), *Treatise on the police and crimes of the metropolis*. Montclair, NJ: Patterson Smith.

Tobias, J. (1979) *Crime and Police in England 1700–1900*. London: Gil and Macmillan.

Tulloch, J., Lupton, D., Blood, W., Tulloch, M., Jennett, C. and Enders, M. (1998a) *Fear of Crime Volume 1*. Canberra: Attorney-General's Department Commonwealth of Australia.

Tulloch, J., Lupton, D., Blood, W., Tulloch, M., Jennett, C. and Enders, M. (1998b) *Fear of Crime Volume 2*. Canberra: Attorney-General's Department Commonwealth of Australia.

UK Home Office (2006) 'Crime Reduction Toolkits: Fear of Crime', Vol. 2006.

US Bureau of Justice Statistics (2006) 'Sourcebook of Criminal Justice Statistics Online, 31st Edition', Vol. 2006: US Bureau of Justice Statistics.

van derWurff, A., van Staalduinen, L. and Stringer, P. (1989) 'Fear of Crime in Residential Environments: Testing a Social Psychological Model', *Journal of Social Psychology*, 129 (2): 141–160.

van Dijk, J. and Mayhew, P. (1992) 'Criminal Victimisation in the Industrialised World'. The Hague: Ministry of Justice.

Wade, J. (1972/1829) *Treatise on the police and crimes of the metropolis*. Montclair, NJ: Patterson Smith.

Walklate, S. (1994) 'Can There be a Progressive Victimology?', *Victimology: An International Review*, 3 (1 and 2).

Walklate, S. (1995) *Gender and Crime: An Introduction*. London: Prentice Hall/ Harvester Wheatsheaf.

Walklate, S. (1998) *Understanding Criminology: Current Theoretical Debates*. Bristol: Open University Press.

Walters, R. (2003) *Deviant Knowledge: Criminology, Politics and Policy*. Cullompton: Willan.

Warr, M. (1984) 'Fear of Victimisation: Why are Women and the Elderly More Afraid?', *Social Forces*, 59: 456–470.

Warr, M. (1992) 'Altruistic Fear of Victimisation', *Social Science Quarterly*, 73 (4): 723–736.

Weatherburn, D., Matka, E. and Lind, B. (1996) 'Crime Perception and Reality: Public Perceptions of the Risk of Criminal Victimisation in Australia', *Crime and Justice Bulletin*, Vol. 28: NSW Bureau of Crime Statistics and Research.

Weber, L. and Bowling, B. (2002) 'The policing of immigration in the new world disorder' *Beyond September 11: An anthology of dissent*. London: Pluto.

Welch, M. (2003) 'Trampling human rights in the war on terror: implications to the sociology of denial', *Critical Criminology*, 12: 1–20.

White, R. and Haines, F. (1996) *Crime and Criminology: an Introduction*. Melbourne: Oxford University Press.

Wigg, R. (1967) 'America moves towards national strategy against crime', *The Times*, London.

Williams, F.P., McShane, M.D. and Akers, R.L. (2000) 'Worry About Victimisation: An Alternative and Reliable Measure for Fear of Crime', *Western Criminology Review*, 2 (2).

Williams, L. (2006) 'Every move they make, mum's watching', *The Sydney Morning Herald*, Sydney.

Williams, P. and Dickinson, J. (1993) 'Fear of Crime: Read All About It? The Relationship Between Newspaper Crime Reporting and Fear of Crime', *The British Journal of Criminology*, 33 (1): 33–56.

Wilson, D. and Sutton, A. (2003) 'Open-Street CCTV in Australia', *Australian Institute of Criminology Trends and Issues*. Canberra: Australian Institute of Criminology.

Wilson, E. (1995) 'The Invisible Flâneur', in S. Watson and K. Gibson (eds), *Postmodern Cities and Spaces*. Oxford: Blackwell.

Wilson, J. (1975) *Thinking About Crime*. New York: Basic Books.

Wilson, J. and Kelling, G. (1982) 'Broken Windows', *The Atlantic Monthly*: 29–38.

Wilson, J. and Kelling, G. (1989) 'Making Neighbourhoods Safe', *The Atlantic Monthly*: 46–52.

Wilson, L. (1938) 'Newspaper Opinion and Crime in Boston', *Journal of Criminal Law and Criminology*, 29 (2): 202–215.

Wollongong City Council (2000) *Wollongong Crime Prevention Plan*. Wollongong: Wollongong City Council.

Wood, D. (1984) 'British Crime Survey, 1982 Technical Report'. London: Home Office.

Yin, P. (1982) 'Fear of Crime as a Problem for the Elderly', *Social Problems*, 27: 492–504.

Young, A. (1996) *Imagining Crime: Textual Outlaws and Criminal Conversations*. London: Sage.

Young, A. and Rush, P. (1994) 'The law of victimage in urban realism: thinking through inscriptions of violence', in D. Nelikin (ed), *The Futures of Criminology*. London: Sage.

Young, J. (1987) 'The Tasks Facing a Realist Criminology', *Contemporary Crisis*, 11: 337–356.

Young, J. (1988) 'Risk of Crime and Fear of Crime: A Realist Critique of Survey-Based Assumptions', in M. Maguire and J. Pointing (eds), *Victims of Crime: A New Deal?*, 1st Edition. Milton Keynes, Philadelphia: Open University Press.

Young, J. (1994) 'Recent Paradigms in Criminology', in M. Maguire, R. Morgan and R. Reiner (eds), *The Oxford Handbook of Criminology*. Oxford: Clarendon Press.

Zedner, L. (2000) 'The Pursuit of Security', in T. Hope and R. Sparks (eds), *Crime, Risk and Insecurity*. London: Routledge.

Zedner, L. (2002) 'Victims', in M. Maguire, R. Morgan and R. Reiner (eds), *The Oxford Handbook of Criminology*. Oxford: Clarendon Press.

Zehr, H. (1976) *Crime and the development of modern society*. New Jersey: Rowman and Littlefield.

Zielinski (1995) 'Armed and Dangerous: Private police on the March', in *Covert Action Quarterly*, Fall (accessed at http://www.mediafilter.org/cap/CAQ54p.police.html on 19/06/2001).

Zirker Jr, M.R. (1967) 'Restoration and Eighteenth Century', in Studies in English Literature, 1500–1900, Vol. 7, No. 3, pp. 453–465.

No Author

(1856) 'Police' *The Times*, London, 9 September: 9.

(1870) 'Lord Derby at Manchester', *The Times*, London, 18 January: 10.

(1875) 'The Social Science Congress', *The Times*, London, 7 October: 6.

(1934) 'Lynching Spirit Laid to a Fear of crime', *The New York Times*, New York, 22 January: 9.

(1963) '"Gordon Riots" Fear as Crime Rate Keeps Rising' *The Times*, London, 30 May: 9.

(1966) 'Millions In Fear From Crime. Says Mr. Johnson', *The Times*, London, 10 March: 8.

(1966) 'Crime is Top Problem in District, Area's Negroes and Whites Agree', *The Washington Post*, Washington, DC, 2 October: 1.

(1969) 'From Warren to Burger', *The Times*, London, 27 May: 9.

(2004a) 'Law and Order Survey 2004', *The Daily Telegraph*, Sydney, 3 June: 13, 14.

(2004b) 'Law and Order Survey Results', *The Daily Telegraph*, Sydney, 12 July: 1 & 4.

(2004c) 'Terrorist attack fears mounting', *The Daily Telegraph*, Sydney, 12 July: 4.

(2005) 'Terror hotline hits 24,000 calls', *The Age*, Melbourne, 24 August: 4.

(No Date) 'Tips when shopping and carrying handbags', *Westfield Shoppingtown*.

Index

abnormal fear of crime 125–6
Aboriginal people 155
actuarial risk of victimisation 20, 120,
    122–3, 126, 128, 183
administrative criminology 7, 86–92,
    96, 101, 103–5
administrative project 119, 134
Adventures in Criminology
    (Radzinowicz) 7
advertising
    of gated communities 165, 174–5
    by insurance companies 169–70,
        184
    by mobile phone companies 187
    by private security companies
        169–70, 178–9
advice literature
    access to 142
    governmental 99, 136–7, 141–3,
        150, 160–1
    on national security and risk of
        terrorism 160–1
    NRMA Neighbourhood Watch
        147–9
    NSW Police 143–5
    on risk of victimisation in
        governance of fear of crime
        136–7
    sources 141–3
    and type of *fearing subject* 142

Westfield 144–7
    for women 99, 142, 150
Afro-Americans 72, 152, 155
age 90, 91, 116–17
    see also children; elderly people;
        young men; young people;
        young women
Alison, Sir Archibald 35–8
'amplified' fear of crime 83, 91, 94
anger about crime 109
Anglo-Australians 155, 156
anti-terrorism legislation 159, 167
anxieties and concerns
    in mid-late 18th century Western
        Europe 27–8, 29, 31–33
    in 19th century Western Europe
        33–7, 45–8
    in 1960s USA 59–61, 65–7, 69–70
    in 1970s UK 88
'anxiety,' terminology 19, 69, 123,
    124
    see also emotions
Argana, Marie G. 71
Armstrong, G. 180
Arrigo, B. 120
aspirational classes 26–7, 172, 173
asylum seekers 156–7
Atkinson, R. 177
Australia
    anti-terrorist legislation 159

news media reports on fear of
crime in USA 84
newspaper reports of violent
crime 184–5
police 30–2, 33, 177
politicisation of fear of crime 84
poor law abolition 34–5
private security 176
radical criminology 93–6
research literature on fear of crime
83
science of police 30–2
social unrest 34, 35
Thatcher government 85, 92, 96,
100, 101
victim surveys 86–91, 96, 105–8
(*see also* British Crime Survey
(BCS))
women's movement initiatives 98
United Nations 49–50
University of Michigan (UoM) 64, 65
urbanisation 26–7, 36–7
USA
anti-terrorist legislation 159
black riots 73
criminological research centres
88–9
ethnic minorities 152, 155
fear of terrorism 156, 157
feared subject 155
gated communities 172, 175
'Great Society Program' 62–3, 74
history of fear of crime (*see*
history of fear of crime in USA;
prehistory of fear of crime in
USA in 20th century to mid
1960s)
information on risk of
victimisation 133
insurance companies 184
knowledgeable society 57–61, 76
mobile phones 186
mugging 94–5
new right governments and law
and order 100, 101
police 178
prehistory of fear of crime in 20th

century to mid 1960s 48–9,
50–2, 60
private security 178
Reagan administration 100, 101,
102
right realism 102
secrecy 58, 64
September 11 2001 terrorist attacks
157, 159–60
'war on crime' 156, 159
'war on terror' 156, 157, 158–60,
161

victim surveys
and anger *versus* fear of crime
109
and emotions 20
and fear of crime 2
and fear of crime feedback loop
77–8
in history of fear of crime in USA
64–8, 70, 71–2, 82, 120, 202
and left realism 105–7
measurement of fear of crime 5,
125
question design 11, 88, 90–1, 118
and risk of victimisation 20, 67,
70, 83
and sex roles 126–7
UK 86–91, 96
and women as victims of crime
117–18
by women's magazines 99
see also British Crime Survey
(BCS); fear surveys; opinion
poll surveys
victimology 71, 76
victims
irresponsibility 146–7
women 97–100, 116
young people 196, 197
see also risk of victimisation
Victims of Personal Crime (Gottfredson
and Garofalo) 82
violent crime
fear of, in victim surveys 2
mass media reports 188–9